WESTERN FRUIT BERRIES & NUTS
HOW TO SELECT, GROW AND ENJOY

Robert L. Stebbins
Lance Walheim

Executive Producer: Richard Ray
Contributing Editor: Robert Woolley
Photography: Michael Landis

Produced by Horticultural Publishing Co., Inc.:
Art Director: Richard Baker
Associate Editor: Michael MacCaskey
Research Editors: David Loring, Randy Peterson,
    Stephen Dudley
Copy Editor: Al Horton
Production Editor: Kathleen Parker
Design: Judith Hemmerich, Lingke Oei
Typography: Linda Encinas
Illustration: Gayle Cunningham, Roy Jones, Robert
    L. Stebbins
Additional Photography: Maxine Thompson,
    Steven Spangler, Dr. Robert Norton
Photographic Assistant: Richard B. Ray
Cover Photo: Michael Landis

For H.P. Books:

Publishers: Bill and Helen Fisher
Executive Editor: Carl Shipman
Editorial Director: Rick Bailey
Editor: Scott Millard

ISBN: 0-89586-078-3
Library of Congress
Catalog Card Number: 81-82134
©1981 Fisher Publishing, Inc.   Printed in USA

Published by H.P. Books
P.O. Box 5367, Tucson, AZ 85703
(602) 888-2150

Fruit Gardening in the West   3

Growing Fruit, Berries and Nuts   23

Which Fruit, Berry or Nut?   73

Fruit Gardening in the West

Fruit gardeners in the western United States share an activity that is both rich in tradition and refreshingly new. Many of their gardening techniques are centuries old, handed down from Spanish missionaries who were the first to realize the exciting potential of western climates, soils and waters. The great migration of easterners who followed these missionaries found the West full of opportunity but remarkably different from their homeland. Many of their time-honored horticultural practices had to be altered. Western fruit growing became a science of its own, constantly more exciting and ever more localized.

Today, from the arid Southwest to the moist Pacific Northwest, commercial orchards and home gardens produce an incredible amount of fruit. No place in the world supports such a variety and abundance. The West truly is the Mecca of the fruit grower.

As thousands of Western gardeners can attest, growing fruit at home can be very satisfying. Can you think of anything more flavorful than a peach or apple picked at peak ripeness from a tree in your own back yard? There's special satisfaction in knowing that you've chosen one of the finest-tasting varieties and nurtured it faithfully from a young tree to bearing age. Nothing from the supermarket tastes as fresh or pleases the palate as fruit you've carefully grown yourself.

LET YOUR GARDEN DO MORE FOR YOU

Taste isn't the only pleasure in fruit gardening. Many fruit plants are as beautiful as they are bountiful. Spring blossoms of apricots and plums are as colorful and fragrant as any ornamental. Cooling shade from a pecan or walnut tree is as pleasant as the best ash or sycamore. It makes sense to take advantage of these ornamental edibles. Why not grow versatile, attractive plants that give you an abundant harvest?

This is all part of a new philosophy in gardening: *Let your garden do more for you.* Realize the potential of your garden space or landscape. With proper planning and

selection, anyone can grow practical, productive, fruit-bearing trees or plants. The idea of gardening efficiency is an underlying philosophy in this book. Information contained here will help you plan and establish a more beautiful, rewarding and productive garden—no matter where you live in the West.

TRIED AND PROVEN INFORMATION

Material in this book has its inspiration in the pioneering work of Reid M. Brooks and Claron O. Hesse. Their understanding of western climates and appreciation of the needs of the home gardener provide the foundation for much of the information available on growing fruit in the West.

This book also benefits greatly from the work of hundreds of university experts, breeders and extension agents. They have expanded our knowledge of horticulture and helped home gardeners achieve success. Progressive nurseries have also contributed much to the home fruit grower by offering plants that produce fruit of superior quality and flavor. Without the willingness of breeders, agents and nurseries to share the most up-to-date information on varietal introduction, cultural practices and climate adaptation, this book would not have been possible.

IMPORTANCE OF ADAPTATION

Westerners can grow such a wonderful range of fruit because there are so many different climates. However, each fruit has its own climatic requirements. Each area of the West will not be able to grow all the fruit described in these pages. Choosing fruit types and varieties that are adapted to your area is the first step in successful fruit culture. This is an important consideration and a major point of emphasis throughout this book.

'Shiro' Japanese plum

Left: Nothing surpasses the juicy flavor of fruit fresh from the tree. Stand back and enjoy.

Climate and Fruit Behavior

Climates exist on large and small scales. The 19 western fruit zones described in this chapter represent large climate differences. These differences are determined by many factors such as elevation, latitude, longitude, mountain ranges, sunshine, rainfall and large bodies of water. Climate zones are the basis for variety recommendations in this book. Use the information given for your climate zone as a general guide to your fruit gardening.

MICROCLIMATES

On a small scale, climates vary in your own back yard. *Microclimates* are small climates that differ from the general surrounding climate. Understanding and using these microclimates are the first steps toward growing fruit not normally recommended for your climate zone. Using microclimates to the best advantage allows you to beat the odds against success dictated by large, unchangeable climate factors.

You experience different microclimates with nearly every step you take outdoors. Bright glare reflecting from a white wall, cool shade of a large tree, moist wind blowing off a small lake—these are factors that influence climates of small areas. Such microclimates can differ dramatically from the general climate within a large zone.

THE SUN AND MICROCLIMATES

By far the greatest factor influencing microclimates is *solar radiation* from the sun. You can manipulate the sun's rays to benefit your fruit trees and other garden plants. But first you need to understand the basic principles of *insolation*, *absorption* and *reflection*.

Briefly, *insolation* refers to solar energy's penetration of the earth's atmosphere as heat and light rays or radiation. *Absorption* refers to heat retained by materials struck by radiation. *Reflection* refers to radiation bouncing off of materials.

Radiation and absorption—Radiation comes in two forms: short waves and long waves. Radiation travels from the sun in the form of short waves. These waves do not heat the atmosphere, but are absorbed or reflected in varying degrees by all materials they hit. These include soil, plastic, foliage, canvas and water. Consider the percentages of heat absorbed by the substances shown on page 8.

At night, short waves absorbed by materials during the day are reradiated as long waves. Long waves differ from short waves in that they warm the atmosphere.

During daylight, absorption of short waves is greater than reradiation of long waves. The amount of absorption depends on the density and color of the object. A white wall will *reflect* more radiation, which can then be absorbed by other objects. Trees which have high heat requirements, such as grapefruit or peach, benefit from this reflection. A dark wall will *absorb* more radiation. After sunset, radiation of long waves is greater than solar radiation. The dark wall, which has absorbed more short waves than the white wall, will reradiate more warmth at night.

A straw mulch will reflect much of the sun's heat. Knowledgeable gardeners remove the mulch in spring to allow the sun's rays to warm the soil. In summer they replace the mulch to cool the soil.

Trapping reradiation—On a clear, still night, reradiated heat escapes directly into the atmosphere and is lost. Under these conditions enough heat can be lost to cause a *radiation frost*. Radiation frosts are very common in the West. Another type of frost, the *freeze frost*, occurs when masses of arctic air move into an area. This type of frost is common in the colder regions of the West.

Cloud cover creates a canopy that prevents reradiated heat from escaping and usually prevents radiation frosts.

The *greenhouse effect* can be used for cold protection or to provide additional heat. It occurs because short-wave radiation can pass through glass or plastic but long-wave radiation cannot. A structure covered with glass or plastic allows short waves from the sun to enter. Short waves are trapped through absorption or through reradiation by long waves. The result is that the inside temperature becomes higher than the outside temperature.

There are many ways to trap reradiated heat at night to avoid cold damage to plants. For example, heat can be contained under the overhang of a house or underneath a frame covered with plastic.

WATER

Water is the best heat storage reservoir. The ocean absorbs 95 percent of the insolation it receives. It also reradiates heat very slowly, so its day and night temperatures are more constant than those of faster-radiating land surfaces.

Water can be used several ways to increase night temperatures:
• Translucent jugs or plastic tubing filled with water and placed around fruit trees or in greenhouses will radiate heat at night and increase air temperatures.

• Planting next to large bodies of deep water tends to delay bloom in spring. It also moderates extremes of low winter temperatures.

• Watering before an anticipated frost will increase reradiated heat. Wet soil will absorb more heat than dry soil and therefore release more heat at night.

• Sprinklers turned on under trees as temperatures reach 32° F (0° C) will provide some protection against frost. This is because water releases heat as it cools. Also, sprinkling in spring cools the fruit buds and tends to delay bloom. This is a good frost-protection method useful to the home gardener. The University of California recommends placing a sprinkler on each side of a tree and applying water at a rate of a half-gallon per minute. Sprinklers should be turned on when temperatures drop to 32° F (0° C) and turned off when temperatures begin to rise. Sprinkling over trees can be an effective method of frost protection. Water should be applied in sufficient amounts so that ice is constantly forming. Do not apply too much water or the tree will be damaged by the weight of the ice.

Because water absorbs heat when it evaporates, it can also be used for cooling in warm weather. Sprinklers on the windward side of a hedge or screen cool the opposite side.

EXPOSURES CHANGE WITH SEASONS

A walk around your home will give you some insight into the importance of *exposure*. Exposure is the direction—east, west, north or south—that an object faces.

As you walk around the house, you see that the north side receives little sunlight. Depending on the season, it is probably cool and moist the entire day. The west and south sides receive the warmest afternoon sun. The east side receives sunlight in the morning and is shaded during the hottest part of the day.

A similar situation exists with hillsides on opposite sides of valleys. North-facing slopes are generally cooler and wetter than south-facing slopes.

All of this relates to the amount of heat absorbed through direct exposure to the sun. Exposure also influences plant adaptation. A cool, moist spot may be ideal for apples but terrible for grapefruit or figs. Conversely, a south-facing slope may be too hot for apples but will sweeten grapefruit and figs to perfection.

Exposure also changes with the seasons. As the illustration on page 9 shows, the path of the sun changes from summer to winter. A sunny location in summer may be completely shaded in winter.

It takes time to locate the coldest and warmest spots in the garden. Once they are discovered, you can use them to help place your plants correctly.

FROST PROTECTION

Long-time gardeners say they can smell a frost coming. Although you may doubt this, clear winter skies and crisp, still air are reliable signs that a frost can be expected.

Planting frost-tender fruit trees next to dark-colored, south-facing walls that reradiate heat at night goes a long way in providing frost protection. Planting under overhangs or awnings also allows plants to take advantage of trapped, reradiated heat.

'Golden Delicious' apple trained in espalier fashion takes advantage of a warm microclimate. Sunny, light-colored wall reflects heat and increases temperature to benefit tree.

For a small plant, additional protection can be provided. Build a stout wooden frame around the plant and cover the frame with burlap or clear plastic. Be sure the foliage doesn't touch the covering or it will be damaged by the cold. Burning a 150-watt bulb inside the cover will add substantially to the trapped, reradiated heat. Various heaters, such as return-stack heaters that burn diesel oil or room heaters that burn coal oil, can be set among frost-tender trees. These heaters are more feasible with commercial plantings, but gardeners have been known to go a long way to save their valued fruit trees.

Young trees are especially sensitive to cold damage. Insulate tender trunks with several layers of folded newspaper or similar protective material.

COLD AIR TRAVELS LIKE WATER

Because cold air is heavier and denser than warm air, it flows like water down gulleys and valleys. It dams up behind obstacles and settles in low spots. Because of this, plants in valley floors and low spots may suffer from heavy frosts. Sloping land along sides of valleys where cold air can drain away may be frost-free. Such areas above cold valley floors yet below colder, high elevations are sometimes referred to as *thermal belts*. For a thermal belt to be effective, it should be at least 100 feet above the nearest low ground where cold can settle.

If you are worried that your plants may suffer frost

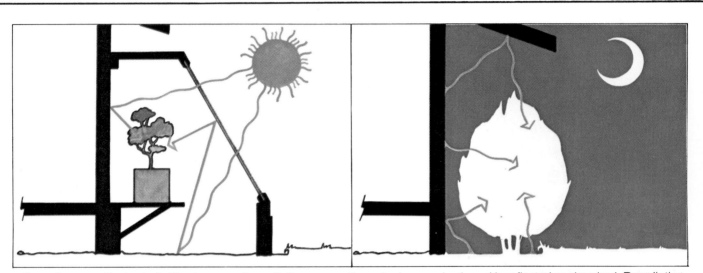

Greenhouse effect—Left: Short-wave solar radiation passes through glass or plastic and is reflected or absorbed. Reradiation by long waves cannot pass through glass or plastic. Trapped long waves heat the air and provide frost protection. Right: Planting next to walls that reradiate heat at night and under overhangs that trap reradiated heat provide some frost protection.

Cold air travels like water—Cold air flows down and away from sloping land, damming up behind objects and settling in low spots. Plant frost-sensitive fruit on sloping land where cold air will drain away.

damage, avoid planting in low spots. If you fear trapping cold air in corners or walled-in yards, simply open gates or provide air drainage through plantings so cold air will flow away. If you live on a hillside, planting early-blooming varieties at the top of the hill and late-blooming varieties at the bottom decreases the likelihood of frost damage.

VULNERABILITY TO FROST

Late-spring frosts are particularly damaging to certain deciduous fruit trees. Frosts may limit where these trees can be grown successfully. As spring advances, vulnerability to frost increases while the likelihood of frost decreases. Apple blossoms, for example, are damaged at 27° to 25° F (about −3° C) when they are closed but beginning to swell. During bloom they are damaged at 29° to 28° F (about −2° C). After petals fall, very small fruit are damaged at 28° to 30° F (about −1° C). Each stage is illustrated on pages 42 and 43. Using late-blooming varieties helps avoid spring frost damage.

Evergreen fruit trees usually begin to grow slowly as winter approaches. During this period, trees gradually become acclimated to cooler temperatures and are less susceptible to cold damage. Excess fertilizer and water in late summer and fall can cause growth flushes of frost-sensitive foliage at a time when frosts are most likely. Withhold late summer watering and fertilizing to induce dormancy where early fall frosts are a problem.

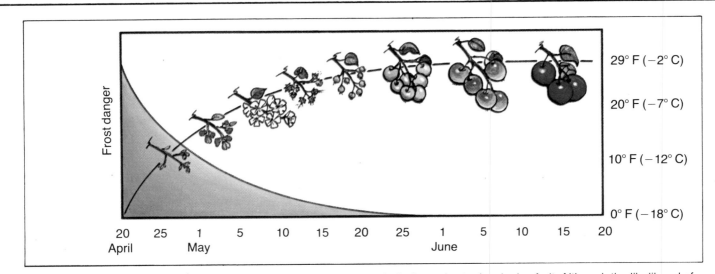

Vulnerability to cold temperatures—Late-spring frosts are particularly damaging to developing fruit. Although the likelihood of frost decreases as spring advances, the fruit's susceptibility to damage by cold temperatures increases.

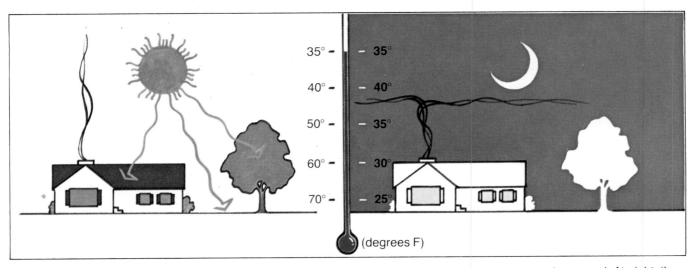

Inversion layer—During the daylight hours when solar radiation is at its peak, the warmest air is near the ground. At night, the reverse is true. Warm air rises, accumulating in an inversion layer some distance above the ground. Cold air settles in low spots.

LIVING WITH THE WIND

Strong winds can dry foliage, damage fruit and decrease air temperatures. Wind protection is often the key to success in many coastal and desert regions.

The best type of wind protection is one that *slows* wind rather than *stops* it. When wind hits a solid, impenetrable object, it tumbles over, swirls and continues. The turbulence caused as it passes often does more damage than the unobstructed wind.

Lattice fences, vines on trellises, screens, hedges and trees allow some wind to pass through or redirect it without severe turbulence. These kinds of windbreaks also allow good ventilation to help prevent mildews.

HEAT AND SUNBURN DAMAGE

Too much heat and very strong sunlight can be as much a problem as not enough. Protection against sunburn is particularly important for bark of young trees that has been exposed through pruning. White latex paint or a protective wrap helps avoid sunburn. Nursery shade cloth or lath will help diffuse the burning rays of the sun. More information on sunburn can be found on page 24.

HEAT

Important fruit qualities are directly related to available heat. Many nuts will not properly fill their shells

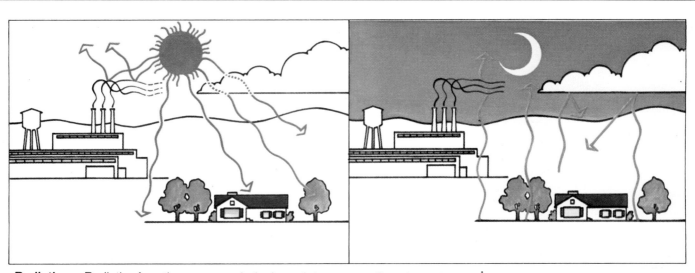

Radiation—Radiation from the sun comes in the form of short waves. On a clear, winter night, reradiation escapes directly into the atmosphere, often causing a *radiation frost*. On cloudy nights, reradiation is trapped by clouds and frosts are unlikely.

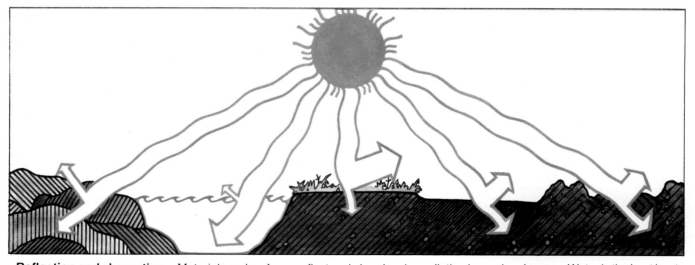

Reflection and absorption—Materials and surfaces reflect and absorb solar radiation in varying degrees. Water is the best heat reservoir, storing 95 percent of the radiation received. Radiation stored during the day is released as heat at night and can provide valuable frost protection.

without high summer heat. Sweetness and ability to ripen properly are also heat related with many fruit. For example, pink grapefruit will only develop its characteristic color and sweetness when grown in hot climates.

Commercial fruit growers pay close attention to heat requirements. Growers who plant orchards in areas where these requirements are met precisely are rewarded with the highest-quality fruit. The same is true for home gardeners.

The principal areas for apple production have average temperatures of 65° to 75° F (19° to 24° C). Areas where the mean temperature ranges above 75° F (24° C) are less adapted to apple production.

The best 'Bartlett' pear districts in the western states have temperatures slightly higher than those considered best for apples. Winter pear varieties will perform well where summer weather is much cooler than required for 'Bartlett'.

Peaches are better adapted to warmer conditons than apples. Peaches grown in regions having mean summer temperatures as low as 65° F (19° C) are usually not as high quality as those grown in warmer regions. Excellent fruit production and quality are obtained in some sections having mean summer temperatures above 75° F (24° C). Today, most of the cling peaches produced in California are grown in regions having high growing-season temperatures.

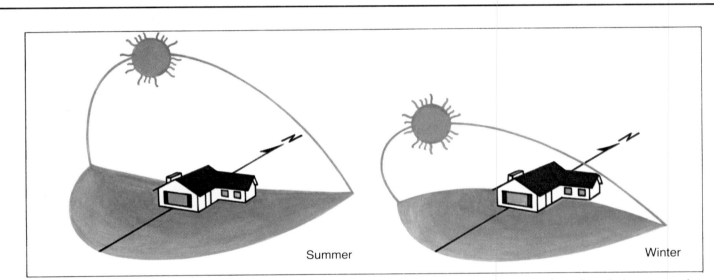

Exposures change with the season—Angle and exposure of the sun change with the seasons. Locations that are sunny in summer may be shady in winter. Keep that in mind when choosing a planting site.

Frost protection—Left: Water is an excellent heat reservoir. It stores radiation during the day and then releases it gradually as heat at night. Right: Plastic covers trap reradiated heat and are excellent for frost protection. An electric light placed under the cover provides additional warmth.

IMPORTANCE OF CHILLING

Exposure to 600 to 1,000 hours of temperatures below 45° F (7° C) is necessary to fully break the rest period of many deciduous fruit. This is known as a tree's *chilling requirement.* If trees are not exposed to sufficient cold, buds do not open or open slowly and unevenly in the spring. Blossom buds of most fruit require slightly less cold than leaf buds. Frequently, blossom buds in southern latitudes will open before leaf buds begin to grow. Unless the leaf system develops shortly after blossoms open, fruit fails to set due to lack of food supply from the leaves.

CHILLING REQUIREMENTS

Here are the numbers of hours required for chilling common deciduous fruit. Fruit varieties of many species are available that require less than normal amounts of chilling. Plant low-chill types where winter chilling is insufficient.

Fruit	Number of hours below 45°F (7°C)
Almond	300 to 500
Apple	900 to 1,000
Apricot	350 to 900
Asian pear	500 to 600
Blackberry	200 to 600
Blueberry	700 to 1,200
Crabapple	300 to 500
European pear	600 to 900
European plum	700 to 1,000
Fig	100 to 350
Filbert	800 to 1,200
Grape	100 to 400
Japanese plum	500 to 900
Peach and nectarine	600 to 900
Pecan	600 to 900
Persimmon	100 to 400
Quince	100 to 450
Raspberry	800 to 1,700
Sour cherry	800 to 1,200
Sweet cherry	800 to 1,200
Walnut	500 to 1,000

COLD TOLERANCE

The most cold-tender part of the tree during the dormant season is the root system. Fortunately, the soil protects the roots so that root injury occurs less frequently than injury to tops of trees. Grass sod, mulch or a heavy cover crop reduces cold penetration. A heavy snow cover is usually sufficient to prevent root injury. In moderately clay-type soils well supplied with moisture, penetration of cold to the root zone is much less rapid than in more open, drier soils.

Trees gradually exposed to cold in autumn and early winter become *acclimated,* a process by which they gain an increased ability to withstand colder temperatures. Fruit tree species acclimate at different rates and have varying temperature ranges they can withstand when fully acclimated.

How fast the temperature falls is at least as important as the lowest temperature reached in determining whether cold damage will occur.

Apples, sour cherries and American plums, when fully acclimated, usually withstand temperatures as low as −30° F (−34° C) without severe injury. Pears, sweet cherries and Japanese and European plums usually tolerate temperatures to −20° F (−29° C). Peaches and apricots are likely to be injured at −15° F (−26° C). Fruit buds of all these fruit may be injured at temperatures somewhat above the limits for severe tree injury. Large differences in hardiness also exist between varieties within a species.

CLIMATE STATISTICS

In defining fruit-growing zones, several climate factors have to be considered. No one factor creates a climate. For example, the growing season in Seattle in western Washington is 255 days. This is the number of days between the average last frost in spring and first frost in fall. Prosser in eastern Washington has a growing season of 157 days. However, Prosser has 2,427 *accumulated heat units.* This is defined as accumulated mean temperatures above 50° F (10° C), multiplied by the number of days per month—April 1 through October 31. Using the same formula, Seattle has 1,882 heat units. Some fruit varieties require more than 1,882 heat units and will not reach maturity in Seattle, even though the growing season is longer than in Prosser.

The percentage of sunny days during the growing season greatly influences fruit adaptation. Freestone peaches in eastern Washington are much sweeter than peaches in western Washington. This is because western Washington has more cloudy days. The percentage of sunshine in Wenatchee, for example, is 80 percent, while in Seattle it is 63 percent.

Climate of the States, prepared by officials of the National Oceanic and Atmospheric Administration, U.S. Department of Commerce, was used as the source for the listings.

When statistics in *Climate of the States* were insufficient, we supplemented with *Climate and Man,* the USDA Yearbook of Agriculture, 1941. The growing seasons it lists are often longer than those listed in *Climate of the States* due to the longer recording period.

GROWING SEASONS MAP

The map of growing seasons on the opposite page is provided as supplemental information to the fruit-growing zones discussed on pages 12 to 21. As previously mentioned, many other factors are involved in defining fruit-growing zones. But length of growing season is still useful in comparing differences between zones and even within zones. Success or failure with many fruit can be predicted by studying this map and the detailed information that follows it.

GROWING SEASONS IN THE WEST

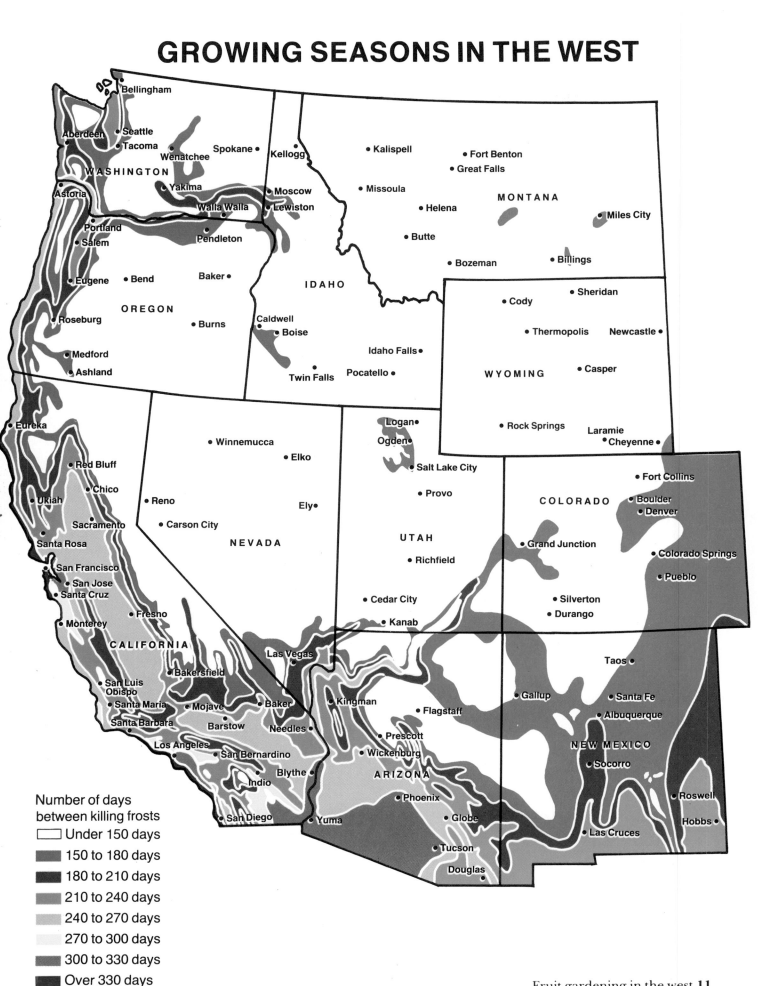

Number of days between killing frosts

- Under 150 days
- 150 to 180 days
- 180 to 210 days
- 210 to 240 days
- 240 to 270 days
- 270 to 300 days
- 300 to 330 days
- Over 330 days

Western Fruit Zones

ZONE 1
Coldest Areas of the West
Less than 150 days growing season

The severity of winter cold may differ drastically in a very small area in Zone 1. Temperatures are modified by slopes, air flow, elevation, latitude and precipitation. The climate of Zone 1 can become the climate of Zone 2 if microclimates are used wisely. See page 4. Most fruit growers in this zone face a growing season of less than 150 days. But a few feet in elevation may account for weeks of frost-free days in many localities. For example, Clarkston, Washington, and Lewiston, Idaho, are located on opposite sides of the Snake River. The weather station in Clarkston Heights reports 158 frost-free days. The station at Lewiston records 179 frost-free days. This is a difference of 21 days in growing seasons within a few miles.

Winter temperatures at Pendleton in northeast Oregon permit growth of a wide range of deciduous fruit and berries. The growing season is 163 days. Climate is far different in central Oregon. County Extension Agent Marvin M. Young writes: "Central Oregon has a very short growing season. It averages from 95 to 100 days in the Madras area, 80 to 90 days in Redmond and Prineville, 80 days or less in Bend. The Tumalo-Sisters area may range from 75 to 80 days, depending on location and closeness to the Cascade Range. Areas south of Bend to LaPine and higher elevations have progressively shorter seasons. Frosts can occur any day of the year.

"In most cases apple, pear, plum, cherry, peach, apricot and other species will survive but often fail to bear fruit.

"Growers in these areas have developed some commonly held probabilities for fruit production:

Apples: once every 4 to 5 years.
Pears: once every 5 to 6 years.
Pie (sour) cherries: most years a partial crop, occasional failure.
Sweet cherries: generally unsuccessful.
Peaches: occasional partial crop. Not dependable.
Wild plums: 2 out of 3 years.
Apricots: unsuccessful.
Strawberries: very successful.
Raspberries: successful.
Blackberries: fairly successful.
Blueberries: fairly successful with special care.

"There can be striking climatic variations within short distances in central Oregon. Air currents, canyon walls and rock outcroppings create microclimates. Some homeowners will have nearly year-round production of some fruit such as apples, while their neighbor may experience failure only a short distance away."

Thomas Bunch, county extension agent at Prineville, Oregon, writes: "We experience freezing temperatures generally every month of the year. It is not uncommon for temperatures to go below 25° F (−5° C) in the last week of June. For example, peach trees produce approximately 12 peaches once every 10 years."

Areas where the growing season is less than 150 days are placed in Zone 1. Zone 2 encompasses area where the growing season is 151 to 180 days. Realize any growing season is an estimate and varies from shorter to longer year to year. Estimates of growing season are accurate roughly 50 percent of the time.

In the climate statistics listed on these 2 pages, many growing seasons are borderline between Zones 1 and 2.

City	Elevation (feet)	Extreme Low	Years of Record	Last Spring Frost	First Fall Frost	Growing Season (days)	% July Sun
Billings, MT	3,567	−19° F (−28° C)	43	May 15	Sep. 24	132	78
Casper, WY	5,338	−41° F (−40° C)	40	May 18	Sep. 25	130	72
Cheyenne, WY	6,126	−38° F (−39° C)	103	May 20	Sep. 27	130	68
Helena, MT	3,828	−42° F (−41° C)	98	May 12	Sep. 23	134	79
Moscow, ID	2,660	−30° F (−34° C)	82	May 12	Sep. 6	117	89
Pocatello, ID	4,444	−28° F (−33° C)	39	May 10	Sep. 29	142	76
Provo, UT	4,470	−35° F (−37° C)	67	May 20	Sep. 23	126	83
Pueblo, CO	4,639	−27° F (−33° C)	23	Apr. 28	Oct. 10	155	78
Reno, NV	4,404	−19° F (−28° C)	90	May 14	Oct. 2	141	92
Twin Falls, ID	3,960	−30° F (−34° C)	53	May 13	Sep. 23	113	83

ZONE 2
Eastern Washington and Mild Winter Areas of Oregon, Idaho, Utah, Colorado and Inland British Columbia
150 to 180 days growing season

This zone includes favorite fruit-growing regions in the Intermountain and Rocky Mountain areas. Most have growing seasons between 150 and 180 days long. In eastern Washington the influence of the Columbia and Snake Rivers is most pronounced in the Wenatchee-Okanogan areas. The warming influence of the Columbia River allows fruit production in areas close to the river.

City	Elevation (feet)	Extreme Low	Years of Record	Last Spring Frost	First Fall Frost	Growing Season (days)	% July Sun
Boise, ID	2,838	−28° F (−33° C)	38	May 6	Oct. 12	159	88
Denver, CO	5,283	−28° F (−33° C)	43	May 3	Oct. 16	166	71
Ellensberg, WA	1,480	−31° F (−35° C)	78	May 4	Sep. 28	147	70
Lewiston, WY	1,413	**	31	Apr. 21	Oct. 17	179	77
Logan, UT	4,608	−25° F (−32° C)	26	May 3	Oct. 15	165	76
Pendleton, OR	1,487	−25° F (−32° C)	37	Apr. 27	Oct. 8	163	81
Salt Lake City, UT	4,222	−20° F (−29° C)	49	Apr. 12	Nov. 1	202	84
Spokane, WA	2,349	−30° F (−34° C)	96	Apr. 25	Oct. 11	169	80
Summerland, BC	1,500	14° F (−27° C)	65	Apr. 25	Oct. 19	176	**
Wenatchee, WA	1,229	−29° F (−34° C)	18	Apr. 14	Oct. 19	188	80
Yakima, WA	1,064	−24° F (−31° C)	68	Apr. 21	Oct. 15	177	67

**Data not available.

You can see that eastern Washington is a land of sunshine compared to western Washington and western Oregon, Zones 3 and 4. The concord grape grows beautifully here, but not so west of the Cascade Range. Apples reach perfection in this climate. This is the land of Washington apples, especially red 'Delicious' and 'Golden Delicious'. Freestone peaches are also much sweeter than peaches in Zone 3. Spring frost is a frequent hazard at lower elevations. Orchards are located on mesas above the valley floors to avoid these frosts.

Although the growing season is longer in Zone 3 than in Zone 2, it lacks the sunshine and heat of Zone 2.

Note the accumulated heat units in central Washington compared to that of western Washington. See page 10 for a definition of heat units.

South Central Washington	Elevation (feet)	Total Heat Units	Growing Season (days)
Hanford	773	3,186	175
Kennewick	392	3,118	187
Kennewick (10 miles southwest)	1,500	2,630	183
Pasco	608	3,199	206
Prosser	840	2,427	157
Walla Walla Airport	1,170	2,853	202
Wenatchee Airport	1,229	2,751	187

Western Washington	Elevation (feet)	Total Heat Units	Growing Season (days)
Aberdeen	12	1,360	197
Buckley	685	1,644	198
Centralia	185	2,035	182
Everett	99	1,586	209
Mount Vernon	14	1,528	209
Olympia Airport	190	1,693	**
Puyallup	50	1,770	160
Seattle-Tacoma Airport	386	1,882	233

ZONE 3
Western Washington and Coastal British Columbia

This is the land of rhododendrons, blueberries and daffodils. It is also the land of high relative humidity, which allows fruit diseases to flourish. Robert Norton of Western Washington Research Station of Mt. Vernon assesses Zone 3: "The area has a long, frost-free season and winter injury is rare. Moderate summer temperatures promote good fruit growth. There is usually enough rain for established trees, yet summers are relatively dry.

"Major insect pests such as codling moth that commonly infest other fruit-growing areas may not require routine control here. Conversely, diseases cannot be ignored. Apple and pear scab, mildew, brown rot of stone fruit and botrytis fruit rot in berries can destroy fruit crops any time from bloom to harvest. Some of these can be controlled by good cultural practices and proper variety selection."

This book will help you with proper culture and selecting the right fruit varieties. But in this zone pay particular attention to soil drainage. Where drainage is restricted, plant on a mound or in a raised-box frame. Never allow water to stand around the crown of a tree. This can cause crown rot.

ZONE 3 (Continued)

City	Elevation (feet)	Extreme Low	Years of Record	Last Spring Frost	First Fall Frost	Growing Season (days)	% July Sun
Bellingham, WA	149	2° F (−17° C)	64	May 8	Oct. 5	150	59
Centralia, WA	185	−16° F (−27° C)	77	Apr. 24	Oct. 23	182	65
Olympia, WA	192	−2° F (−19° C)	36	May 8	Oct. 15	160	62
Seattle, WA	95	3° F (−16° C)	53	Mar. 23	Nov. 18	240	63
*Tacoma, WA	267	7° F (−14° C)	87	Mar. 13	Nov. 18	250	67
Vancouver, BC	10	2° F (−18° C)	45	Apr. 2	Oct. 28	208	63
Victoria, BC	60	3° F (−16° C)	23	Apr. 10	Oct. 31	203	67

*Freeze data from *Climate and Man*.
**Data not available.

ZONE 4
Western Oregon, Willamette Valley and Coastal Areas

The great Willamette Valley and its foothills are famous nursery growing grounds for ornamental trees, shrubs and rhododendrons. It is where the filbert grows to perfection. Most blackberry breeding in the United States is done at Corvallis. Many cherry varieties were introduced in the Portland area at the time the first settlers arrived.

The Oregon coast is much cooler and rainier than the Willamette Valley. Rains in April and May greatly decrease fruit set and increase the danger of fungal and bacterial diseases. On the coast heat units are insufficient in summer to mature many fruit varieties.

Frost is seldom a hazard in the famous, fruit-growing valleys of western Oregon. The mid-Columbian area has a climate intermediate between eastern and western Oregon.

City	Elevation (feet)	Extreme Low	Years of Record	Last Spring Frost	First Fall Frost	Growing Season (days)	% July Sun
Corvallis, OR	255	−14° F (−25° C)	85	Apr. 12	Oct. 31	202	58
Eugene, OR	364	−4° F (−20° C)	38	Apr. 9	Oct. 31	204	60
Portland, OR	21	−2° F (−19° C)	37	Feb. 25	Dec. 1	279	69
Salem, OR	195	−6° F (−21° C)	84	Apr. 14	Oct. 27	197	75

ZONE 5
Digger Pine Belt

This zone includes the intermediate 1,500 to 2,500-foot elevations of the western slope of the Sierra Nevadas and the foothills of California's coastal ranges.

The Digger Pine Belt covers a wide range of climates. It is named for the scraggly Digger pine, which makes its home in these areas. It could be further subdivided into eastern and western halves on either side of the central valleys. The northern boundary is above Redding and the southern boundary is above Bakersfield.

City	Elevation (feet)	Extreme Low	Years of Record	Last Spring Frost	First Fall Frost	Growing Season (days)	% July Sun
Clearlake, CA	1,360	19° F (−7° C)	19	Apr. 10	Oct. 31	204	**
*Nevada City, CA	2,600	−1° F (−18° C)	84	May 19	Oct. 7	141	80
Placerville, CA	2,755	8° F (−13° C)	87	Apr. 28	Oct. 27	182	78
Sonora, CA	1,749	−14° F (−10° C)	69	Apr. 4	Nov. 17	227	85
Weaverville, CA	2,050	−5° F (−20° C)	64	May 27	Sep. 26	122	**
Yreka, CA	2,625	**	74	May 18	Oct. 8	143	**

*Freeze data from *Climate and Man*.

**Data not available.

The fruit gardener in Zone 5 lives in an intermediate area between the hot, central valleys of California and colder, high elevations. On the western side of this zone there is occasional ocean influence.

A definite winter season exists here along with hot summers, which in some places rival the hot weather of the central valleys. Most fruit and nuts produce well, yet late spring frosts may damage the earliest-blooming and earliest-leafing varieties. Above 1,500 feet elevation, in flat terrain where cold air settles, spring frosts may make it difficult to grow almonds and apricots. At higher elevations, other fruit such as grapes and walnuts may be damaged. Apples and pears develop better quality in these areas than in Zone 9 due to colder nights during the growing season.

Although winters are colder at higher elevations, there is also less heat during summer. Pecans will grow above 1,500 feet elevation but the nuts may not fill completely. Chestnuts or filberts should be grown instead.

As you move eastward away from the coastal ranges of this zone, conditions become more arid. Disease problems are less troublesome. But some pests, such as mites, prefer the drier weather.

In many areas, the tender foliage of young fruit plantings will need protection against deer. Gophers and rabbits can also cause damage, especially in isolated, unfenced homesites.

ZONE 6
Northwest Coastal California

In this zone there are many climates—depending on elevation, slope of the land, exposure and distance from the ocean. This is also an area where many types of fruit are grown successfully. It is 'Gravenstein' apple country. You can travel the Gravenstein Highway (Highway 116) from Sebastopol to the ocean and go through some of the finest cider and applesauce country in the world. You'll drive over the Sonoma Farm Trail, well-known for its variety of fruit. Nearby are small nurseries that carry an incredible array of small fruit, including raspberries, currants, gooseberries and even blueberries.

If you travel north on Highway 101, you'll see prime vineyards and some of the oldest wineries in the state.

City	Elevation (feet)	Extreme Low	Years of Record	Last Spring Frost	First Fall Frost	Growing Season (days)	% July Sun
Eureka, CA	60	20° F (−7° C)	91	Jan. 27	Dec. 9	338	52
Fort Bragg, CA	80	29° F (−2° C)	80	Feb. 26	Dec. 9	286	52
*Santa Rosa, CA	167	15° F (−9° C)	89	Apr. 10	Nov. 3	207	65
Ukiah, CA	623	12° F (−11° C)	84	Mar. 26	Nov. 6	225	70

*Freeze data from
Climate and Man.

Ocean influence diminishes as you travel eastward from the coast. It is a limiting factor with fruit that need a lot of heat. However, close to the coast, at elevations above the fog, some fruit can be grown that you wouldn't expect to do well. For instance, near Mendocino, you can find grapes growing on terraced hillsides within a mile of the coast.

The ocean influence does contribute to disease problems. Late-leafing walnuts, scab-resistant apples and mildew-resistant fruit are recommended. Apricots are usually unsuccessful, even in areas where they escape late spring frosts. They are severely plagued by brown rot, which thrives in wet spring weather. Bacterial canker is a real problem along the north coast. Cherry trees usually succumb to canker within five years. It is best to plant resistant varieties.

Low valley floors are very common sites for late spring frosts. The farther inland, the greater the problem. The difference in length of growing season between Eureka and Santa Rosa bears this out. Citrus, apricots, almonds, freestone peaches and nectarines should be planted at least 100 feet above the valley floors where air drainage is better.

ZONE 7
Northwest California with Diminishing Coastal Influence

This zone lies below the Digger Pine Belt and includes Napa, Sonoma and Anderson Valleys, as well as the area around Cloverdale.

In general, these regions are protected from direct ocean influence by mountain barriers. They have warmer summers than Zone 6, so diseases that prosper in moist, coastal air are less of a problem. Winters are colder than in Zone 6. The threat of spring frosts is evidenced by the number of wind machines and heaters that can be seen in the Napa Valley.

The University of California Viticultural Regions, see Grapes, page 145, define the climate changes as one moves from south to north in Zone 7. Napa, Sonoma and Oakville are in Viticulture Region 1, the coolest region. Their climates are cooled by the San Francisco Bay. Fog moderates summer temperatures and winters are not cold, averaging in the mid-40s° F (6° to 8° C).

As you move north up the Napa Valley, summers are warmer and winters colder. Rutherford and St. Helena are in warmer Viticulture Region 2. Calistoga, Cloverdale and Anderson Valley are in still-warmer Region 3. The following statistics show similar relationships:

City	Elevation (feet)	Extreme Low	Years of Record	Last Spring Frost	First Fall Frost	Growing Season (days)	% July Sun
Cloverdale, CA	320	17° F (−8° C)	75	Mar. 4	Nov. 25	266	72
Napa, CA	60	17° F (−8° C)	82	Mar. 14	Nov. 20	251	80
Petaluma, CA	16	28° F (−2° C)	64	Mar. 12	Nov. 20	253	80
St. Helena,* CA	1,780	11° F (−12° C)	70	Apr. 2	Nov. 3	215	75

*Angwin airport.

Fruit requiring high heat—table grapes, jujubes and late-season peaches and nectarines—should only be grown in the warmest sites of Viticultural Regions 1 and 2. Luckily, there is still plenty of winter chilling for apples and pears.

West and south-facing slopes will receive a great deal of heat, even close to Napa. With good air drainage they may be relatively frost-free. Northern and eastern slopes will be wetter and cooler, as evidenced by the greater number of Douglas fir and coastal redwoods.

St. Helena, Calistoga and especially Cloverdale are fine areas for growing hardy varieties of citrus. In fact, many old plantings of 'Washington' navel, grapefruit and Satsuma mandarin still line the streets.

Buckskin disease-resistant cherries and late-leafing walnuts are also recommended for this zone.

ZONE 8
The Many Climates of the San Francisco Bay

Anyone who lives in this area and listens to the nightly news knows the progressive increase in daytime temperatures from foggy San Francisco to sunny Walnut Creek and Livermore. In Livermore, the most easterly point of the Bay area, the climate is more similar to that of the central valleys than to San Francisco. It has a little less heat than the central valleys due to westerly winds and occasional fog, but summers are hot and many fruit are well adapted. The following temperatures dramatically illustrate the differences between cities in this zone.

San Francisco	Average Maximum Temperatures for July
Berkeley	68° F (20° C)
Livermore	91° F (33° C)
Oakland	71° F (22° C)
Palo Alto	78° F (25° C)
Richmond	69° F (20° C)
San Francisco	69° F (20° C)
San Mateo	79° F (26° C)

In coastal areas receiving ocean breezes, early and midseason fruit varieties are recommended. There is insufficient heat to ripen many late varieties. Bacterial and fungal diseases will be troublesome. In fact, some gardeners prune their apricots in summer to avoid bacterial infection, which tends to enter pruning wounds during the wet winter season.

In Berkeley, there is one foggy climate at the Bay level and a warmer, sunnier climate in the Berkeley Hills. In some areas of the hills there are thermal belts where frosts seldom occur. Many subtropicals can be grown in these areas, but deciduous fruit are restricted to low-chill varieties. The foggy areas near the Bay may actually receive more chilling.

Over the crest of the Berkeley Hills—the main obstacle to coastal fog—summer temperatures may jump 15° to 25° F (−10° to −5° C) in Lafayette, Walnut Creek or Livermore. Winter temperatures will also be colder. Site exposure plays an important role, but chilling is generally not a problem. Varieties with higher heat requirements are usually successful.

City	Elevation (feet)	Extreme Low	Years of Record	Last Spring Frost	First Fall Frost	Growing Season (days)	% July Sun
Berkeley, CA	345	25° F (−4° C)	91	—	—	365	**
Kentfield, CA	128	17° F (−8° C)	65	Mar. 10	Nov. 19	254	**
Livermore, CA	400	27° F (−3° C)	106	Mar. 18	Nov. 17	244	**
Oakland, CA	6	25° F (−4° C)	49	Jan. 28	Dec. 29	335	74
*San Francisco, CA	130	27° F (−3° C)	106	Jan. 7	Dec. 29	356	66

*Freeze data from *Climate and Man.*

**Data not available.

ZONE 9
Sacramento and San Joaquin Valleys of California

Name any deciduous fruit and you will find it growing in the great California central valleys and their foothills. Commercially, it is almonds in the Red Bluff-Chico areas, kiwifruit in Chico and peaches in Marysville and Yuba City. Figs are grown in Fresno, oranges in Porterville, olives in Corning and Orland and grapes in Lodi and Bakersfield. High summer temperatures bring these fruit and others to peak quality.

Along the sides of the valleys are areas with good air drainage that are practically frost-free. These areas are ideal for many tender fruit, especially citrus, which might be damaged on the colder valley floors.

Hot weather may pose minor problems in Zone 9. Many red apple varieties require cooler temperatures to develop their characteristic, deep red color. However, even with poor color, red apples will still have good flavor and texture. Yellow and green apples do very well in the central valleys.

Hot weather may also cause pit burn in 'Blenheim' apricots and cause cherries to double. Areas around the Sacramento River Delta are slightly cooler and better suited to varieties that prefer cooler weather.

Fireblight of pears is a problem in the northern and southern ends of the valleys. Rain and high spring temperatures in these regions are perfect for its development. Mites are very prolific in the central valleys.

Late-spring frosts can be a problem with almonds. In low-lying frost pockets, stick to late bloomers such as 'Mission' and 'Thompson'.

City	Elevation (feet)	Extreme Low	Years of Record	Last Spring Frost	First Fall Frost	Growing Season (days)	% July Sun
Bakersfield, CA	495	13° F (−10° C)	71	Feb. 11	Dec. 12	295	95
Chico, CA	185	11° F (−12° C)	108	Mar. 25	Nov. 11	321	96
Colusa, CA	50	14° F (−10° C)	72	Feb. 26	Nov. 20	267	96
Fresno, CA	328	17° F (−8° C)	90	Feb. 15	Nov. 27	285	96
Lindsay, CA	420	18° F (−8° C)	64	Mar. 18	Nov. 16	243	94
Marysville, CA	57	16° F (−9° C)	106	Feb. 13	Dec. 1	291	90
Merced, CA	153	16° F (−9° C)	104	Mar. 10	Nov. 16	251	97
Porterville, CA	383	18° F (−8° C)	89	Mar. 6	Nov. 29	268	94
Red Bluff, CA	342	17° F (−8° C)	99	Feb. 22	Nov. 26	227	96
Redding, CA	425	17° F (−8° C)	102	Feb. 24	Nov. 29	278	96
Sacramento, CA	84	16° F (−9° C)	84	Feb. 19	Nov. 28	282	97
Stockton, CA	22	17° F (−8° C)	22	Mar. 6	Nov. 18	257	97
Visalia, CA	325	13° F (−10° C)	88	Feb. 27	Nov. 29	275	94

ZONE 10
Santa Clara Valley and Fremont Area of California

A few years ago, the Santa Clara Valley boasted commercial crops of pears, apricots, prunes and cherries. Because of urbanization, only a few orchards remain. Now these diverse plantings of fruit exist mainly in home gardens.

In the foothills of Los Altos and Saratoga in the west and Mission San Jose in the east, citrus is grown without regard to hardiness. Many subtropicals thrive in the Santa Clara-San Jose areas—witnessed by many large, bearing avocados that were planted years ago. Still, there is sufficient chilling for most deciduous fruit.

There is less summer heat in this area than in either Zone 7 or 9. Compare these average July high temperatures of Fresno in Zone 9, St. Helena in Zone 7 and San Jose and Los Gatos in Zone 10:

Fresno	81° F	27° C
St. Helena	71° F	22° C
San Jose	82° F	28° C
Los Gatos	68° F	20° C

Fruit such as apricots, which grow best in mild weather, have better quality in Zone 10 than in the hotter central and coastal valleys. There is also less threat of frost, which can damage early-blooming varieties.

City	Elevation (feet)	Extreme Low	Years of Record	Last Spring Frost	First Fall Frost	Growing Season (days)	% July Sun
*Gilroy, CA	194	**	20	Mar. 31	Nov. 20	214	80
*Los Gatos, CA	365	21° F (−6° C)	91	Feb. 3	Dec. 16	316	72
*San Jose, CA	365	18° F (−8° C)	71	Feb. 10	Dec. 6	299	72
Santa Clara, CA	71	19° F (−7° C)	40	Feb. 18	Nov. 28	283	72

*Freeze data from *Climate and Man.*

**Data not available.

ZONE 11
Coastal and Inland Valleys of Central California

Many fruit that are now popular in California were introduced by Spanish missionaries in the 17th and 18th centuries. The mission gardens were testing grounds for every deciduous and evergreen fruit of Spain. Zone 11 originally had nine of these missions.

ZONE 11 (Continued)

Edward J. Wickson remarked in his book, *California Fruits* (10th edition): "It is of no little interest to ascertain how great a variety of fruits was grown in these mission orchards. Vancouver, in 1792, found a fine orchard at Santa Clara, with apple, peach, pear, apricot and fig trees, all thrifty and promising." He also describes at the Mission Santa Buena Ventura apples, pears, plums, figs, oranges, grapes, peaches and pomegranates.

In home gardens in this zone, fruit can be planted according to individual climates and microclimates. Commercially, apples are still grown in the Watsonville area, grapes in the Paso Robles area, and grapes and apples near San Luis Obispo.

Close to the coast, such as around Santa Cruz, disease problems are very serious in stone fruit. Apricots are difficult to grow. Peach leaf curl runs rampant due to constant reinfection. In general, early and mid-season varieties are most successful due to lack of heat later in the year. Conversely, some areas may not have enough chilling for many varieties of apple and cherry, so low-chill varieties are recommended.

Farther inland to areas such as Paso Robles, summers are much hotter and winters are colder. Climate begins to resemble that of the central valleys of Zone 9. San Juan Batista is usually the cut-off point for strong coastal influence. At high elevations spring frosts can be a problem.

The climate near San Luis Obispo is generally warmer than near Santa Cruz. As you drive from San Luis Obispo to the coast, avocados and tender citrus can be seen. Fruit that prefer cooler temperatures, such as pears, reach higher quality in Santa Cruz than in San Luis Obispo.

ZONE 12
Cool Winter Interior of Southern California

Southern California has very complex climate patterns. They are influenced by the ocean, periodically by the desert's Santa Ana winds, and by elevation.

In each zone, climate variations can be expected. If you live on a hillside facing south, you may be able to grow subtropicals, even in the coldest areas.

In the coldest areas of southern California and at all high elevations, deciduous fruit requiring winter chill can be grown. Climates may change drastically in a few miles as elevations vary from 100 feet to more than 2,000 feet. For example, the low-elevation climate of San Diego, Zone 14, permits the growth of many subtropical fruit. At Julian, Zone 12, a short distance from San Diego but at 3,000 feet elevation, apples are a featured fruit. Other upper-elevation apple zones in southern California include Yucaipa in the Riverside area and Lake Hughes north of Newhall. Warm air often drifts up from nearby deserts to cause early bloom in these mountain areas. This makes many fruit subject to spring frost damage.

In warmer areas, special low-chill varieties of apples, cherries, pears and peaches must be selected. Even these varieties are subject to delayed foliation. Flower buds bloom irregularly. Leaf buds begin growth irregularly and may not develop foliage until several weeks after the normal time. Following warm winters, such fruit trees will stagger into bloom and bear little if any fruit.

In establishing zones, we have listed cities with comparable temperatures and growing seasons.

City	Elevation (feet)	Extreme Low	Years of Record	Last Spring Frost	First Fall Frost	Growing Season (days)	% July Sun
Hollister, CA	280	15° F (−9° C)	40	Feb. 22	Nov. 28	279	**
Salinas, CA	85	18° F (−8° C)	40	Mar. 13	Nov. 30	262	60
*San Luis Obispo, CA	315	20° F (−7° C)	83	Jan. 30	Dec. 13	320	65
Santa Cruz, CA	130	20° F (−7° C)	105	Feb. 27	Dec. 3	279	**
Santa Maria, CA	254	24° F (−4° C)	35	Mar. 11	Dec. 5	269	**
Watsonville, CA	95	34° F (1° C)	71	Mar. 2	Nov. 21	267	**

*Freeze data from *Climate and Man.*

**Data not available.

City	Elevation (feet)	Extreme Low	Years of Record	Last Spring Frost	First Fall Frost	Growing Season (days)	% July Sun
Corona, CA	510	**	64	Mar. 6	Dec. 7	276	**
*Newhall, CA	1,243	10° F (−12° C)	16	Mar. 12	Nov. 8	241	**
Redlands, CA	1,318	18° F (−8° C)	85	Feb. 25	Dec. 7	285	**
San Jacinto, CA	1,535	7° F (−14° C)	83	Mar. 24	Nov. 12	233	**

*Freeze data from *Climate and Man.*

**Data not available.

ZONE 13
Warm Winter Interior of Southern California

Marine air and interior air alternately occupy this zone. One day may be foggy and cool, the next sunny and warm. Here are some climate statistics of cities in this zone:

City	Elevation (feet)	Extreme Low	Years of Record	Last Spring Frost	First Fall Frost	Growing Season (days)	% July Sun
Claremont, CA	1,201	19° F (−7° C)	83	Mar. 11	Dec. 7	271	**
*Los Angeles, CA	100	28° F (−2° C)	42	Jan. 3	Dec. 28	359	82
*Pasadena, CA	864	21° F (−6° C)	70	Feb. 3	Dec. 13	313	**
Riverside, CA	840	21° F (−6° C)	96	Mar. 10	Nov. 21	257	81
San Bernardino, CA	1,125	17° F (−8° C)	86	Mar. 14	Nov. 25	256	82

*Freeze data from Climate and Man.

**Data not available.

Desert influence is stronger in southern cities such as Riverside and San Bernardino. The average, maximum temperature in Riverside in July is 96° F (35° C) compared to 89° F (32° C) in Pasadena. The average, maximum temperature in San Bernardino in July is 100.4° F (38° C).

Climates of Los Angeles and other cities in the Los Angeles basin are more dramatically moderated by the Pacific Ocean. Frost-free days are greater, but summer temperatures are lower.

Many gardens in this zone provide an ideal environment for all subtropicals. The exceptions are gardens not considered frost-free.

In this zone there is an average of 400 to 600 hours of chilling. There may be as many as 700 in a single year but fewer than 400 in a warm year. Deciduous fruit production is therefore unpredictable even with low-chill varieties. Cold troughs in inland valleys do provide more chilling.

ZONE 14
Subtropical Belt of Southern California

This zone is often within sight of the ocean. It stretches from the foothills above Gaviota through Saticoy and Camarillo in the Oxnard coastal plain and through Los Angeles proper and its low foothills. It extends south to Fallbrook, Vista, La Mesa and San Diego.

This climate is made up of warm thermal belts bordered by cooler valleys and hilltops. Here we find the warmest, mildest winters north of the Mexican border. Accumulated chilling is usually too low for many deciduous fruit, but it is the best climate for subtropicals in the western United States.

Ocean air influences this climate most of the time. Proximity to the ocean is critical for many subtropicals. Farther inland there is more heat but a greater threat of frost.

City	Elevation (feet)	Extreme Low	Years of Record	Last Spring Frost	First Fall Frost	Growing Season (days)	% July Sun
Chula Vista, CA	9	**	55	—	—	365	**
La Mesa, CA	530	37° F (3° C)	43	—	—	365	**
San Diego, CA	13	25° F (4° C)	106	—	—	365	67
Santa Ana, CA	115	38° F (3° C)	61	—	—	365	79
Vista, CA	510	32° F (0° C)	15	—	—	365	**

**Data not available.

ZONE 15
Coastal Southern California

Zone 15 represents the mild, marine climates found on the beaches and coastal plains of southern California. Extending from Point Conception to the Mexican border, this climate always reflects ocean weather, except during the season of the hot, inland, Santa Ana winds.

Coastal climates vary depending on their wind protection, elevation and distance from the ocean. The many eucalyptus windbreaks near Ventura demonstrate the importance commercial citrus growers place on buffering cool, coastal winds. Windbreaks can change a cool climate that is ideal for lemons into a warmer climate suitable for 'Valencia' oranges. For the home gardener, this means that locating a variety on one side of the house or the other can make the difference between success and failure.

Zone 15 can become quite narrow in areas where coastal hills and bluffs extend nearly to the beach. These narrow strips are cut through by river drainage and bottomlands. They can have unusually cold winter weather when cold air drains down from coastal uplands. Avocado and tender citrus are often damaged when this occurs. This cold air does not occur frequently enough to provide necessary chilling for deciduous fruit.

Although Santa Barbara and Carpinteria are on the coast, their climate is influenced by the Channel Islands. These two cities exhibit more of an inland-type climate without cold winters.

Fruit selection in this temperate zone is limited to low-chill varieties. The moist, ocean air also encourages certain bacterial and fungal diseases. They are not usually as severe in southern California as along the central coast.

City	Elevation (feet)	Extreme Low	Years of Record	Last Spring Frost	First Fall Frost	Growing Season (days)	% July Sun
Laguna, CA	35	33° F (10° C)	46	—	—	365	**
Long Beach, CA	34	36° F (2° C)	19	—	—	365	**
Newport, CA	10	37° F (3° C)	55	—	—	365	**
Oceanside, CA	10	34° F (1° C)	25	—	—	365	**
San Diego, CA	13	25° F (−4° C)	106	—	—	365	79
Santa Barbara, CA	9	23° F (−5° C)	93	Jan. 27	Dec. 17	338	65
Santa Monica, CA	15	43° F (6° C)	39	—	—	365	**

**Data not available.

ZONE 16
Medium to High Deserts of California

There is no abrupt line dividing medium and high deserts of California. Consider the climate in the desert towns of Mojave, California City, China Lake, Lancaster and Palmdale, of which Lancaster is typical:

City	Elevation (feet)	Extreme Low	Years of Record	Last Spring Frost	First Fall Frost	Growing Season (days)	% July Sun
Lancaster, CA	2,355	23° F (5° C)	4	Mar. 31	Oct. 31	215	93

Lancaster's temperatures are lower than those for the intermediate deserts of Arizona, Zone 18. There is

enough winter cold in California's interior desert for practically all deciduous fruit. This is not always true for Zone 18.

Some of the elevations in the medium desert are as follows:

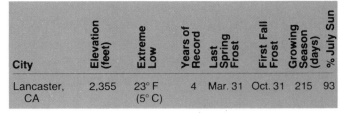

City	Elevation (feet)
Apple Valley	2,935
Barstow	2,105
Boron	2,410
Boulder City	2,525
California City	2,400-2,900
China Lake	2,300
Edwards AFB	2,300
Lancaster	2,355
Las Vegas	2,006
Mojave	2,787
Palmdale	2,549
Randsburg	3,530
Ridgecrest	2,300
Twentynine Palms	1,980
Victorville	2,858

Summer heat is high but nights are cooler than in the intermediate deserts of Arizona. Wind protection is essential in all desert areas. In isolated locations windbreaks are an important part of gardening. In March, April and May, winds exceeding 40 miles per hour can be expected. In a windy year there may be 12 to 14 days of such spring winds. August, September and October are quiet months.

The Antelope Valley is buffered from desert extremes by its proximity to the San Gabriel Mountains. Soils are also better there than in deserts to the east, where they tend to be more alkaline. Sometimes unusually warm spring weather in the Antelope Valley causes early bloom. When followed by cold weather, frost damage results.

ZONE 17
Low Deserts of California and Arizona

These deserts are subtropical. This zone includes Palm Springs, Borego, Indio, Brawley, Salton Sea, El Centro, Coachella, Palm Desert, Desert Hot Springs and Blythe in California. It also includes Yuma, Casa Grande and Phoenix in Arizona.

Some favorite fruit grown here are citrus, olives, grapes, figs, pecans, pomegranates, early peaches and dates. This zone is the home of the USDA Date and Citrus Experiment Station at Indio. Near Phoenix, in areas such as Sun City, citrus is widely used as a landscape plant.

Although this zone is subtropical in nature, it is quite

different from the coastal subtropical belt. High summer temperatures and rapid fluctuations in weather rule out many fruit that can be grown in Zone 14.

Spring winds are often a problem in the Palm Springs and Indio areas. They damage flowers and young fruit on deciduous and evergreen trees.

City	Elevation (feet)	Extreme Low	Years of Record	Last Spring Frost	First Fall Frost	Growing Season (days)	% July Sun
Blythe, CA	268	5° F (−15° C)	68	Feb. 2	Nov. 29	290	**
Brawley, CA	−100	19° F (−7° C)	68	Jan. 29	Dec. 20	314	**
Casa Grande, AZ	1,415	17° F (−8° C)	65	Mar. 8	Nov. 19	256	90
Indio, CA	11	13° F (−10° C)	99	Feb. 14	Dec. 3	292	**
Palm Springs, CA	425	18° F (−8° C)	79	Feb. 8	Dec. 6	301	90
Phoenix, AZ	1,117	16° F (−9° C)	41	Feb. 14	Dec. 6	295	94
Yuma, AZ	206	22° F (−5° C)	31	Jan. 13	Dec. 26	347	89

**Data not available.

ZONE 18
Intermediate Deserts of Arizona

This is the climate zone of Tucson, Wickenburg, Florence and Safford. It is characterized by hot summers, relatively mild winters and frequent winds. Tucson and Wickenburg have typical climate statistics:

City	Elevation (feet)	Extreme Low	Years of Record	Last Spring Frost	First Fall Frost	Growing Season (days)	% July Sun
Tucson, AZ	2,584	6° F (−14° C)	85	Mar. 15	Nov. 22	252	78
Wickenburg, AZ	2,095	11° F (−12° C)	67	Mar. 21	Nov. 18	242	**

**Data not available.

Although Tucson has more cold weather than Phoenix, it is not sufficient to chill most deciduous fruit. However, plums do well in this area and low-chill peaches and apricots are most satisfactory. Citrus, olives, dates, figs, grapes and strawberries are also grown.

In the interior areas of Arizona, commercial groves of pecans fill more than 13,600 acres, apricots 280 acres, pistachios 100 acres, and lemons, tangelos and tangerines more than 22,000 acres.

ZONE 19
High Elevations of Arizona and New Mexico

The University of Arizona Extension Service says this about the 3,000 to 4,500-foot elevations of Arizona and New Mexico: "At lower elevations, lack of winter chilling may cause erratic spring bloom and poor fruit set. At the upper end of the elevation scale, near 4,500 feet, spring frosts may damage bloom and small fruit of many varieties. Spring frost hazard varies by site and from season to season. Air drainage is the most important variable during potential frost periods."

The ideal elevation in this zone for most deciduous fruit is between 3,000 and 4,500 feet. Above that range you must plant late-blooming or bloom-hardy varieties, or have excellent air drainage to be successful with stone fruit.

Apples do well throughout the high elevations of Arizona and New Mexico. Above 6,000 feet annual crops on most fruit trees are not predictable. Peaches, pears, apricots and blackberries are not recommended at all above 6,000 feet.

High-elevation areas of Arizona and New Mexico often have high concentrations of chlorides and boron in the soil. Check with your county extension agent for identifying and treating soil problems.

City	Elevation (feet)	Extreme Low	Years of Record	Last Spring Frost	First Fall Frost	Growing Season (days)	% July Sun
Albuquerque, NM	5,307	−10° F (−23° C)	75	Apr. 16	Oct. 29	196	76
Bowie, AZ	3,770	**	52	Apr. 2	Nov. 7	219	**
Carlsbad, NM	3,230	−17° F (−27° C)	29	Apr. 2	Nov. 7	220	75
Clovis, NM	4,280	**	64	Apr. 16	Oct. 31	198	**
Deming, NM	4,301	−7° F (−22° C)	16	Apr. 16	Nov. 2	200	80
Douglas, AZ	4,098	−7° F (−22° C)	29	Apr. 9	Nov. 6	211	85
Flagstaff, AZ	7,006	−14° F (−25° C)	79	Jun. 8	Sep. 26	110	90
Globe, AZ	3,710	**	3	Apr. 3	Nov. 3	214	**
Kingman, AZ	3,539	**	11	Apr. 6	Nov. 10	218	**
Roswell, NM	3,669	−29° F (−34° C)	6	Apr. 9	Nov. 2	208	75
Sante Fe, NM	6,800	−13° F (−25° C)	6	May 3	Oct. 15	165	78
Taos, NM	6,965	**	63	May 22	Sep. 30	130	**

**Data not available.

Growing Fruit, Berries and Nuts

Culture, pest control, propagation, pruning and small space techniques

Walk with an experienced fruit grower through his garden. He pokes the soil with a stick to check for soil moisture. He grabs a handful of soil and squeezes it to determine texture. He touches leaves, notes their color and turns them over to look for pests and disease. He inspects fruit, possibly thins a few and moves on. He knows, as you should, that success in growing healthy and productive fruiting plants depends on observation.

Observing and caring for plants regularly are steps toward fruit gardening success. But a chapter on fruit culture can only give guidelines. No book can predict exactly which successes or failures lie ahead. Use this chapter as a framework to help interpret your observations and to judge plant response. Combine it with more specific information in other parts of this book, especially the sections on individual fruit.

You should understand the roles different climate factors play in your region. Many problems can be avoided by simply planting fruit types and varieties that are well adapted to your area. Note the various microclimates around your garden and home. Choosing the right planting site can mean the difference between success and failure. See page 4.

SOILS

Three requirements are necessary for root growth: *moisture, air* and *nutrients.* Soil composition influences how much of these three ingredients are made available to plants. The type of soil also affects common cultural practices such as watering and fertilizing. Before planting any plant, it pays to have a basic understanding of your soil type.

Left: Regular watering, periodic applications of a balanced fertilizer and proper pruning will help ensure fruit gardening success.

Soils can generally be classified by texture as *clay, loam* or *sandy:*

Clay soils are composed of small mineral particles that cling tightly to moisture and nutrients and leave little room for air. A handful of moist, clay soil feels greasy or sticky and squeezes through your fingers in ribbons. Overwatering is a problem in clay soils because drainage is usually poor. If the root area remains saturated, roots will drown. They will also be susceptible to bacterial and fungal diseases.

Sandy soils are composed of larger mineral particles. Water and nutrients pass through sandy soils quickly. If you grab a handful of moist, sandy soil and squeeze it into a ball, it will crumble when released. There is plenty of air for root growth but close attention must be paid to watering frequency. Sandy soils dry out faster than clay soils. Fertilizers must also be applied more frequently.

Loam soils have a texture somewhere between clay and sandy soils. They contain large and small mineral particles and usually ample amounts of organic matter. Loam soils retain moisture and nutrients but still allow for good aeration and drainage. If you squeeze a handful of loam soil, it will form a loosely packed ball.

IMPROVING SOILS

The only way to improve the aeration of a heavy clay soil or increase the water and nutrient-holding capacity of a sandy soil is by adding organic matter. Peat moss, compost or shredded bark are common soil amendments. Unfortunately, many fruit trees root deep—up to 4 to 6 feet or more. Soil can be improved easily for shallow-rooting fruit such as strawberries or blueberries. For most fruit trees it is nearly impossible to work organic matter to the full depth of the roots.

DRAINAGE

Your soil will probably not be a perfect loam. Luckily, most fruit adapt to different soils as long as there is good drainage and nutrient requirements are met. Waterlogged, poorly drained soils can be fatal to cherries, peaches, almonds, walnuts, citrus and avocados. Apples, pears, plums and quince are slightly more tolerant but constantly wet soil is bad for any plant.

Before planting, check drainage of your planting hole as described in the instructions on page 28. If the soil drains poorly, consider alternatives. Plant elsewhere or plant in containers or raised beds. Information on growing fruit in containers and raised beds can be found on page 71.

In some areas of the desert Southwest there are impenetrable soil layers below the surface known as *caliche* or *hardpan.* These layers impede drainage as well as root growth. If they are not too thick, caliche and hardpan can be broken through with a hand-held auger or jackhammer, creating a drainage *chimney*.

WHEN TO PLANT

Deciduous trees, vines and shrubs can be planted any time during their *dormant season*—the time between leaf fall in autumn and the swelling of new buds in spring.

Remember this general rule when you plant: Establish the root systems of deciduous plants as early as possible before top growth begins in the spring.

In the Pacific Northwest and cold-winter areas, plant in fall or spring. Each planting period has advantages. If there is danger of the soil freezing, spring planting is best. In areas where the soil does not freeze, fall planting allows roots a longer period to become established before growth begins in spring.

In most parts of California and Arizona, January and February are the best months to plant deciduous fruit. The ground has been moistened by winter rains. More rains usually follow to settle plants naturally and keep roots moist.

Evergreen plants, especially frost-tender types such as citrus and avocado, should be planted in spring shortly after the last frost. They then have the entire growing season to become established before cold weather comes in fall.

Summer planting is usually not recommended. High heat puts too much strain on new plants and constant watering is a necessity.

HOW TO PLANT

Fruiting plants are usually purchased bare root or in containers. Sometimes they can be purchased with rootballs wrapped in burlap. This is referred to as *balled and burlapped* (B&B). Each type—bare root, container or B&B—has slightly different planting procedures.

Deciduous fruit are usually purchased bare root. Most are grown in open fields and dug during their second or third dormant season. All soil is knocked away from the roots after digging.

Bare-root plants are easily shipped. Companies that sell fruit plants through mail order catalogs usually pack the bare roots in moist wood shavings and enclose them in plastic for shipping. In retail nurseries bare-root plants are often stored in large bins of moist wood shavings or soil. If they are not sold by the time growth begins in spring, they are potted and sold in containers.

Bare-root plants should be carefully protected from the time of purchase to planting. Do not let roots dry out. Pack them in moist wood shavings, peat moss, soil or similar material. Store in a cool, shady spot until planting.

Fruit trees that are purchased in containers or B&B are planted in the same manner. When planting B&B, do not remove the burlap. Roll the edges of the burlap down the sides of the rootball. When the ball is planted the burlap should be completely covered with soil. The burlap will decay naturally. Be careful not to break the rootball when planting B&B plants.

Step-by-step instructions for planting bare root, container and B&B fruit are given on pages 26 to 29.

BACKFILLING THE PLANTING HOLE

It is important to establish the roots of plants in *native soil,* the soil present on your lot, as soon as possible after planting. Unless your soil is very sandy or heavy clay, it is best to fill the planting hole with the same soil that you took out. If you have a heavy clay or light, sandy soil, blend two parts native backfill soil with one part organic material such as compost, peat moss or shredded bark. If you are planting from containers, this 2:1 mix provides a transition between the usually lightweight container soil mix and native soil. For bare-root plants, this improved soil is a better rooting medium for establishing plants.

Do not mix fertilizer in the hole or backfill soil. Direct contact with fertilizer will burn tender young roots. Fertilizers should be sprinkled on top of soil around the plant and watered in after planting but are usually not necessary the first year. For more on fertilizing, see page 30.

PRUNING AND STAKING YOUNG FRUIT TREES

Young fruit trees and shrubs should be pruned after planting to compensate for roots that were cut or damaged during planting. Cutting back one-third or more is not too drastic. How to prune young fruit plants is described in detail on page 48.

Most young fruit trees will not need staking after planting. Older container trees or those transplanted from another location can be supported with two stakes, one on each side of the tree. Strips of cloth, plastic tree tape or twine enclosed in a piece of old garden hose can be used to loop around the trunk about two-thirds up the tree. Anchor to the stakes on each side.

A tree will become stronger and support itself sooner if allowed to sway somewhat with the wind. Check ties often to make sure they have not become too tight. Trees can be girdled by ties that constrict the trunk.

PREVENT SUNBURN

Trunks and branches of newly planted fruit trees are especially susceptible to sunburn. Steps should be taken to prevent exposure to intense sunlight. When planting, direct the outward curve of the graft union toward the southwest. The inward curve is particularly

Avoid problems caused by poor soils and overwatering. Grow fruit trees such as this genetic dwarf peach in containers with a lightweight soil mix. For more on container culture, see page 71.

susceptible to sunburn. This orientation points it away from the hottest sun.

If you live in a region where summers are hot, paint the trunk of the tree with white latex paint, tree paint or whitewash after planting. This prevents sunburn, cools the tree and decreases the likelihood of premature leafing out in spring. Painting the lower part of the tree an inch or two below the soil surface to just above the bud union also helps prevent borers from entering the bark.

In the hottest areas of the West, such as the California and Arizona low-elevation deserts, it is advisable to paint trunk and branches for maximum sunburn protection.

WATERING

For many fruit, watering practices are directly related to fruit quality. Peaches, plums, citrus, apricots, strawberries, blackberries and others bear smaller, less-juicy fruit if not given adequate water. Drought-stressed plants are also more susceptible to insect and disease problems.

Overwatering can be as hazardous as underwatering. Soggy, poorly drained soils can kill many fruiting plants. Cherries, citrus and avocados are particularly susceptible.

Watering frequency—How often to water depends on many things. Young plants with small root systems require close attention to water needs.

Planting Container-Grown Trees

1. Dig hole slightly larger than rootball. Check for drainage as shown in step 2 of bare-root planting, page 28.

2. If native soil is very sandy or heavy clay, blend one-third organic soil amendment with backfill soil.

5. Place tree in hole making sure it rests slightly above surrounding soil level. Direct outward curve of graft union toward the southwest to avoid sunburn.

6. Fill in hole with backfill soil. Make sure tree is not planted too low.

3. Add enough backfill soil to hole so tree will rest slightly above surrounding soil level.

4. Remove tree from container. Cut or free any badly circling roots. Metal containers may have to be cut at the nursery.

7. Build a water basin slightly larger than the rootball. Paint trunk with white latex paint to guard against sunburn.

8. Water tree thoroughly. Make sure tree has not settled too deep. If it has, raise by gently sliding a shovel underneath the rootball and lift it to proper height.

Planting Bare-Root Trees

1. Dig hole just large enough to accommodate roots.

2. Fill hole with water twice to check drainage. If hole has not completely drained in a reasonable time, 12 to 24 hours, you may have to find another site.

3. If native soil is very sandy or heavy clay, blend one-third organic soil amendment with backfill soil. Form a small mound in bottom of hole and spread roots over mound.

7. If planting more than one tree in a hole, position trees equal distances apart and slant them slightly outward.

8. Fill hole with soil. Do not put fertilizer directly in hole or it may burn tender roots.

9. Lightly tamp soil around roots. Check for proper planting depth.

4. Prune off any roots that are dried, broken, discolored or too long.

5. Where gophers are a problem, place a small cylinder of chicken wire in the hole. See page 41.

6. Place tree in hole at its original planting depth. The original soil line will appear as a dark to light color change on trunk below bud union.

10. Make a watering basin slightly larger than planting hole.

11. Paint trunks with white latex paint to guard against sunburn.

12. Water trees thoroughly and re-check planting depth. If trees have settled too deep, gently lift them by lower trunk until they are raised to proper height.

Soil type influences how often you have to water. As mentioned on page 23, sandy soils dry out faster than clay soils. Overwatering and poor drainage are constant threats in clay soils.

Climate plays a significant role in watering frequency. Hot areas such as the desert Southwest naturally require more frequent watering than cool, moist regions such as the Pacific Northwest.

If you live in Phoenix or Tucson, watering is a year-round affair. Winter rains in these areas rarely provide enough water. Even dormant deciduous trees need some soil moisture in winter or their roots may die.

In Seattle, watering may only be needed to supplement year-round rains. Poor drainage is much more likely than drought stress.

Shallow-rooted fruit such as strawberries will need more frequent watering than deep-rooted trees such as peaches or plums. Some fruit such as pomegranates and figs are more drought tolerant than other fruit. More specific information on water requirements can be found in the individual fruit descriptions.

Develop a watering schedule—To develop your own watering schedule, you need to survey all the variables just mentioned. Watch for weather changes and vary your watering accordingly. Learn the water requirements for your plants and recognize the signs of drought stress. Off-color, grayish foliage and wilting leaves are dramatic signals of water need. Unfortunately, once plants have reached this stage, they will probably drop much of their fruit.

Follow these tips for more efficient watering:

• **Water deeply and infrequently**—Lightly sprinkling dry soil does little to supply moisture to roots. Commercial orchards sprinkle-irrigate for as long as 12 to 24 hours to completely saturate the root area to a depth of more than 6 feet. This might sound wasteful, but commercial growers repeat this practice only two or three times a season, depending on climate and weather.

Shallow-rooted fruit will need more frequent and less-deep watering. Poking the soil with a stiff wire or stick will give you some idea of water penetration. The depth the wire or stick moves easily into the soil is approximately the depth of water penetration.

• **Direct water to the roots**—Water travels straight down, not outward. Build watering basins to cover the entire root area. Basins should extend out slightly past the *drip line,* an imaginary line extending to the outer edge of the plant canopy. For trees susceptible to collar rots, such as citrus, cherries and avocados, build a second, small basin around trunk to keep water *away* from trunk. Do not mound soil against trunk.

Small fruit such as strawberries and blueberries or trellised fruit such as blackberries or raspberries should be planted in mounded rows or raised basins.

Water is then channeled directly to roots. See illustrations on page 154.

• **Use drip irrigation**—This watering system applies water very slowly where it is needed most—to the plant's root zone. Many types of drip irrigation are available that conserve water and do a thorough job of watering. Consult your nurseryman or extension agent for advice.

• **Use a mulch**—Mulching is a very effective way to conserve moisture. A *mulch* is a layer of material that covers the soil. It can be *organic,* such as compost, sawdust, bark, wood chips or straw, or it can be *inorganic,* such as black plastic or stone.

In addition to conserving moisture, mulches cool the soil, an important benefit in hot climates. In cold winter areas mulches can prevent alternate freezing and thawing of soil, which causes plants to heave from the ground.

Mulches also help prevent weeds and soil compaction due to foot traffic. Organic mulches decompose to improve soil texture.

The depth of mulch applied depends on the material used. Organic mulches can be up to 6 inches deep. Mulches that hold moisture should be kept out of contact with trunks of fruit trees. Constant moisture against the trunk promotes disease.

FERTILIZERS AND MINERAL ELEMENTS

Plants require certain chemical elements for normal growth. These essential elements are carbon, oxygen, hydrogen, nitrogen, phosphorus, potassium, calcium, magnesium, manganese, copper, iron, zinc, sulfur, boron and molybdenum.

The first three elements—carbon, oxygen and hydrogen—are supplied by carbon dioxide in air and water from soil. The second three—nitrogen, phosphorus and potassium—are known as *fertilizers.* The remaining are classed as *minor elements,* because plants require them in small amounts. They are generally available in soils everywhere in sufficient quantities.

Fertilizers are classed as *natural organic* or *chemical inorganic.* Natural fertilizers include manures and plant and animal by-products. Chemical fertilizers are salts containing the elements nitrogen, phosphorus or potassium.

Chemical fertilizers may be simple, containing only one of the fertilizer elements. Or they may be complete, made from salts of all three fertilizer elements. The content of essential elements in complete fertilizer is given in a formula on the bag. The elements in the mixture are always given in the same order—nitrogen, phosphorus and potassium. For example, an 8-6-6 formula indicates 8 percent nitrogen, 6 percent phosphorus and 6 percent potassium.

Organic fertilizers vary in content of essential elements. For example, barnyard manure is between 1/2 and 1-1/2 percent nitrogen and 1/2 and 1 percent phosphorus and potassium. Fish meal is 10 percent nitrogen and 6 percent phosphorus but contains no potassium. Blood meal is 12 to 14 percent nitrogen but contains neither of the other two major elements. Cottonseed meal is 6 to 9 percent nitrogen, 2 to 3 percent phosphorus and 1 to 2 percent potassium.

The most economical fertilizer is the one that costs the least per pound of essential elements. Fertilizer recommendations are usually made in *pounds of actual nitrogen*. To determine how much *actual nitrogen* is in a quantity of fertilizer, multiply its percentage of nitrogen by the total pounds of fertilizer. For example, a 10-pound bag of complete fertilizer with a formula 10-4-4 contains 1 pound of *actual nitrogen* (.10 x 10 = 1.00). For cost comparison, you can see that a pound of actual nitrogen is supplied by the following: 5 pounds of ammonium sulfate (21-0-0); 3 pounds of ammonium nitrate (34-0-0); 10 pounds of a complete fertilizer with a formula 10-4-4; or approximately 100 pounds of a good manure. The cheapest of these is as effective for plant growth as the most expensive.

Nitrogen is the first fertilizer element. Experience has shown that most fruit plants respond by increased growth and production to proper applications of nitrogen. Plants deficient in nitrogen have light yellowish foliage, make poor growth and produce small, poor-quality fruit. Symptoms are general. No definite patterns, spots or death of plant parts occur.

Infertile soils, where plant growth is poor, may require annual applications of about 1 to 1-1/2 pounds actual nitrogen per mature tree per year. On more fertile soils less nitrogen will be needed. For small fruit plants, an application of approximately 1/5 to 2/5 pound of actual nitrogen per 100 square feet provides ample fertilization.

Young fruit plants, less than 5 years old, should receive one-fourth to one-half the rate of mature plants. The time of nitrogen application is generally not important. Fall or winter is the traditional period, well before spring growth. If trees are deficient, maximum response will be gained by fall or winter application. If trees have received an annual application of fertilizer for several years, summer applications maintain adequate growth just as well as winter applications.

Soil type and rainfall may dictate the best method of applying nitrogen fertilizers. Light, sandy soils may benefit more if fertilizers are applied two times a year, using half the total amount each time. One application would normally be made in the winter or spring season, the other in summer. This minimizes leaching or washing away of soluble nitrogen salts from such soils.

Heavier soils in areas of high rainfall may also benefit from this method. Rains may leach soluble salts below the root zone of plants. However, a single application is sufficient for soils in most areas.

Fruit trees should not receive excessive amounts of nitrogen fertilizers. Vegetative growth will be greatly stimulated but fruit will be watery, lack sugar and aroma and color will be poor.

A fruit tree will compete for nutrients if grown in a garden site, in a lawn or near other plants. Fertilizer requirements of nearby plants must be considered. They may be using a large portion of the fertilizer applied. The best way to determine fertilizer needs is to *watch for plant growth*. If plants are growing satisfactorily, nitrogen requirements are being satisfied.

Phosphorus is the second fertilizer element. Foliage of deciduous or evergreen trees low in phosphorus becomes dull and bronzed in late summer. Affected citrus fruit are below-average quality and have enlarged, puffy skins. Stone fruit that have adequate phosphorous normally exhibit brighter color, firmness and earlier maturity. Phosphorus deficiency, although rare and difficult to recognize, can be corrected with an application of superphosphate. Apply 1 pound per inch of trunk diameter, cultivate into soil and water.

Potassium, the third fertilizer element, is found to be deficient in only a few locations. Your trees will seldom benefit from applications of this element. Deficiency of potassium has been noted most frequently in European plum, prune, olive and almond. European plums show leaf scorch and dieback of shoots is common. Olive leaves become yellowish, shoot tips die, and growth is weak. Almond leaves are small and boat shaped, with less growth than normal. Crops are greatly reduced.

Potassium deficiency may be corrected on almonds and olives by applying rather massive doses of potassium sulfate to the soil under the tree. Apply 15 to 25 pounds, depending on size of tree. A single application may be effective for several years. Work the material down in the soil. Potassium is quickly fixed—tied up chemically—by the soil and does not readily leach into the lower soil layers explored by the roots.

Theoretically, potassium deficiency of European plum and prune should be cured by the same treatment. But the treatment has not proved effective, even though evidence concludes that potassium deficiency is responsible for the symptoms described. If you find that your soil is deficient in potassium, prune trees severely from the time of planting and thin fruit heavily. This limits the fruiting area and ensures a light crop, which seems to be the best corrective measure. Heavy soil applications of potassium salts should also be made. Following these steps often delays the onset of potassium deficiency.

Minor fertilizer elements—Minor elements most often deficient are zinc, iron, manganese, boron and copper. Boron may also cause trouble if present in excess.

Zinc is often deficient throughout the West. Apples, most of the stone fruit, nut trees and grapes have been known to suffer from lack of zinc in many soils, especially sandy soils. In young trees, severe deficiencies are characterized by stunted growth, with tufts or rosettes of small, yellow or mottled leaves at the tips of bare shoots. There is often a noticeable delay in development of spring foliage, absence of crop and dieback of twigs or branches. In old trees, the only noticeable signs may be pale or yellowish foliage, smaller than normal leaf size and poor crops. The inhibition of terminal growth may cause lateral buds to grow. The lateral buds in turn develop small, chlorotic leaves. This gives a typical rosette of deformed twigs and foliage, which is pronounced on pecan trees.

Zinc applied to deficient soils is often quickly and effectively fixed—tied up chemically in the soil so that it is not available to the tree. If small quantities are needed, methods other than application to the soil are generally advised.

A zinc sulfate spray can be applied to tree limbs in the dormant season. Rate of application the first year should be 2-1/2 pounds per 10 gallons of spray. Follow successive years with the same spray at a ratio of 1 to 2-1/2 pounds per 10 gallons. Depending on the severity of the deficiency, this will usually provide a cure. A foliage spray of zinc oxide at the rate of 1/2 pound per 10 gallons of water applied in the spring is also helpful.

Cherry and walnut may fail to respond to these sprays. They must be supplied with zinc by driving small, triangular pieces of galvanized iron or glaziers' zinc points into the branches. Space them about 1 inch apart. Use ten pieces for each inch of branch circumference. Thus, a branch 3 inches in circumference will require thirty pieces. Drive them through the bark and into the sapwood parallel to the length of the branch. This treatment is usually effective for several years.

A soil application of zinc sulfate may also be used as a permanent treatment. It is the simplest to apply. Dig a circular trench 14 inches deep about 2 to 4 feet from trunk, depending on tree size. Place 10 pounds of zinc sulfate plus another 1 pound for each inch of trunk diameter in the trench. Tree roots will pick up enough zinc from this local, highly concentrated application to satisfy their needs for several years.

Correct zinc deficiency in grapes by painting on pruning cuts a solution of 1-1/2 pounds of zinc sulfate per gallon of water just after pruning.

Iron is sometimes chemically bonded in the soil so that plant roots cannot absorb it. The affected plant shows typical yellowing of the foliage, called *chlorosis*. Chlorotic leaves are normal size, unless the deficiency is extreme. Leaves turn yellow except veins remain green.

Alkaline and lime soils most commonly bond iron in this unavailable form. Because applications of lime make soils more alkaline, such chlorosis is often called *lime-induced chlorosis*. All plant species may be affected. Fruit plants such as blueberries, which require acid soils, will inevitably show chlorosis if planted in alkaline soil. Because soils have a great *fixing power* for iron, rendering it unavailable to plants, applications of iron salts will not cure the trouble. Adding sulfur to soil will make it more acid and may help in overcoming iron deficiency, but this is seldom effective. Iron chelates are most effective in correcting iron chlorosis. Chelates must be applied frequently and are most readily absorbed when sprayed on young, expanding foliage. See page 33.

Almond, apple, apricot, citrus and walnut most commonly show symptoms of manganese deficiency. It can be identified by diffused, yellow areas between the leaf veins, which remain green. Later in the season, yellow areas may turn red or dark brown. Only in extreme cases will there be a dieback of the top of tree. Quantity or quality of fruit is not affected, but the crops will be limited if branches die.

Normally, a mild case of manganese deficiency is not worth correcting. However, severe cases need treatment. Spray on foliage a mixture of 1 pound of manganese sulfate and 1 pound of hydrated lime with a teaspoon of casein spreader dissolved in 10 gallons of water. This should correct the problem for one season.

Boron is a very minor element. It is essential to normal plant development, although excess can cause severe disease symptoms.

Limited regions in the West are deficient in this element, most frequently in high rainfall areas of the Northwest. Deficiency of boron has been noted in apple, apricot, olive, pear and walnut. Young twigs may die back in severe cases. Skin of apples and pears show undue russeting and cracking. Brown, cork-like areas appear in the flesh, especially near the bottom end of the fruit. These corky flesh spots have given boron deficiency the common names *cork spot* and *drought spot* in apples and pears.

Boron deficiency of olive shows mainly as deformed fruit. Affected fruit areas, usually toward the tip, are dark colored, shriveled and variously deformed. The names *monkey-face*, *sheep-nose* and *shrivel-tip* have been

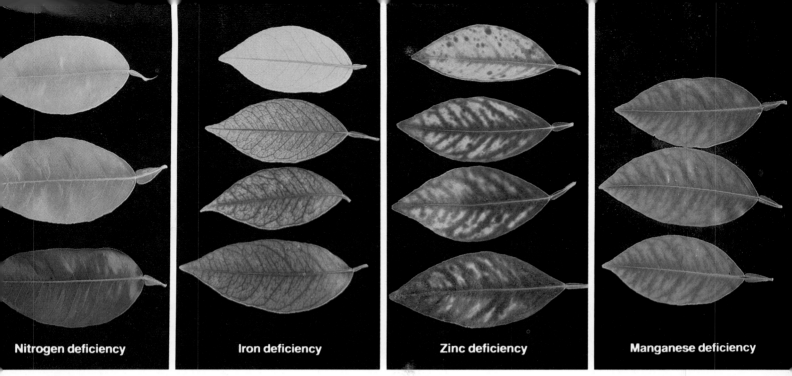

Nitrogen deficiency   **Iron deficiency**   **Zinc deficiency**   **Manganese deficiency**

The above deficiencies in citrus leaves are typical for most fruit trees. Nitrogen deficiency causes symptoms in older, lower leaves first. Iron, zinc and manganese are usually present in sufficient quantities in most soils. Deficiencies are caused by plant's inability to absorb these minerals. Soil pH, water conditions and temperatures strongly affect the availability of minerals. Deficiency symptoms of iron, zinc and manganese generally occur in newest growth first. Other symptoms of mineral deficiencies can be found on pages 31 and 32.

applied to these symptoms. Terminal shoot buds often die, resulting in short, bunchy, twig growth from lateral buds. By late summer, leaves may become yellow toward the tips.

Boron deficiency is readily corrected by applications of borax or boric acid to the soil. Apply 1/2 to 1 pound of borax under the canopy of tree. If boric acid is used, apply 1/3 to 2/3 pound. Apply any time during the year. A single treatment should last two or three years. Do not repeat the treatment until signs of deficiency reappear. Too much boron may injure the tree.

Excess boron is found in many soils and adversely affects almost all fruit plants. Some fruit are more sensitive than others—apricots, bush-type fruit and walnuts are particularly subject. Boron excess commonly causes a marginal scorch of leaves, accompanied by upward cupping of leaves and black spots in the leaf blade. These leaf symptoms are found on blackberry, fig, gooseberry, grape, pecan, raspberry, strawberry and walnut. High concentration of other salts sometimes results in similar symptoms, but the scorch is more likely to start from the tip of the leaf.

Apricot, nectarine, peach and plum show boron injury on current season's growth. Look for dying back of the tips, accompanied by cracked and corky bark that may exude gum. Shoots of apricot and plum will also have greatly enlarged nodes.

Apple, cherry and pear seldom show typical symptoms as given above. Soil and leaf analyses may be necessary to determine if excess boron is causing the problem.

Excess boron must be leached from soil with water to correct the difficulty. Water containing more than 1.5 parts per million (ppm) of boron may permit accumulation in the soil until it becomes excessive.

Copper deficiency, *exanthema*, is less common than deficiencies of the minor elements just mentioned. Its symptoms are quite similar to those given for zinc deficiency and commonly appear on the same plants. Copper deficiency is easily corrected by applying 1 to 5 pounds of copper sulfate to the soil under the tree. Copper deficiency rarely appears on deciduous trees given an annual spray of Bordeaux for disease control.

CHELATES

The quickest way to clear up micronutrient deficiencies of zinc, manganese, copper and iron is to apply them in chelated form. Chelates sprayed on deficient leaves will usually correct the deficiency, but sprays often need to be repeated frequently. Chelates are most readily absorbed by young, expanding foliage.

SALTY SOILS

Excesses of nonessential elements or salts in the soil may cause trouble. Excess salts characterize so-called saline soils. Sodium may sometimes be present in amounts that harm plants. Leaves die from the tip or margins and tree grows poorly because of loss of leaf surface. Limbs may eventually die and sunburn of exposed limbs may hasten the death of the tree. As with excess boron, the only means of correcting excesses of salts or elements is by leaching with water.

Pests and Diseases

Most fruit growers no longer try to eliminate all pests. Instead they seek to maintain a balance between the "bad guys" and the "good guys"—that is, between the pests and the pests' natural predators. You too might view the pest problem as a matter of balance. A certain number of pests exist on plants, but they provide food for the predators that hold them in check. As long as nature maintains a balance and the pests stay under control, the garden remains healthy.

Occasionally, you may need to supplement natural gardening practices with more specific measures. But home fruit growers have an edge on commercial growers, who have to observe fairly rigid standards of quality control. As long as you don't mind an occasional wormy apple or a chewed leaf, you may seldom need to spray.

KEEPING PESTS AND DISEASES IN CHECK

1. Grow healthy plants. Diseases and pests are most likely to gain a foothold in plants that are weak and unhealthy. For example, boring insects are commonly found in neglected trees. The strong sap flow in vigorous, healthy trees quickly plugs the bored holes and sometimes kills the insects. Prune and thin fruit to allow maximum sunlight and ventilation. This not only maintains general health of plants, but discourages many rot and mold diseases. Cultivating the soil improves aeration and drainage, essential to good health. It also destroys many dangerous larvae that inhabit the top soil layers.

2. Develop a sharp eye for problems. An experienced gardener inspects his garden closely and often, using a hand lens to spot tiny pests such as spider mites. He usually finds trouble before it can develop into epidemic proportions.

3. Keep your garden clean. Remove rotting fruit from tree and ground. Clean up fallen leaves and debris regularly and remove any sickly growth. By following these practices you will be removing spores, larvae and eggs of pests that may cause problems later.

4. Be aware of potential problems within your climate area and the weather conditions that trigger them. If you know what may happen beforehand, you will know *what* problems to look for and *when*. This book and your county extension agent can help you with the specifics.

5. Choose fruit varieties resistant to pests and diseases common to your climate area. Note the list of varieties in this book that can be grown without special attention. Fruit charts also indicate which varieties are resistant to particular problems and if they are suited to growing in certain climate zones.

6. Use a soap-and-water solution to control minor problems. One tablespoon of liquid dishsoap in a gallon of water can be used as a spray to combat minor infestations of aphids and mildew. Soap and water applied early often prevent large problems and drastic solutions later.

7. Encourage and introduce beneficial insects. See the illustrations on page 36 and note the University of California listing of commercial sources.

8. Apply an appropriate pesticide. If natural controls fail, determine which pest or disease is present and which spray or dust will control it. Follow directions on the pesticide container to the letter. The illustrations of common pests and diseases on pages 38 to 41 will help you identify plant problems.

FRUIT THAT REQUIRE LITTLE OR NO CARE

Blueberry	Pistachio	Carissa
Pomegranate	Feijoa	Quince
Fig	Jujube	Loquat
Macadamia	Acerola cherry	Olive
Capulin cherry	Pecan	Lychee
Persimmon	Black walnut	Guava (Chilean or regular varieties)

DORMANT OIL SPRAY

A few words should be said about a special category of sprays—*oil sprays*. Dormant oil spray is the *first and only* spray of the year for many successful gardeners. It is

Peach leaf curl, enemy of peach growers, can be controlled by one, timely dormant spray. See page 40.

combined with water and applied to deciduous fruit trees in winter, when pests are dormant. The oil coats many insects or their overwintering eggs or cocoons long enough to smother them.

DIFFICULT PROBLEMS

Unfortunately, a few pest and disease problems are next to impossible to solve. If a plant is infected with one of the following pests or diseases, replacement is sometimes the best remedy.

Rots—Rot diseases usually affect tissues beneath bark around the lower trunk, causing mold-like fungal growth or a moist decay to girdle the tree. Most common are oak root fungus, crown rot and root rot. Root rot is particularly threatening to avocados.

Rots flourish in excessively wet, heavy soils. If you water properly and provide drainage, your plants are not likely to become infected. Resistant rootstocks for many fruit have been developed to help prevent rot diseases.

Virus and Mycoplasms—These two types of diseases cause similar damage. Peculiar deformities or discolorations of leaves, fruit or stems are symptoms. There is no practical control for the homeowner.

Nematodes—These microscopic, eel-like worms live in nearly every type of soil, but particularly in sandy soil. Nematodes live by parasitizing plant roots. There is virtually no control beyond preplant soil fumigation, so start with nematode-resistant rootstocks to prevent infestations.

THE GARDENER'S ARSENAL

The following chart lists and compares some of the more readily available chemicals approved for use in the home garden. Treat these chemicals with extreme care and use according to directions on the label.

GENERIC NAME	TRADE NAMES	USES	REMARKS
BACILLUS THURINGIENSIS	Dipel, Thuricide, Biotrol.	Codling moth, peach twig borer, leaf rollers, Oriental fruit moth, red-humped caterpillar.	Biological control—timing is critical. Affects only caterpillars and larvae. Apply when pests are young. Works slowly and does not kill every caterpillar. Nontoxic to people.
BENOMYL	Benlate.	Scab, brown rot, bacterial leaf spot, powdery mildew.	Often combined with Captan. Some fungi beginning to show resistance and immunity. Safe to handle. Spray up to harvest.
BORDEAUX (Copper sulfate and lime)	Many.	Peach leaf curl, bacterial leaf spot.	Mix with dormant spray. Can be used right up to harvest.
CAPTAN	Orthocide, Captan.	Scab, brown rot, bacterial leaf spot, cherry leaf spot.	Safe to handle and can be sprayed up to harvest. Use a wetting agent/spreader.
CARBARYL	Sevin.	Pear slug, codling moth, Oriental fruit moth, leaf roller.	Highly toxic to honeybees and beneficial mites. Moderately toxic to people. Wait one day after spraying before harvest.
DIAZINON	Spectracide.	Borers, pear slug, leafhopper, scale, aphids, codling moth.	Causes russeting on green and yellow apples. Strongly toxic—wait 20 days after spraying to harvest.
DICOFOL	Kelthane.	Spider mites.	May require a second spray 7 days later. Moderately toxic to people and very toxic to predatory mites. Wait 14 days after spraying to harvest.
DORMANT OIL	Volk oil.	Leaf roller, scale, spider mites, aphids, codling moth.	Most important spray of the year. Very low toxicity. Do not apply to walnuts.
FIXED COPPER (Copper sulfate*)	Many.	Brown rot, peach leaf curl, bacterial leaf spot.	Similar to but more stable than bordeaux. Use a wetting agent. May injure some trees.
LIME-SULFUR	Dormant Disease Control, Orthorix, Lime-sulfur.	Scab, peach leaf curl, bacterial leaf spot, powdery mildew.	Best for peach leaf curl. May discolor painted surfaces. Do not apply in hot weather or to apricots.
LINDANE	Killbore.	Borers.	Long residual quality gives effective borer control. Highly toxic to people. Wait 60 days before harvesting sprayed fruit.
MALATHION	Cython.	Pear slug, walnut husk fly, leafhopper, scale, aphids, codling moth.	All-purpose, low-toxicity spray. Highly toxic to honeybees and moderately toxic to many beneficial insects. Harvest after one week. Has injured 'McIntosh' and 'Cortland' apples, sweet cherries, certain European grapes and 'Bosc' pears.
METHYOXYCHLOR	Marlate.	Leafhoppers, codling moth, scale crawlers.	Very low toxicity to people, but very toxic to fish. Wait one day before harvest.
SULFUR	Many.	Brown rot, scab, powdery mildew, mites.	Oldest known fungicide. Safer than lime-sulfur in hot weather.

*Copper oleates not effective.

Beneficial Insects

These insects live by feeding on insects that we usually classify as pests. Look for them at work in your garden. University of California Extension price bulletin 4096, $3.00, lists commercial sources of beneficial insects. See address, page 189.

Parasitized aphid—This dead aphid served as the food source for a tiny, parasitic wasp. Circular holes with hatches are actually escape hatches, cut by the immature wasp as it emerged. Look for parasitized aphids to determine if biological agents are at work in your garden before using chemical controls.

Lady bugs—This well-known beetle feeds on many pests but exhibits a particular taste for aphids, especially during their larval stage. A growing lady beetle can consume over 40 aphids per day. If not treated properly, lady beetles will leave your garden quickly. Read directions on container carefully.

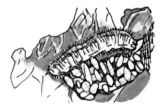

Parasitized caterpillar—White objects attached to this caterpillar are wasp cocoons and the caterpillar is their food source. Soon, this cabbage worm will die and other wasps will emerge to lay eggs on other caterpillars.

PESTS AND DISEASES BY CLIMATE ZONE

	Aphids	Bacterial Canker	Bacterial Leaf Spot	Borers*	Brown Rot	Codling Moth	Crown (collar) Rot	Fireblight	Peach Leaf Curl	Leaf-hopper
SEVERE PROBLEM IN ZONES:	6-17	3,4,6-8 11	All	6-15,17	3,4,6-8 10,11,14,15	All but 3,4	All	6,9	All	All
TREE FRUIT										
Apple	●		●	●		○	●	○		●
Apricot	●	○		●	○		●	●		●
Cherry	●	●	○	●	○		●	●		●
Citrus	●	●	●	●			○			
Crabapple	●		●	●		●	●	○		
Fig										
Peach/Nectarine	●	●	●	●	○		●		○	●
Pear	●	●	●	●	●	○	●	○		
Persimmon				●		●				
Plum/Prune	●	●	●	●	○	●				
Pomegranate										
NUTS										
Almond		●	○	●	○		○			
Chestnut							●			
Filbert										
Pecan							●			
Pistachio							●			
Walnut	●	●				○	●			
BERRIES										
Blackberry	●		●							
Currant	●		●	●						
Gooseberry	●		●	●						●
Grape	●									●
Raspberry	●							●		●
Strawberry	●		●				●			
SUBTROPICALS										
Avocado							●			
Kiwifruit			●				●		●	
Loquat	●		●				●		●	

*Peach Tree Borer, Peach Twig Borer, Shothole Borer, Raspberry Crown Borer, Flatheaded Borer

○ — Denotes particularly severe problem.

Lacewings—Lacewing larvae eat more than adults and often consume caterpillars more than twice their size.

Trichogamma wasp—The best known of the egg parasites, trichogamma wasps attack over 200 different pest species, including codling moth, cane borers and leaf rollers. They lay eggs on their prey, using them as a food source until eggs hatch.

Mites—Shown are two of several species of beneficial predatory mites that feed on pest fruit mites. Predatory mites are usually larger and more mobile than pest mites.

Aphinus melinus—Shown here laying eggs on a citrus red mite. Citrus red mite is one of the more serious citrus pests.

PESTS AND DISEASES BY CLIMATE ZONE

	Leaf Rollers	Mites	Oak Root Fungus	Oriental Fruit Moth	Pear Slug	Powdery Mildew	Root Rot	Scab	Scale**	Verticillium Wilt	Walnut Husk Fly
SEVERE PROBLEM IN ZONES:	6-17	7-17	All	7-15	9-12	3,4,6	All	3,4,6	6-17	All	7-15
TREE FRUIT											
Apple	●	○	●	●		●	●	○	●	●	
Apricot	●	●	○	●			●		●	●	
Cherry	●	●	●		●				●		
Citrus		●	●	●	○				●		
Crabapple	●	●	●	●		●	●	○	●		
Fig							●				
Peach/Nectarine		●	●	○					●		
Pear	●	○	●		●	●	●	○	●		
Persimmon	●	●							●		
Plum/Prune	●	●	●	●					●	●	
Pomegranate		●									
NUTS											
Almond		○	○			●		●		●	
Chestnut			●			●	●				
Filbert			●			●					
Pecan			●			●					
Pistachio		●	●							○	
Walnut		●	●						●		○
BERRIES											
Blackberry		●	●			●			●	●	
Currant			●			●			●	●	
Gooseberry			●			○			●		
Grape	○	○	●			○					
Raspberry		●	●			●				●	
Strawberry	●	●	●			●				●	
SUBTROPICALS											
Avocado		●	●				○			●	
Kiwifruit	●	●	●						●	○	
Loquat			●								

**Hard shell scale (San Jose, Oystershell, Citrus red)   ○ — Denotes particularly severe problem.

Insect Problems and Solutions

Peach tree borer

Damage by Pacific flathead borer

Pacific flathead borer

Cross-section of borer damage

BORER

General decline in tree vigor, accompanied by numerous holes in trunk and lower branches. Holes may be surrounded by a sappy sawdust. Peach twig borers attack new shoots and may cause their sudden death. Cane borers do the same to young canes.

Control—Twig borers: First, rely on dormant oil spray. If infestation gets out of hand, spray with carbaryl when dead twigs appear. Tree borers: Healthy, vigorously growing trees discourage borer attack and are your best defense. Protect newly planted trees from sunburn by painting trunks with white latex paint. Avoid any external tree injuries and remove badly infested trees or dead wood nearby. Spraying trunk and lower branches with lindane until runoff offers additional protection, as does *Bacillus thuringiensis* and Sevin. Cane borers: Pull and destroy infected canes and drench crown of plant with diazinon.

Adult shothole borer

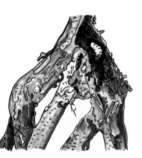

Raspberry crown borer

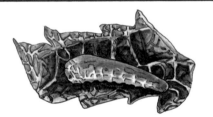

Pear slug larva on damaged leaf

Mature pear slug borer

PEAR SLUG

Green, slimy-looking maggots that eat leaf tissue between veins, leaving a lacy patch.

Control—Cultivate soil in early June and mid-August to kill emerging adults. Spray malathion, diazinon or carbaryl at petal fall (cherries and pears) and preharvest (pears). Not usually a major pest every year.

WALNUT HUSK FLY

Blackened areas on developing walnut husks. Dark sap may exude from blackened area. Nutmeats not affected.

Control—Spray malathion in early August and again in late August as adult flies emerge. If you use a protein fly bait with mixture you can mix malathion at half strength.

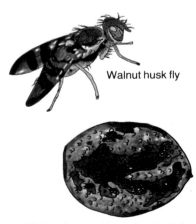

Walnut husk fly

Walnut damaged by walnut husk fly

Common leafhopper and damage

Grape leafhopper

LEAFHOPPER

Slender, active, wedge-shaped insects feed on the undersides of leaves. Badly damaged leaves look speckled and may be host to several insects, which quickly hop away when disturbed. Leafhoppers spread many destructive virus diseases.

Control—Usually not necessary if less than 20 on one leaf. If infestation becomes serious, spray malathion, methoxychlor or diazinon.

FRUIT TREE LEAF ROLLER

Deep, russeted scars on young and mature fruit. Leaves may be webbed together, forming a cavity. A small caterpillar lives and feeds therein, relatively well protected from its enemies.

Control—Dormant spray kills overwintering eggs. *Bacillus thuringiensis* is very effective against worms if sprayed as worms hatch, usually around colored bud. Be sure to force spray into rolled leaves. Sevin is also effective.

Damage to pear

Leaf roller larva and damaged fruit tree leaf

Damage to young pear

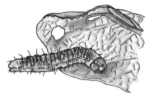

SCALE

Decreased plant vigor due to presence of many, small, immobile, shell or disc-shaped insects. They encrust twigs and larger branches. Sometimes scale attack ripe fruit.

Control—Oil spray at dormancy is a must! If scale persist, try malathion, methoxychlor or diazinon but you must spray when the "crawlers" appear. Look for the young, yellowish crawlers in late spring as they leave the protective shell of the mother scale and scatter over the plant. Check with a hand lens.

San Jose scale

APHIDS

Colonies of small, plump insects suck fluid from new leaves and shoots. Aphids secrete a sweet substance that forms a black, sooty mold and attracts ant colonies. Infected tree parts often curl and disfigure. White, cottony tufts indicate woolly apple aphid.

Control—Spray with malathion, diazinon or plain, soapy water when infestation gets too heavy. Prune infected shoots heavily.

Apple aphid

Woolly apple aphid

European red mite colony

SPIDER MITES

Growth declines and trees appear pale green from a distance. Speckled, bronze leaves may show many, tiny, spider-like insects scurrying over the surface and across small webs stretched between leaf axils.

Control—Dormant oil spray kills eggs. Spray Kelthane or sulfur when seen and again one week later. Mites thrive in dry, dusty environments. Prevent water stress and hose down foliage periodically with water.

CODLING MOTH

Principle cause of wormy apples. Look for holes on surface of fruit surrounded by brownish debris. Young and mature fruit are attacked.

Control—Dormant oil spray may suffocate codling moth pupae that choose to overwinter in cracks on the tree surface. Look for their cocoons and hand-pick them from the tree. Spray *Bacillus thuringiensis,* malathion, methoxychlor, diazinon or carbaryl at colored bud stage. See illustration page 42. Repeat twice more after petal fall, two weeks apart.

Apple damage by codling moth

Codling moth adult

Codling moth larva

Oriental fruit moth

ORIENTAL FRUIT MOTH

Wormy fruit, particularly around the pit and stem end of peaches. The culprit is a pinkish worm about 1/2-inch long when full grown. It may mine twigs and shoots like the peach twig borer. It differs in color from the chocolate-brown twig borer.

Control—Spray carbaryl once or twice between fruitlet and preharvest, as needed. *Bacillus thuringiensis* is also effective.

Larva and damage to peach

Disease Problems and Solutions

BACTERIAL CANKER

Water-soaked lesions and gummy cankers on trunk and lower branches, followed by dying back of girdled branches. Blossoms and young fruit may show blighted or blackened infection.

Control—Remove and destroy girdled branches after leaf fall. Use sharp tools and disinfect blade after each cut with regular household bleach. If entire tree trunk is badly infected, it may be best to remove tree.

FIREBLIGHT

Individual terminal shoots and blossoms wither as if scorched by fire.

Control—When the first symptoms appear, cut out and destroy infected shoots at least eight inches below the lowest visible sign of infection. Disinfect tools with household bleach after each cut. Because tender shoots are primarily affected, prune and fertilize carefully to discourage excessive shoot growth.

VERTICILLIUM WILT

Sudden, peculiar, die-back of leaves on a branch from the bottom towards the top. On fruit trees, sapwood underneath bark often turns black. New canes and leaves of small fruit often wilt and turn a grayish blue.

Control—Not much can be done to eradicate the disease, but well-maintained trees often recover. Avoid planting near susceptible hosts, such as strawberries and tomatoes or where such plants were once located.

SCAB

Dark, corky patches infect developing leaves and fruit. Many scabs are scattered over fruit surface. They grow together into an ugly, irregular infection. Very serious in wet regions.

Control—Rake and destroy fallen leaves before bud break. Old leaves are the primary source of scab spores. Plant apple varieties that resist scab. Spray captan, lime-sulfur, sulfur or benomyl at colored bud, petal fall and fruitlet stages. Warm, wet spring weather favors scab infection and may call for additional sprays. Spray thoroughly underneath and around tree.

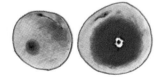

BROWN ROT

Firm, light brown, spoiled areas on ripening fruit, begins as a small spot, which rapidly spreads over fruit surface. Fruit dries leather-hard, forming a "mummy" that sometimes remains on tree. Blossoms may also be infected. Thrives under wet conditions.

Control—Be sure to pick up and destroy all "mummies." Prune to encourage air circulation and thorough spray coverage. Spray captan, sulfur, benomyl or fixed copper at colored bud stage, again at pre-harvest. May have to repeat after wet weather.

PEACH LEAF CURL

Profuse leaf distortion begins shortly after blossom. Infected leaves look thickened and blistered, take on a reddish brown color and fall by late spring.

Control—Protective fungicide must be sprayed prior to bud break or shortly after leaf fall. Use bordeaux, lime-sulfur, or fixed copper sprays.

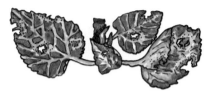

BACTERIAL LEAF SPOT (SHOTHOLE)

Circular, purple spots dry and fall away, leaving leaf with a speckled, shot-hole effect as if blasted by a shotgun.

Control—Spray captan, bordeaux, benomyl, fixed copper or lime-sulfur at fruitlet stage, again at leaf fall.

POWDERY MILDEW

Fuzzy, felt-like white patches cover undersides of young leaves and terminal shoots. They stunt growth and cause leaves to yellow and fall.

Control—Plant trees in full sun. Prune to encourage air circulation. Because roses harbor mildew spores, remove or relocate any roses near fruit garden. Lime-sulfur, sulfur, Karathane or benomyl sprayed at colored bud, petal fall and fruitlet stages gives maximum control. Do not use Karathane on cherries.

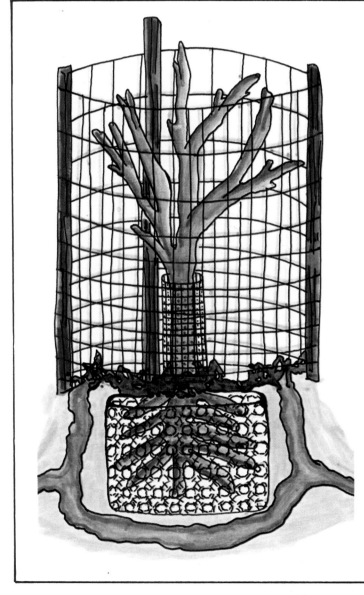

Wildlife Pests

Deer—Deer have been known to strip leaves from young trees, sometimes eating unprotected trees back to the main trunk. Commercial deer repellents, blood or bone meal, tankage (a feed supplement available at most feed stores) and even human hair have been known to repel deer when suspended from trees in small cloth bags. The material must be renewed about every two weeks.

Wire fences and deer-proof cages are excellent deer control devices. In areas where deer are known to be a problem, erect a cage of field fence, completely encircling young trees. Support cage with three stout posts. If you have planted a large garden, then consider reliable but expensive deer fencing. The fence must be at least 6-1/2 feet high.

Birds—Birds become a problem near harvest time, particularly on cherries. A nylon mesh net stretched over the tree before harvest minimizes bird feeding.

Commercial bird repellents are available and work especially well on cherries.

Gophers and Moles—These underground dwellers often destroy young trees by gnawing on roots. When planting, protect roots by lining planting hole with 1/2-inch wire mesh. Set a few traps from time to time for additional protection. The family cat will also catch a fair share. Between these three control methods, you should be able to minimize damage.

Rabbits and Mice—Above-ground rodent pests harm trees by gnawing at bark and leaves within their reach. Protect trees by installing a 1/4-inch wire mesh or plastic collar around tree trunk when you plant. Plastic types are designed to expand as tree grows, but wire guards can girdle tree if they are not removed and refitted each year. Both effectively prevent damage from mice and rabbits.

Keep brush and snow from piling too near tree. Brush conceals rodents from their natural enemies and provides cover right up to tree trunk. Snow may pile high enough to allow rabbits to reach lower branches unless it is kept cleared away.

Pest and Disease Timetable

The following illustrations depict seven major changes that occur in the life of a deciduous fruit. These changes span seven months, from early spring to late summer. They will help you understand the growth cycle of a deciduous fruit. Use the timetable to act on problems that commonly appear after a certain stage, before they get out of control.

Stage 1—Dormant (Winter)

This is a fruiting spur as it has appeared since leaf fall. Soon buds will begin to swell, a hint of the coming bloom. It is important that any pest control activities be completed *before* buds begin to swell.

Maintenance—Now is the time to plant new bare-root trees. Paint tree trunk and install gopher and rodent protection. Prune existing trees to allow maximum sun and air penetration. Hand pick codling moth cocoons tucked away in cracks or underneath loose bark.

Sanitation—Rake leaves left over from last season. They may harbor apple scab spores.

Chemical—Spray dormant oil, covering every twig, nook and cranny. Now is the last chance to spray for peach leaf curl.

Aphid eggs

Dormant

Stage 2—Colored Bud (Early Spring)

This is a critical stage in controlling diseases. Fruiting buds have just begun to open and reveal colorful, tightly wrapped blossom tips. Bud color will vary among fruit types. If you haven't pruned or planted, colored bud stage is your last chance.

Maintenance—Treat any sunburned or injured branches before new foliage obscures them.

Biological—Now is a good time to release the first brood of beneficial insects. If you choose a strict biological control strategy, do not spray insecticides at any stage. You will probably destroy your biological insect population.

Pear bud

Apple bud

Colored Bud

Stage 3—Full Bloom (Early Spring)

Buds have now opened and put forth clusters of delicate, fragrant blossoms. This attracts thousands of pollinating bees. Never spray insecticides during this stage, or you may destroy the bees. Watch for early hatches of pest caterpillars. If weather is warm and wet, be on the lookout for fireblight damage. These are conditions that promote the disease. Most of all, sit back and enjoy the show!

Full blossom of apple

Full Bloom

Stage 4—Petal Fall (Early Spring)

At this stage, much has happened to form the new crop. Blossoms have lost their petals. Bees and other insects have pollinated the flowers. Now is the time when eggs of many insects begin to hatch. Codling moth, leaf rollers, Oriental fruit moth and twig borers are among the first caterpillars to appear. Aphids often attack lush new terminal growth.

Maintenance—Look for withered shoots, possibly victims of fireblight or twig borers.

Sanitation—Prune and burn any shoots infected with fireblight. Watch for this disease later in the season.

80% petal fall on apple

Petal Fall

Stage 5—Fruitlet (Spring)

The young fruit crop should be fully visible and well on the way to becoming ripe. Once again, examine trees for insects, checking young fruit and foliage for recent damage from larvae. Powdery mildew, scab and shothole diseases usually attack at this stage, especially if weather has been wet.

Maintenance—Pull new weeds growing next to trunk. If you lay the weeds over the soil they act as a natural mulch.

Chemical—Spray a fungicide after any late rains, especially if you live in a humid climate. Spray a second insecticide cover if fruit and foliage damage is exceptionally widespread.

Weather—The weather during the next few weeks will determine how severe many diseases will be. Wet weather may bring on rots, molds and mildew.

Pear

Fruitlet

Stage 6—Preharvest (Summer and Fall)

Fruit are now about three weeks from harvest. If you have diligently followed pest and disease control, immediate problems may only be a sudden onset of brown rot, botrytis rot, birds and later generations of insect pests. Now is the time to begin thinking about pest and disease problems you may face next season.

Maintenance—Summer pruning, fruit thinning, cultivation and careful irrigation can influence pests and diseases at this stage. Look for scale crawlers that normally appear about this time. If birds are a problem, erect netting or provide for other means of keeping them away from fruit.

Sanitation—This is important to future pest and disease control. Removing dropped fruit now will pay off next season. Thin fruit that show external damage before removing healthy ones.

Chemical—Get a jump on next year's problems by spraying a protective fungicide cover. If biological control measures are not keeping pace, an insecticide spray will protect your remaining fruit. Check the label for the recommended number of days between sprays and harvest BEFORE you spray. Always wash fruit before eating.

Weather—Hot, dry weather in desert and inland areas may sunburn fruit. If necessary, install a shade cover. These conditions also encourage spider mites. Wash dusty foliage with water to keep populations down. Apply a miticide if infestations are particularly serious.

Pear

Preharvest

Stage 7—Leaf Fall (Fall)

The crop has now been harvested and weather has probably turned colder. Trees respond to this change by dropping their leaves and "hardening up" for the cold winter.

Maintenance—If your area receives abundant rainfall, prepare watering basins around trees to ensure good drainage away from trunk. Also keep snow from piling against tree.

Sanitation—Remove and destroy any diseased or injured limbs. Be sure to paint wounds with a sealing compound. Remove dropped, rotted fruit and fruit remaining on trees. Clear brush and debris away from trees.

Chemical—Spray for peach leaf curl and bacterial shothole.

Leaf Fall

Well-pruned apple tree.

Pruning

To gain an appreciation for the need to prune, consider what a fruit tree will become if it is not pruned. Without pruning, most fruit trees outgrow their allotted space, become dense and unsightly, resist efforts at spraying and picking, break apart and become unfruitful. Proper pruning keeps the tree within bounds. The tree can be sprayed, thinned and picked using a ladder of moderate height. In the case of dwarf trees, you can pick standing on the ground. The skillful fruit gardener shapes trees so they carry a heavy load of good fruit from top to bottom. Pruning, limb bending, tree support, fruit thinning and fertilizer use are all employed in a coordinated program. All these promote high production of good-quality fruit.

TOOLS FOR PRUNING

Use a solidly constructed ladder of sufficient height to prune large fruit trees. Climbing high in the tree to make cuts is risky to yourself and to tree limbs. Most fruit trees can be pruned from a 10 or 12-foot ladder. Get one with a third leg, not the leaning type. While it is sometimes convenient to make a few cuts high in the tree with a pole saw or pole lopper, it is difficult to do detailed pruning entirely with such tools.

The lopper is the single most useful pruning tool, followed by hand shears or "snippers." A pruning saw is needed for larger cuts.

Correct tools are essential to proper pruning. Pictured below are a bow saw (a) for large limbs, and a handy folding saw (b) for smaller limbs. Pruning shears come in many forms. Gear-driven pruners (c) and lopping shears (e) are best for larger branches. Hand pruners (d) are used on smaller branches. Hedge shears (f) are ideal for keeping fruiting hedges such as citrus or pineapple guava under control.

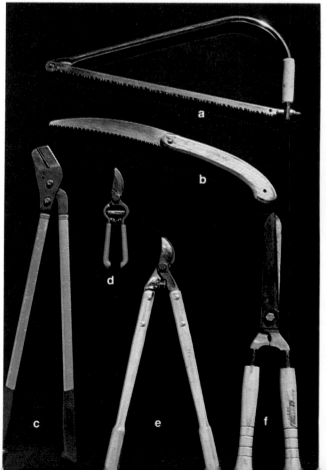

The above peach tree is pruned low so it can be sprayed, thinned and harvested easily.

TRAINING FRUIT TREES

Training includes all techniques used to shape the tree: limb spreading, tying, staking, pinching and pruning. The objectives of training are to establish the basic tree shape, develop a strong limb structure and encourage fruiting at an early age. Improper training or lack of training can result in severe breakage, freeze injury and poor form after the tree has grown to maturity.

A PRUNER'S GLOSSARY

To understand training, it will be helpful to know the names of the parts of a fruit tree and some pruning terms. See illustrations at right and top of page 46.

Shoot—Length of branch growth in a single season. In summer, it is the current-season growth. In winter, it is growth made the previous season. A ring of small ridges, the *bud scale scars*, appears at some point along the branch. This marks the start of last season's growth.

Spur—Short shoot that bears flower buds terminally, on the end, or laterally, on the sides.

Root sucker—Shoot that arises from the root system, generally below ground.

Sucker and watersprout—Terms sometimes used interchangeably. They refer to a long shoot that appears on the trunk or a major limb, usually in locations where a shoot is not desired. Some people reserve the term *sucker* for a long, unwanted shoot that arises on

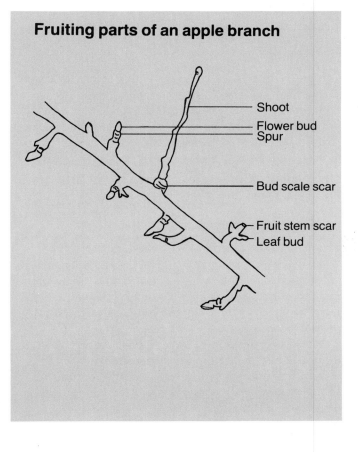

Fruiting parts of an apple branch

- Shoot
- Flower bud
- Spur
- Bud scale scar
- Fruit stem scar
- Leaf bud

Pruning anatomy

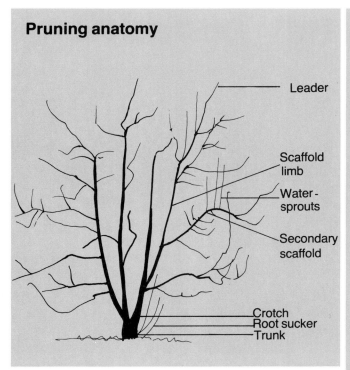

Leader

Scaffold limb

Water-sprouts

Secondary scaffold

Crotch
Root sucker
Trunk

the trunk or very close to it. *Watersprouts* arise on the upper sides of smaller limbs, generally arching toward the horizontal.

Scaffold limb—Large limb that forms part of the framework of the tree.

Leader—Uppermost portion of a scaffold limb. This portion determines a limb's future direction of growth. The *terminal* is the tip of the leader.

Buds—Formed on the sides or ends of shoots in leaf *axils,* the angle formed as a leaf joins a shoot. Buds may contain only leaf *primordia,* plant tissue that will develop into a leaf. Or, they may contain only flower primordia or a mixture of both.

Deciduous—Trees that drop their leaves in autumn.

Head—Part of a tree from which the main scaffold limbs originate.

Crotch angle—Angle formed between the trunk and the main scaffold limb.

Heading and thinning—All pruning cuts can be classified as either *heading* or *thinning.* Heading means cutting off part of a shoot or limb rather than removing the entire shoot or limb at a branch point. Thinning means removal of an entire shoot where it originates.

These two treatments have opposite effects. Heading increases the number of new shoots formed but thinning decreases it. *Pinching* is removal of part of a shoot while it is still growing, and is really a form of heading.

Thinning reduces the number of new shoots

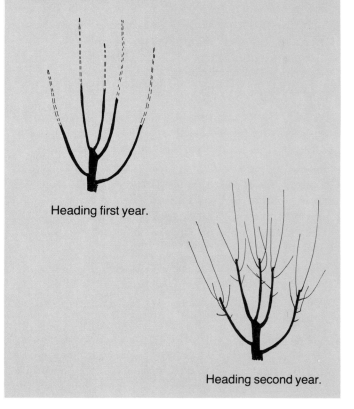

Thinning first year.

Thinning second year.

Heading increases the number of new shoots formed

Heading first year.

Heading second year.

Apical dominance

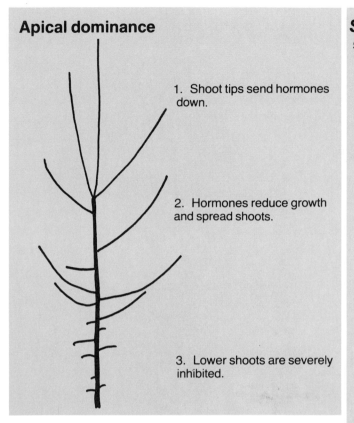

1. Shoot tips send hormones down.

2. Hormones reduce growth and spread shoots.

3. Lower shoots are severely inhibited.

Spreading modifies apical dominance and strengthens crotches

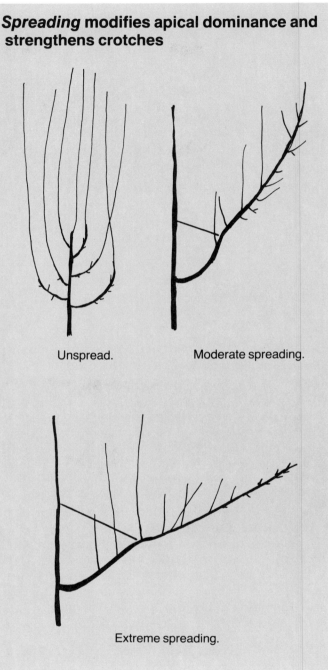

Unspread.

Moderate spreading.

Extreme spreading.

Apical dominance—Influence of the growing shoot tip on buds and other shoots below it. The shoot tip sends a message in the form of a chemical hormone that moves downward with gravity. This message prevents the growth of most lateral buds below the tip and reduces the growth of lower shoots.

Apical dominance determines which buds will grow and which won't. It is the principal way a tree organizes its growth. Removal of the shoot tip by heading will remove the inhibition of lateral buds, allowing them to form shoots. Thus, heading increases the number of new shoots formed. Thinning, removal of branches where they originate, preserves the apical buds of the remaining limbs and shoots, thus reducing the number of new lateral shoots. Heading is used to increase branching and to shorten and stiffen limbs. Thinning is used to direct and modify growth.

Some fruit trees lose apical dominance because the shoot terminates in a flower bud or because the terminal bud dies at the end of a growing season. The intensity of apical dominance varies considerably between species and between varieties within a species.

Apical dominance is modified if the shoot is bent downward, either artificially or naturally by the weight of leaves and fruit. Buds on the upper sides of bent shoots tend to grow into shoots. An upright limb produces the longest shoots near its apex. Moderate limb spreading, 30 to 60 degrees from vertical, reduces the vigor of shoots near the apex while increasing the number of shoots formed and the length of those farther from the apex. Wide spreading exaggerates this difference but may reduce the total number of shoots formed.

Healing a wound—Natural healing depends on the growth of bark fed by leaves located *above* the wound. For this reason, large stubs will not heal over. Cut close to the remaining limb to avoid leaving stubs.

Growth habits

Freely branching, semiupright habit.

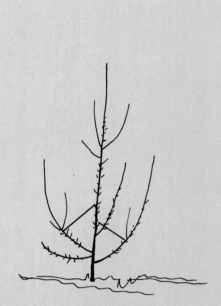

Spur-type growth habit.

Growth habit—Tendency of a tree to grow upright, semispreading or spreading. It may be vigorous, of medium vigor or dwarf. It may have few or many branches.

Fruiting habit—Position of flower buds and the age of the branch they are borne on. They may be borne terminally as with apples and pears, or laterally as with peaches, cherries and plums. Fruit buds are found on current season's growth, as with grapes and citrus. They can also appear on shoots of the previous season, as with peaches. Apples, pears and cherries appear on spurs that are many years old.

Pruning reduces the overall size of the tree and the size of pruned parts relative to unpruned ones. The remaining parts, especially near the pruning cuts, grow more vigorously. Pruning young trees is necessary for training, but it reduces the amount of fruit borne in the early years. It may also delay the time of first fruit crop. Most pruning is done in the dormant season after danger of fall or early winter freezes has passed. Pruning in early summer is devitalizing but useful in training. Late summer pruning helps control excess tree vigor.

TRAINING TECHNIQUES

When tree is dug at the nursery, most of the roots are pruned off. Even if your tree came in a container, it was probably dug from the field with great loss of roots. To compensate for this loss, it is necessary to prune off about half the tree's top at planting time. Trees with 1-year-old tops, branched or unbranched, and 2-year-old roots are more likely to grow well after transplanting than are trees with tops 2 or more years

Pruning new fruit trees

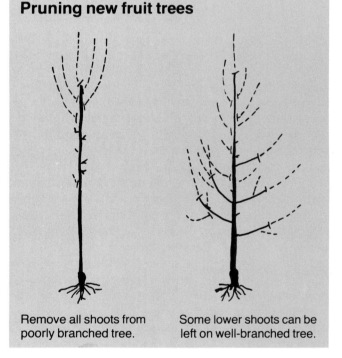

Remove all shoots from poorly branched tree.

Some lower shoots can be left on well-branched tree.

old. Unbranched nursery trees should be headed about 24 inches above ground after planting. Make sure not to cut below bud union. A few well-placed branches may be kept on nursery stock but head the side branches to an outward-pointing bud about 3 to 6 inches from the main trunk.

Early in the first and second summer after planting you can direct growth to the shoots that will become main scaffold limbs by pinching or removing unwanted shoots. Use spring-type clothespins to spread shoots that form narrow angles with the trunk. This is

Vase-shape training

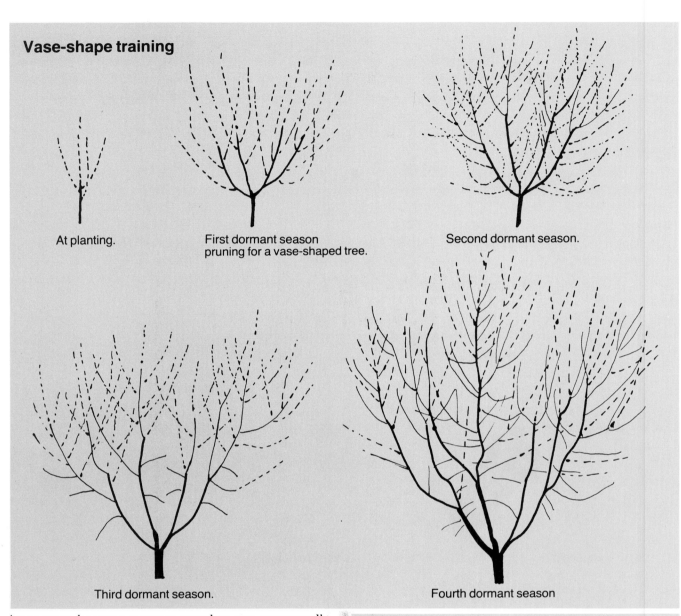

At planting.

First dormant season pruning for a vase-shaped tree.

Second dormant season.

Third dormant season.

Fourth dormant season

important because narrow crotches are structurally weak and will break easily when the tree is older. Don't develop all the scaffold limbs from one spot on the trunk because this also makes a weak tree. Ideally, scaffold limbs should be spaced 6 to 8 inches apart vertically.

On windy sites it may be necessary to stake the tree until it is strong enough to stand alone. Don't tie the trunk so tight to the stake that it cannot move. The trunk will thicken and gain strength due to movement imparted by wind.

The most common training system is the *vase shape* or *multiple leader*. From 3 to 5 well-placed shoots are selected as soon after planting as practical. Others are suppressed through heading or removed. Head shoots in the dormant season about 2 feet from the crotch. Branching is developed toward the outside of the tree, giving it an overall vase or goblet shape.

Shoots selected for scaffold branches can be strengthened by spreading with a clothespin.

Central leader training

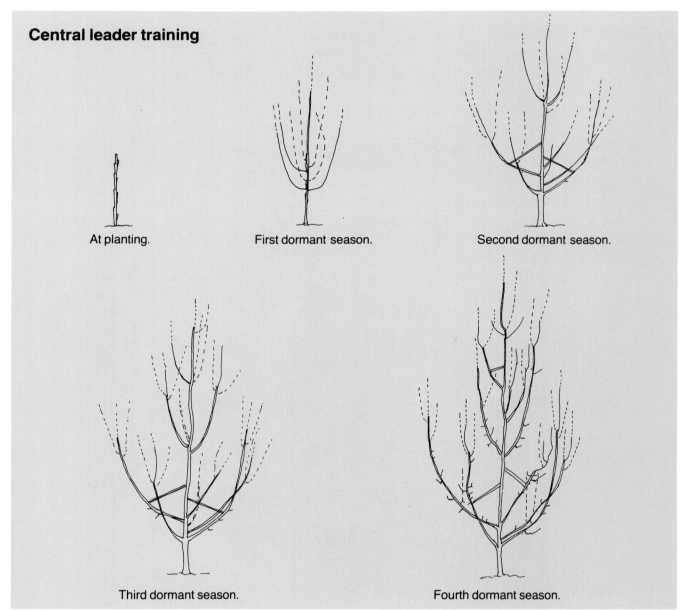

At planting.

First dormant season.

Second dormant season.

Third dormant season.

Fourth dormant season.

In *central-leader training,* all side limbs are developed from a central axis like a Christmas tree. Central-leader training is used to confine a tree to a small space, especially if it is dwarf or semidwarf. This method is much less practical to use with large trees.

Training to a central leader is accomplished as follows. First, establish the dominant position of the central leader by removing or spreading competing shoots. Remove or pinch back shoots that compete with the central leader during summer. Head the central leader each year at about 3 feet above the highest *whorl* of branches. This is the central axis from which side limbs develop. Use wooden limb spreaders to develop side limbs at about a 45 to 60-degree angle from the central leader. Some fruit trees will not need spreading because side limbs form naturally at wide angles. If

the tree becomes too tall, gradually remove the central leader and redevelop the tree in a vase shape.

A *modified central leader* system of training is used for many nut trees such as walnut, pistachio and pecan. This method develops the main scaffold branches high enough to walk under. In this method one dominant shoot, the leader, is trained to a stake the first season of growth. Other shoots are removed or shortened to 2 or 3 buds. In the following dormant season the leader is headed at about 6 feet and scaffold branches are selected near this height the following summer. After the scaffold branches are chosen, training proceeds in the same manner as for central leader training.

More information on pruning can be found in descriptions of the individual fruit.

Maintain fruiting wood throughout the tree

By promoting upright limbs high in tree and by pruning hardest in upper, outer portions, fruiting wood is maintained throughout tree.

PRUNING THE YOUNG, BEARING TREE

Pruning a young tree can encourage growth at the expense of fruiting. Therefore, prune the young bearing tree lightly, if at all. Some pruning is usually required to keep the tops from overloading with fruit and breaking off. With young, vase-shaped trees, it is often helpful to encircle the scaffold limbs with a rope or strap so the weight of fruit can't pull them too far down. Occasionally, when a tree has been stunted by drought or insufficient mineral nutrition, pruning by heading restores vigor.

Some pruners attempt to spread the tree by heading the leaders to outward-growing shoots. This is termed *bench cutting* because it creates a bench-like appearance due to apical dominance. See page 52. However, as the leader grows, it turns inward again, defeating the purpose of the bench cut. The point where the leader was bench cut is structurally weak and may bend excessively or break under a load of fruit.

It is better not to bench cut but to maintain strong lateral branches back to the leader. Develop widespreading side limbs from the scaffold limb. Eliminate limbs growing inward. When outward-growing side limbs set a good crop, they will pull the entire scaffold limb outward, causing the tree to spread. Always prune one side of a forked limb more severely than the

Bench cutting

Bench cutting to outward-growing limbs is not usually effective in spreading branches.

Development of a side limb by maintaining a straight axis from the leader *is* an effective method of spreading branches.

other. Equal forks are weak and tend to prevent light from penetrating the center of the tree.

The upper and outer portions of the tree grow more than the inner, lower portions because they receive more light. Unless reduced by regular pruning, tops will easily overgrow and shade out the lower and inner parts of the tree. Pruning the upper-outer portions after shoot growth has stopped in summer will let light into the lower portions and maintain more even vigor throughout the tree.

In hot climates, be careful not to expose the bark of main scaffold limbs to direct sunlight or they will be sunburned. Don't leave horizontal limbs in the tops of

trees because they will produce many suckers and shade out lower wood.

The height of a tree is maintained at a constant level by cutting out all but one of the strong shoots that develop at the point of heading. Head this shoot about one-third to one-half of its annual growth.

The amount of pruning required for renewal of fruiting wood depends on the fruiting habit of the species. Peaches, which bear only on shoots of the previous season, require heavy annual pruning. Those species that bear on long-lived spurs need less pruning. The sections on each individual fruit contain more information on fruiting habits.

Pruning a mature tree

In a well-pruned tree, heavy structural limbs (the dark part of tree trunk and limbs in illustration) make up the lower portions of the tree. The upper portions contain maximum fruiting wood.

PRUNING MATURE TREES

A well-pruned, mature fruit tree is a beautiful sight. It is short enough to be pruned, thinned and picked from a relatively short ladder. It produces fruit of good size and quality from the tops of the scaffold limbs all the way to the trunk. It is structurally strong so little or no artificial support is needed to prevent breakage or excessive spreading under a load of fruit. Openings in the tree canopy permit penetration of light and chemical sprays to the interior. These openings also provide spaces in which to set a ladder for harvesting and pruning.

In mature fruit trees the lower portions tend to become weak and produce only a few fruit of poor quality. The uppermost parts tend to produce vegetative growth. Between these two extremes of growth and poor fruiting is a *zone of equilibrium* where most of the crop is borne. This zone of equilibrium moves upward and outward in the tree as new fruiting wood develops on the upper, outer portions. The shaded weak zone and the overly vegetative zones tend to enlarge at the expense of the zone of equilibrium.

Techniques of pruning mature trees are aimed at maintaining a large zone of equilibrium between growth and fruiting. This is achieved largely by pruning harder in the upper, outer portions of the tree. This allows light to pass down between the limbs, illuminating leaves on fruiting shoots and spurs along the sides of main scaffold limbs. A good pruning job involves a large number of well-placed, small cuts. The return in fruit is well worth the time expended. Although most of the work can be done with loppers, a few saw cuts may be required. Hand shears are convenient when working in close quarters.

Start by clearing out a place in the tree to set a ladder. Then climb to the top and reduce the terminals to single, upright, headed shoots. Starting in the top will help you envision the passage of light through the tree. Remove watersprouts, except where they may be needed to replace fruiting wood. Remove or cut back horizontal or downward-hanging branches in the

Balanced fruiting zone

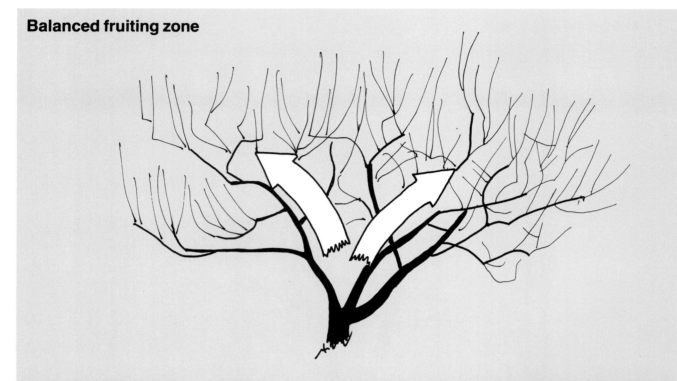

Pruning counteracts the tendency of the fruiting zone of a tree to move upward and outward. It creates an equilibrium between foliage growth and fruit development which results in fruit production throughout the tree.

upper-outer portions of the tree. Reduce the ends of all secondary scaffold limbs to a single upright shoot. Reduce one side of equal forks and shorten branches on the sides of secondary scaffold limbs so light can pass toward the tree center. Remove limbs that cross through the center of the tree. Prune to open the center of vase-type trees. Don't let one limb come out directly over another but direct it slightly to one side.

Move downward through the tree, pruning more lightly as you go. Remove old, fruiting wood and leave younger wood. Keep replacement leaders growing on scaffold limbs. Cut back to new leaders as the outer portions of scaffold limbs become horizontal or drooping. Thin out shoots to desired spacing and lightly head the longer ones.

Most fruit gardeners tend to prune younger trees too much and mature trees too little. If shoots that grew near last year's pruning wounds are very vigorous, perhaps the pruning was too severe. In that case, a light thinning of the more vigorous shoots may be all that is required. But if the tree has received little or no pruning for a year or more, much more severe pruning is needed. A vigorous annual pruning is a good way to contain a fruit tree in its allotted space.

Leader replacement

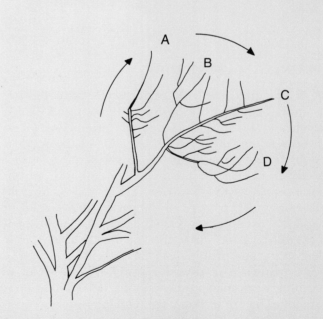

As limbs mature, they tend to bend outward from weight of fruit thus pulling leaders away from upright. Old leader D can be removed and replaced after developing C, then B and finally A as new leaders.

Espaliers

An *espalier* is a plant trained in a flat, horizontal manner, often against a wall or fence. Espaliers can be formal or informal. Many formal espaliers are fashioned in intricate patterns. Pruning, pinching, bending and tying are all used to guide the plant's limbs and branches along a trellis, wire or other support.

Espalier training is an effective way of growing fruit in a limited space. Espaliered plants make attractive garden dividers, and can be grown compactly against a sunny wall or fence.

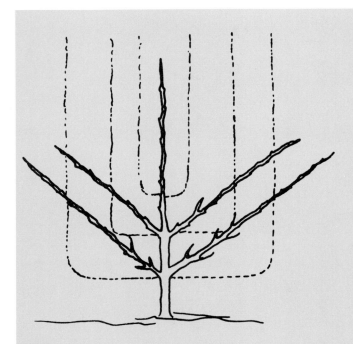

Informal espaliers make use of fan-shaped framework.

Formal espaliers can be trained in geometric patterns.

Espalier pears to save space or create interesting geometric patterns.

Propagating Your Own Varieties

Few gardening practices are more rewarding than propagating fruit varieties of your own choosing. There are many practical reasons to propagate your own trees. You may wish to have two or more varieties on the same tree. Or you may want to achieve a succession of ripening dates, or provide for cross-pollination. After planting a particular variety, you may find it does not do well in your locality. Instead of giving up, you can graft or bud a more desirable variety onto the existing tree.

Details of a few standard methods of propagating are given here. Chances are you will rely on your nurseryman for young trees. Therefore, the steps involved in propagation of trees to the stage at which they are sold in the nursery are not discussed. Most trees available at nurseries consist of a seedling rootstock that has been budded or grafted to a fruiting variety.

LAYERING

Simple layering—One of the simplest of all propagation methods is *layering*. In simple layering, a branch attached to the parent plant is bent so that it lies on the

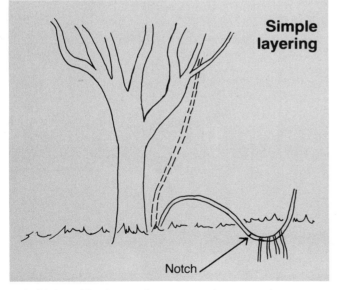

Simple layering

Notch

Left: Cleft grafting is one of many ways to propagate your own selection of varieties. See page 65.

ground. This is done during the dormant season or early in spring. To induce rooting, the branch is notched at the ground line before burying. All except the branch tip is then covered with soil. The following dormant season a section of the branch, which now bears roots and a shoot, is cut free and planted elsewhere in the garden. Filberts are usually propagated in this manner. Carissa, pomegranate and grape can be layered but other methods are also used.

Air layering—Some subtropical fruit can be *air layered*. This method is similar to regular layering but is done higher in the tree. To air layer, notch a branch and hold it open with a wooden wedge. Surround the notch with moist sphagnum moss, peat or similar moisture-holding material. Enclose in a plastic wrap and keep the material moist. When roots form, cut the branch below the rooted area and plant.

Tip layering—Canes of trailing blackberries, dewberries and black raspberries naturally droop to the ground. If a tip is covered with soil, roots will form. This is called *tip layering*, which is the usual method of propagating these plants.

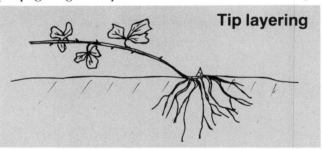

Tip layering

Trench layering—This is an extension of simple layering. In winter the main shoot of a young plant or branch of an older plant is selected. It is bent so that all but the tip is laid in a trench about 4 inches deep. Notched stakes or pieces of heavy wire may be used to hold down the layered branch. The trench is gradually filled with fine soil, adding a little every couple of weeks until the following summer. At the next dormant season, the rooted branch or shoot is cut free for transplanting.

Trench layering is used for hard-to-root species such as apples, pears, plums and cherries. Some varieties of these species do not root well and results may be erratic. Trench layering is a way to propagate plants that otherwise cannot be grown on their own roots. In some cases it may be simpler to plant a seedling or another plant of the desired species, or to topwork by using budding or grafting methods described later in this section.

Mound or stool layering—This method is used to propagate gooseberries, currants, quince and vegetatively propagated dwarf apple rootstocks. The mother

Mound layering

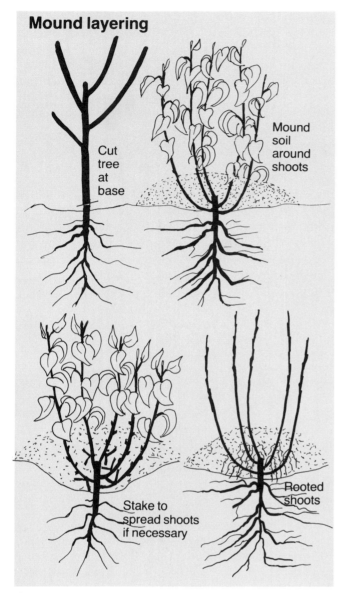

Cut tree at base

Mound soil around shoots

Stake to spread shoots if necessary

Rooted shoots

Cuttings should be long enough to include 2 buds and are usually 6 to 14 inches in length. The bottom cut is made straight across the stem, just below the lower node or joint where a bud is located. The top cut is made about an inch above the upper bud. If buds are numerous along the stem, less attention need be paid to these details. In general, cuttings root most readily near the nodes.

Cuttings are planted in winter if soil can be worked readily; otherwise, they can be stored. Keep them in damp soil, sand, peat moss, sawdust or other shaded, cool, moist places. They can then be planted whenever soil can be dug, but before growth starts in spring.

Plant cuttings vertically so the upper bud is just above the soil surface. Space 2 or 3 inches apart in a row. Keep them moist and weed-free during the following summer season. Those that root will be ready for planting the following winter.

Softwood cuttings—A few fruit plants, notably olive and citrus, can be propagated satisfactorily from *softwood cuttings*—cuttings made during summer from current season's growth. Special beds and care are needed for success. Rooting softwood cuttings usually involves using a greenhouse and a mist system. Mist systems apply a fine spray of water at fixed intervals, which keeps humidity very high and prevents cuttings from drying out. You may do better to stay with the more easily handled hardwood cuttings.

Root cuttings—Red raspberries may be propagated by means of *root cuttings*. Pieces of root are cut into 2 to 4-inch lengths and placed horizontally in trenches about 4 to 5 inches deep. They may also be planted vertically as with stem cuttings. In this case, the top of the cutting should be at ground level. Pull a little soil over the cutting to form a small mound.

plant is cut off close to the ground during winter. As shoots emerge from the stump in spring, cover the base of the shoots with enough soil to ensure that they are kept moist with occasional watering. Some of these shoots will root. They can then be separated from the mother plant the following dormant season.

CUTTINGS

Stem cuttings or slips—These are sections of stems removed from mature plants. They are used to propagate many plants, including grapes, currants, gooseberries, figs, quince, olives and pomegranates.

Hardwood cuttings—For fruit plants, *hardwood cuttings* are generally used. These are cuttings made in winter from mature wood of the previous season's growth. Fig and olive may be more successfully propagated from cuttings made of 2 or 3-year-old wood.

Rooting hardwood cuttings

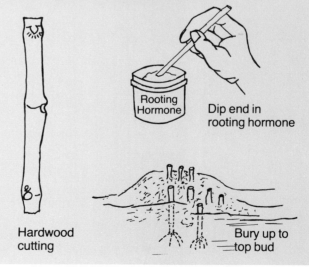

Hardwood cutting

Rooting Hormone

Dip end in rooting hormone

Bury up to top bud

Certain chemicals, described as growth-regulating substances or plant hormones, aid the rooting of cuttings. Indolebutyric acid (IBA), available in a powder form, is most effective in inducing rooting. IBA is particularly useful with difficult-to-root species. It is available under several trade names.

Strawberries are propagated from their *runners*—slender, trailing stems that form leaves at every other node. If the soil surface is kept moist and leafy nodes are buried under a thin layer of soil, they will root. Rooted runner plants can be dug during winter and cut free. Everbearing varieties may form runners sparingly or not at all. If no runners form, divide *crowns* of old plants where stems and roots come together, into two or more parts.

Propagating strawberries by runners

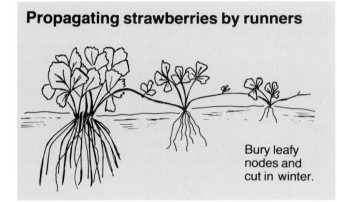

Bury leafy nodes and cut in winter.

Root suckers of red raspberries and 'Stockton Morello' cherry, a rootstock for cherries, are produced naturally from the underground portion of mature plants. They may be dug, removed from parent and planted during winter.

Digging root suckers for planting

Dig during dormant season.

BUDDING

The most common method of propagating fruit trees is by *budding*. It consists of inserting a single bud under the bark of a plant in such a manner that bud and stock unite and grow. This is the method used by nurserymen to grow familiar, named varieties on seedling rootstocks that may be unfamiliar. For the gardener, it is a way of topworking to change a tree or part of a tree to another variety.

Budding is usually done with varieties belonging to the same species or between closely related species. Plum on peach rootstock, both *Prunus* species, is a common match. Another example is 'Rio Oso Gem' peach on 'Elberta' peach. Lemon, orange and grapefruit can be propagated on the same tree. A pear bud could not be made to grow on an apricot tree, nor a cherry on an apple. They belong to different, unrelated species. Page 69 includes information on the degree of compatibility among common fruit species.

Some rootstocks are compatible with several fruit types. Peach, almond, apricot and plum, for example, will grow on a single peach rootstock. With several types of fruit on one rootstock, it may be difficult to maintain good control of diseases and pests, and keep a proper balance in pruning. You will have to weigh the advantages and disadvantages.

Quite often, budding is used to introduce a pollinizing branch to a tree such as filbert, almond or sweet cherry. These fruit need a pollinizer for the production of a crop when only a single tree is growing in a location. You should be careful to choose an appropriate pollinizer. Consult the variety charts in this book.

For all budding, both on deciduous and evergreen species, it is essential that the *cambiums* of the rootstock and bud be in contact. Cambium is the thin layer of cells found between the bark and the wood. Cambium is moist to the touch and produces new bark and new wood season after season.

Budding is usually done when the bark *slips*, which means you are able to peel the bark easily from the wood, exposing the cambium. This usually occurs after periods of active growth from spring to late summer. The bark on older wood tightens earlier in the season than on younger, vigorous shoots.

Spring budding—To do budding in March or April, known as *spring budding*, you must first select budwood in the winter from the variety you want. Keep it in cold storage until you bud. A few shoots of last year's growth, 1/4 to 1/2 inch in diameter, will yield many buds. These branches can be stored in your refrigerator. Place them in moistened newspaper and enclose all in waxed paper to prevent drying.

If you plan to bud later in the growing season, you will be able to select buds from the current season's growth.

Summer or fall budding—If budding is done in late June, July or August, the bud will unite with the stock but it will not usually grow into a shoot until the following spring. This is called *summer* or *fall budding*. Before the buds begin to start spring growth, cut the parent branch back to the bud itself. Otherwise, the bud may not grow.

After the first growing season, the resulting branch may be pruned as you would any other branch. Start your training program the first winter or dormant season in order to form the branch framework you desire.

For most deciduous species fall budding is better. Buds may be forced into growing as soon as they have united with the stock in the fall. Or buds may be left dormant until the following spring. *Forcing* is accomplished by cutting back or pruning the branch above the bud. Some foliage should be left until the bud is well started. For this reason the branch is generally cut back in two or three steps. The final cut is made just above the bud. When spring budding is done, the buds may be forced the same summer.

Evergreen fruit trees can be budded whenever the bark is slipping.

T-budding

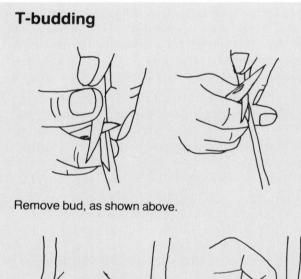

Remove bud, as shown above.

After making T-cut in stock, place bud in T and wrap with rubber budding strips.

T or shield bud—This is the most common way to bud both deciduous and evergreen species. It is a fairly simple operation. The spot where the bud is to be inserted should be free of any growth for a space of 2 to 3 inches. Bark should be as smooth as possible in that area. Make a vertical cut about an inch long through the bark to the wood. Next, with the knife blade slanted slightly toward the first cut, make a transverse cut at the top of the vertical cut, forming the letter **T.** Your horizontal cut should slightly open the two flaps of the vertical cut.

Take budwood directly from a tree of the variety you wish to propagate. This should be done at the time you wish to do your budding. An exception is spring budding, as mentioned before, where budwood has been cut and stored in a refrigerator. Be sure that you select budwood from a healthy tree, one free of any virus or disease.

Remove leaves from one stick of the budwood by cutting through the *petiole,* or leaf stalk, about 1/4 inch from the shoot. No harm is done if the petiole is removed entirely, but the short stalk is a convenient handle for inserting the bud.

Select a well-formed, mature bud. Remove bud from budstick by slicing in under bark, upward toward bud. Start cut 1/2 inch or more below bud. Cut into wood. Extend cut about 1/2 inch above bud. Upon completion of cut, your thumb should be holding bud and *shield,* the small section of the bark, to the knife blade.

Carry the shield to the T cut and insert the bottom of it into the top of the T. Push it down until the entire portion of the shield is encased by the flaps of the cut. This procedure places the cambium of the bud next to the cambium of the stock.

Rubber budding strips, approximately 1/4 inch by 4 inches, are used to press the bud tightly against the stock. They may be purchased at nurseries. Start wrapping the bud at the top of the T by lapping the first loop over the loose end of the rubber strip. Continue wrapping the stock with the remaining stretched strip of rubber until you have used up most of the strip. Then insert the end of the strip under the last loop, which should be at or below the lower cut of the T. This procedure will hold the bud tightly in place and you will not have to tie any knots in the rubber strip. Moistened raffia strips, nurseryman's tape or string may be used in place of rubber budding strips.

A growth union will take place in about 10 days if budding has been successful. The bud ties must be cut as soon as any signs of constriction appear. Cut budding strips or tape on the side opposite the bud shield. Buds inserted from mid-May to mid-June may make some growth the same season. Growth can be forced by

Patch budding

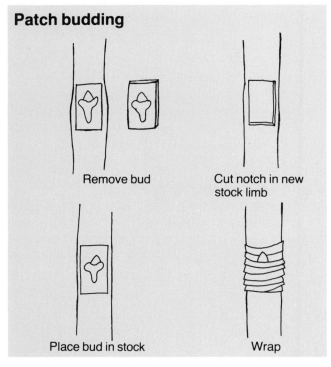

Remove bud

Cut notch in new stock limb

Place bud in stock

Wrap

cutting back to 3 to 6 inches above the bud 3 or 4 days after budding. After 3 or 4 inches of growth of the bud, cut the stock back to just above the bud growth.

Patch or flute bud—Thick-barked species such as walnut and pecan are more easily budded using the *patch* or *flute bud*. Budwood of these species is generally much larger, 1/2 inch to an inch in diameter, than species that are T-budded. However, the T or shield bud is the simplest and most satisfactory method for budding nearly all fruit trees.

To make a patch or flute bud, cut a square or rectangular patch including a bud from a budstick of the variety to be propagated. Slip it from the budstick by pressing near the bud from opposite sides with both thumbs. This will ensure the removal of a small core of wood with the bud. Without the core, the bud will fail to grow.

A piece of bark exactly the same size and shape of the patch is then removed from the stock limb. The patch containing the bud is inserted and tied. If the bark of the stock is considerably thicker than that of the bud, shave the stock bark down so that the tie presses the bud firmly against the stock.

I or modified H bud—For exceptionally thick-barked stock limbs, a modification known as *I* or *modified H budding* is sometimes used. Cut the bud as described for patch budding. Instead of removing a similar patch from the stock limb, make straight cuts the shape of an H laying on its side (**I**). Lift the two flaps on either side of the vertical cut and insert the patch beneath. Trim down the overlay of bark and tie the

bud. Care should be taken to see that the patch does not buckle while being tied.

Chip bud—Grapes are usually budded only after the first year's growth. A method called *chip budding* is used. Chip budding is done in late summer or early fall, as soon as mature buds from light brown canes are available. As with other budsticks, remove leaves and keep canes moist and cool unless the budding is done immediately.

Cut the bud from the cane by making a cut deep into the wood. Start just below the bud and cut at a 45-degree angle downward. Make a second cut, starting a little more than 1/2 inch above the bud. Cut downward in a straight line to meet the lower cut, about 1/8 inch or more from the surface of the cane. Make a similar cut in the stock cane just above the ground line. This cut should be slightly more angled so that the chip containing the bud fits firmly. Tie in the same way as for other buds. Cover the bud with a layer of moist soil to a depth of 4 inches or more.

The next spring, as buds on the top canes start to swell, uncover the propagated bud. If it has united with the vine, cut off the top of the vine to within an inch or so of the bud. During the following summer train the developing shoot upward by tying it to a stake. Remove all suckers developing from the stock. If you start a grape cutting with the intention of eventually budding it, you can make it "suckerproof" by removing all buds but the topmost.

Chip budding can also be done on other deciduous fruit and is a useful technique for spring budding before the bark slips from the cambium.

Chip budding

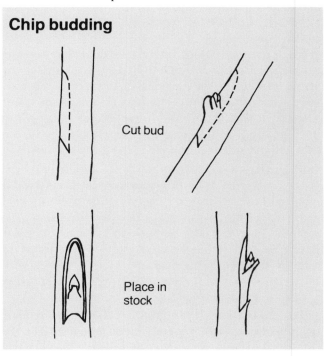

Cut bud

Place in stock

GRAFTING

Older trees and vines that have thick-barked lower branches too large for budding may be changed to other varieties by one of several methods of *grafting*. Grafting means to add a living piece of one plant, usually a stem or branch, to another closely related plant. The process is a little more involved than budding, but some people find it easier to do.

Two general methods of grafting are described here: *bark graft* and *cleft graft*. They are applicable to all fruit trees and require the simplest tools. Professional grafters may use other methods but often prefer these.

Deciduous trees are grafted any time from late winter until after bloom time. Many evergreen trees can be grafted any time of the year, but spring is usually preferred.

For all methods of grafting, a piece of propagating material, *scionwood (scion),* must be selected to be grafted on the parent stock. Scionwood should include two or three buds above the cut necessary to fit the scionwood to the stock. Scionwood is somewhat larger in diameter than budwood, usually 3/8 to 3/4 inch in diameter.

Deciduous-fruit scionwood must be dormant. It is selected in the winter and stored, if necessary, as described for dormant budwood in spring budding. See page 59. The wood should be fully mature, with vigorous buds showing. Avoid flower buds.

Evergreen scionwood is obtained at the time grafting is to be done. It too can be stored for short periods if more convenient. Leaves should be removed as described for budwood. Scionwood should be mature and of good size for the species, often taken from 2 or 3-year old growth. Tip growth should be discarded, although the base of vigorous new growth may be satisfactory.

Nurse branches, which provide shade, protection and nutrients, are sometimes left on deciduous and evergreen trees that are being grafted. A nurse branch is left ungrafted until the neighboring scions are well started, at which time the nurse branch is cut off or itself grafted. In selecting a nurse branch, choose one that will provide some shade to the grafted limbs.

Bark graft—A satisfactory method for all fruit species is the *bark graft*. When deciduous trees are *topworked* (changed to a different variety) by this method, bark grafting is limited to the spring when the bark peels easily from the wood. Scionwood must be dormant. Evergreen trees can be bark grafted whenever the bark is slipping. This may be any time of the year. However, the preferred time for most evergreen species is in the spring.

To make a bark graft, saw off the trunk or main framework branch at a convenient height. Make the cut perpendicular to the length of the branch.

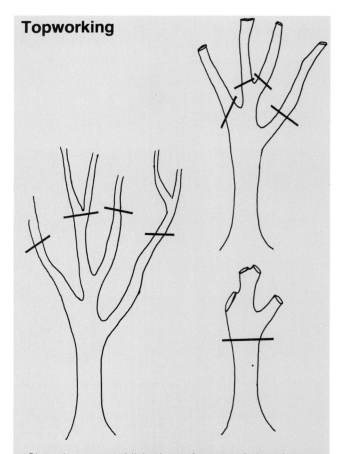

Topworking

Changing an established tree from one fruit variety to another is called *topworking*. It usually includes the use of bark grafts. To prepare a tree for topworking, begin making cuts in the top of the tree and work your way down.

Branches 2 to 4 inches in diameter are preferred. Larger branches heal too slowly. With a knife, make two parallel cuts through the bark, beginning at the saw cut and running lengthwise down the branch for about 1 to 3 inches. The cuts should be as far apart as the scionwood is wide. Pull back the flap of bark made by the two cuts. Make a slanting cut on the scionwood, nearly through wood, about 2 to 2-1/2 inches from the bottom. On the opposite side, at the bottom of the scionwood, make a shorter, tapering cut. Insert this scion into the flap of bark on the branch (stock). Only a little of the longer cut surface should extend above the top of the stock. Using two or three small nails or brads 5/8 to 1-inch long, nail the flap tight to scion and wood of the stock. Seal all cut surfaces with grafting wax.

One, two, three or more scions may be inserted on each stock, depending on the size of the stock. If two or more are placed on the stock, follow the after-treatment for cleft graft described later in this section. Larger and older trees should be topworked by grafting the main branches. If a graft fails to grow, the shoots rising from the stump may be budded.

Bark grafting

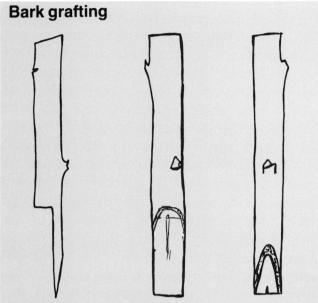

Cuts shown from 3 different angles on how to prepare scionwood for bark graft.

Scion in proper position

Side bark graft—A modification of the bark graft that is very helpful with such trees as macadamia, cherimoya and avocado is the *side bark graft*. Using this method, the grafted limb is not cut off at the time of grafting. The graft is made in much the same manner as described for the common bark graft. But at the top of the parallel cuts in the limb, a triangular piece of bark about three to four times the diameter of the scion is removed. The base of the triangle is toward the bottom. The parallel slits for the scion are centered in the middle of the base of the triangle.

The scion is cut and attached to the stock limb as shown in the side bark graft above. After it has united and started growth, the grafted limb is cut back heavily. About a year later it can be cut back to the scion.

Side bark graft

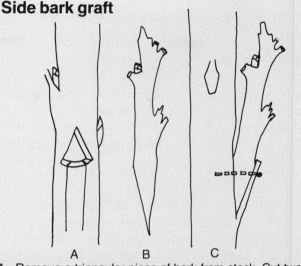

A. Remove a triangular piece of bark from stock. Cut two parallel lines from the base of the triangle.
B. Make one long slanting cut and one short slanting cut in opposite sides of scion.
C. Place scion in stock. Secure with small nails and cover with grafting compound.

Side graft

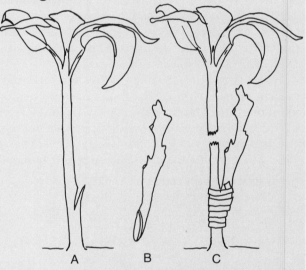

A. Make a long, slanting cut in stock. Leave top of stock in place.
B. Take scion from branch not actively growing. Make one long slanting cut. Remove leaves.
C. Place scion in stock so cambiums touch. Wrap spirally with rubber budding strips. Begin at the bottom and work up. Cut stock in 3 or 4 weeks to force scion growth.

Make a sloping cut opposite the scion to aid in healing.

For trees too small for side bark graft, use *side graft* as illustrated above.

With the side bark graft, as with other grafts, all cut surfaces on stock and scion should be well covered with a grafting compound. Cover the graft at the time it is made and when the stock is cut back to the scion.

Cleft graft—The *cleft graft* is one of the most popular and usable methods for deciduous trees but is rarely used on evergreens. You can use this method if the trunk or any of its branches are from 2 to 4 inches in diameter. Saw the trunk or branch off at the height you wish to insert the scions. One graft may take 1, 2, 3 or more scions, depending upon the size of branch or trunk. With a hatchet or thick, long-bladed knife, split the stump lengthwise through the center. This cut must be held open with wedges placed on either edge of the split.

Cut the lower end of each scion to form a long, tapering wedge. These sloping cuts should be at least 1-1/2-inches long, with at least 2 buds above the cut. The usual length of a scion is 4 to 5 inches.

Place the scion into the wedge of the stump (stock) so that the cambium of the scion touches the cambium of the stock. This means that the scion should be tilted outward somewhat so that the cambiums touch each other by crossing. This is particularly important if the stock has thick bark. When the scions are in position with cambiums touching, remove the wedging implement. The pressure of the stock coming together will hold the scions firmly in place. Because there are so many cut edges to dry out or allow entrance of diseases or pests, immediately cover all the cut surfaces with a generous amount of grafting wax. Be sure to place a dab of wax on the top cuts of the scions, too.

Cleft grafting is usually done in January or February when the stock is completely dormant. It can be done over a longer period than the somewhat simpler bark graft. Cleft grafts may be made after the stock has started growth if the scionwood has been collected earlier and kept completely dormant in cold storage.

Crown graft—Old grape vines may be grafted using the cleft graft. Step-by-step photographs of how to cleft graft can be seen on page 65. The method is called *crown grafting* because it is done at or below the ground line, near the plant's crown. The procedure is exactly the same as cleft graft, but first remove the soil to expose the straight part of the trunk above the roots. Make a split in the same manner as a cleft graft, but somewhat shorter than you would for a branch of a tree. Insert scions into splits, as with cleft graft. Cover scions completely with moist soil, taking care not to disturb the grafts. The following spring when the scions begin growing, remove all watersprouts or long, succulent growth from the stock. If the new growth from the scions becomes long, support it by tying to stakes set in the ground.

Whip graft—A third type of grafting is called *whip grafting*. It is very useful for small trees and is commonly used to graft selected varieties to seedling rootstocks. With whip grafting, scion and stock must be the

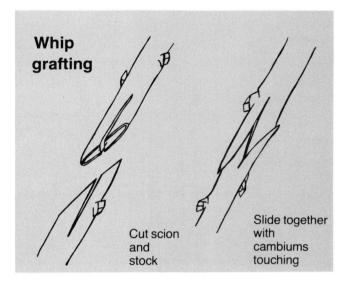

Whip grafting

Cut scion and stock

Slide together with cambiums touching

same size. Wedge cuts are made in scion and stock and they are slid together as shown above. Make sure cambiums are touching and wrap carefully with rubber budding strips or elastic tape.

PROTECTING GRAFTS

Wounds made in grafting need protection against drying and entrance of wood-rotting organisms. For this purpose a compound called *grafting wax* is used. Many types of grafting waxes are available from nurserymen or orchard supply dealers.

Cold asphalt emulsions are also satisfactory and easy to apply. Be sure that asphalt is not washed off by rains before it has had a chance to set. After 24 hours asphalt is usually able to withstand moisture. Apply generously and make a second application if cracks or openings develop.

The easiest-to-use grafting compounds are polyvinyl acetate-based plastics. Before they have dried, they are water soluble. After drying they form a tough, flexible, waterproof coating that will not crack.

True grafting waxes must be melted but shouldn't get too hot. These waxes harden immediately and are not affected by rain. You may also use a hand wax. It is worked and molded by hand. Apply it with your fingers instead of a brush or paddle. Although hand waxes are not commonly used, the results are satisfactory.

Grafts on deciduous trees seldom need protection beyond use of a grafting compound at the time the graft is made. Walnut grafts are an exception and benefit from added protection. Because they are usually grafted late in the spring, walnut grafts are exposed to higher temperatures and more intense sunlight. A common method of protecting these grafts is to tie a paper bag over the scions. It is essential to provide ventilation by tearing or punching small holes in the bottom corners of the bag and along the edges

Cleft Grafting

1. Cut or saw trunk or branch at level you want to insert scionwood.

2. Split stock with a knife or hatchet.

3. Choose dormant scionwood that is about 3/8 to 3/4 inch in diameter and carries at least 2 or 3 buds.

4. Keep cut in stock open with a wedge or knife. Cut end of scionwood to form a tapering wedge at least 1-1/2 inches long.

5. Place scionwood into cut in stock so cambiums of each are touching. Cover union with tape and wax.

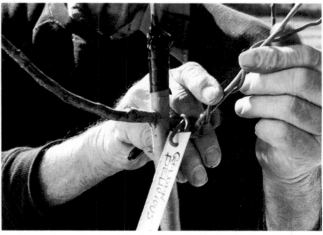

6. Use a long-lasting label to identify the grafted variety.

near the stock. White-washing newly set walnut scions also seems to provide extra protection.

It is common to wrap the scions of evergreen grafts. First, apply grafting compound on all cut surfaces. Wrap a piece of muslin around the top of the stock, covering the cleft or lifted bark of the stock. Pull the wrap tight and tie. This protects against drying if the grafting compound cracks. It also helps hold the scions

firmly in place. After tying with muslin strips, apply another coat of grafting compound. Cover the whole surface around the scions, including the muslin.

Paper bags may then be tied over the scions in the same fashion as described previously. Bags protect the scions and young growth from sunburn. Remove the paper bags when new growth from the scions reaches the bottom of the inverted bag.

PROPAGATION CHART

VARIETY	SEED	COLD STRATI-FICATION DAYS REQUIRED	HARDWOOD CUTTINGS	SOFTWOOD CUTTINGS AND WHEN TO TAKE	LAYERING	ROOT SUCKERS	REMARKS
TREE FRUIT							
APPLE	Yes.	60.	Yes, some varieties.	No.	Stool, trench.	Yes.	Almost any apple can be layered, including dwarfs and rootstock-types.
APRICOT	Yes.	80 to 90.	No.	No.	No.	No.	Rootstocks can be grown from seed.
CHERRY, SOUR	No.	None.	No.	No.	No.	Yes.	Some rootstocks propagated by rooted suckers.
CHERRY, SWEET	Yes.	189.	No.	No.	Trench.	Yes.	Some rootstocks propagated by rooted suckers.
CITRUS	Yes.	None.	No.	Yes, under mist in late spring.	No.	No.	Rootstocks with specific soil and climate adaptations can be grown from seed.
CRABAPPLE	Yes.	30 to 60.	Yes.	No.	Yes.	Yes.	Chilling requirement for seed varies from 30 to 60 days, depending on species.
FIG	Yes.	None.	Yes.	Yes, under mist year-round.	Air.	Yes.	Year-old watersprouts near base of tree produce most vigorous trees. Hardwood cuttings should be taken from 2 to 3-year-old wood.
OLIVE	Yes.	None.	Yes.	Yes, late spring.	No.	Yes.	Olive can be propagated in more ways than other fruit trees.
PEACH	Yes.	70 to 105.	No.	Yes, some varieties in midspring.	No.	No.	Rootstocks with specific soil and climate adaptations can be grown from seed.
PEAR	Yes.	60 to 90.	No.	No.	Stool, trench.	Yes.	No apparent advantage to stool layering.
PERSIMMON	Yes.	60 to 90.	No.	No.	No.	No.	Duration of cold stratification depends on species.
PLUM AND PRUNE	Yes.	90 to 150.	Yes, some plums.	No.	Trench.	Yes.	Japanese plums root easily from hardwood cuttings. Prunes do not. Prunes sucker more and can be propagated from rooted suckers. Prune seed require longest stratification.
POMEGRANATE	Yes.	None.	Yes.	Yes, under mist.	Yes.	No.	Easily propagated from hardwood cuttings.
QUINCE	Yes.	None.	Yes.	No.	Stool.	Yes.	Usually propagated from hardwood cuttings.
BERRIES							
BLACKBERRY	No.	None.	No.	Yes, under mist in summer.	Tip.	Yes.	Growth rate of erect blackberries is much greater from root cuttings.
BLUEBERRY	Yes.	None.	Yes.	Yes, late spring.	No.	Yes.	Hardwood cuttings are difficult.
CURRANT	Yes.	90.	Yes.	No.	Stool, trench.	No.	Usually propagated from hardwood cuttings.
GOOSEBERRY	Yes.	90.	Yes.	No.	Stool, trench.	No.	Usually propagated from hardwood cuttings.
GRAPE	Yes.	None.	Yes.	No.	Tip.	No.	Varieties are not true to type when grown from seed.
RASPBERRY	Yes.	None.	No.	Yes, under mist.	Tip.	Yes.	Can be propagated by root cuttings.
STRAWBERRY	Yes.	None.	No.	No.	No.	No.	Easily propagated by seed or runner. Runners must be disease-free.
NUTS							
ALMOND	Yes.	65.	No.	No.	No.	No.	Very little success with cuttings.

USING THE PROPAGATION CHART

Selected fruit varieties are usually grafted or budded onto a rootstock with desirable characteristics. These characteristics are transferred to the variety and include such traits as dwarfing, disease or insect resistance, wider climate or soil adaptation or increased vigor. Many berries or vines are commercially propagated by rooted cuttings or root cuttings.

Some plants produce seedlings that are identical to the parent. Others are much less predictable. Seedlings may be dramatically different from parent in plant form or fruit quality. Many seeds require a period of *cold stratification*, exposure to cold temperatures, before they will germinate. This is satisfied by keeping seeds in the refrigerator for the period designated in the chart.

PROPAGATION CHART

VARIETY	SEED	COLD STRATI-FICATION DAYS REQUIRED	HARDWOOD CUTTINGS	SOFTWOOD CUTTINGS AND WHEN TO TAKE	LAYERING	ROOT SUCKERS	REMARKS
CHESTNUT	Yes.	None.	No.	No.	No.	Yes.	Although not completely true to type, commonly grown from seed.
FILBERT	Yes.	60 to 180.	No.	No.	Stool, trench.	Yes.	Produces many suckers. Seed chilling requirement depends on species.
MACADAMIA	Yes.	None.	No.	Yes, under mist any time.	No.	No.	Partially hardened, 4 to 5-inch cuttings with 2 whorls of leaves best.
PECAN	Yes.	30 to 60.	No.	Yes, under mist.	Trench, air.	Yes.	Seedlings used as rootstocks.
PISTACHIO	Yes.	30 to 60.	No.	Yes.	No.	No.	Nonedible varieties used as stock for edible varieties.
WALNUT	Yes.	30 to 156.	No.	No.	No.	No.	Seed chilling requirement depends on species.

SUBTROPICALS

VARIETY	SEED	COLD STRATI-FICATION DAYS REQUIRED	HARDWOOD CUTTINGS	SOFTWOOD CUTTINGS AND WHEN TO TAKE	LAYERING	ROOT SUCKERS	REMARKS
ACEROLA CHERRY	Yes.	None.	Yes, spring-summer.	Yes, under mist in June.	Air.	No.	Seed is sometimes not fertile.
AVOCADO	Yes.	None.	No.	Yes, late spring.	No.	No.	Difficult to propagate by softwood cuttings.
BANANA	Yes.	None.	No.	No.	No.	No.	Best-tasting bananas produce few seed. Propagate by rhizome suckers.
CAPULIN CHERRY	Yes.	None.	Semi-hardwood, under mist.	No.	No.	No.	Plant fresh seed only. Variable from seed.
CARISSA	Yes.	None.	No.	Yes, late spring.	Yes.	No.	Cuttings will grow in greenhouse any time, but summer is best.
CHERIMOYA	Yes.	None.	No.	No.	No.	No.	
FEIJOA	Yes.	None.	No.	Yes, late fall.	No.	No.	Difficult to propagate by softwood cuttings.
GUAVA (Psidium)	Yes.	None.	Yes.	Yes, late spring.	Yes.	Yes.	Layering is sure and easy. Suckers transplant readily. Softwood cuttings should be started only in greenhouse.
JABOTICABA	Yes.	None.	No.	No.	No.	No.	Variable from seed. Grafting difficult.
JUJUBE	Yes.	None.	No.	No.	No.	Yes.	Root suckers are easiest.
KIWI	Yes.	30 days or more.	Yes, January.	Yes, late spring.	No.	No.	Superior varieties grafted to seedlings make stronger root systems. Plant cuttings also used.
LOQUAT	Yes.	None.	No.	Yes, in fall.	No.	No.	Plant fresh seed only.
LYCHEE	Yes.	None.	No.	No.	Air.	No.	Seed highly variable. Air layering is usual technique.
MANGO	Yes.	None.	No.	No.	Air.	No.	Do not permit seed to dry out. Remove seed from husk before planting. Plant kidney bean-shaped seed with hump at soil level.
PAPAYA	Yes.	None.	Yes.	Yes, year-round.	No.	No.	Mountain papaya roots easily from cuttings.
PASSION VINE	Yes.	None.	No.	Yes, under mist year-round.	Air.	No.	Roots easily when cuttings are semihardwood with buds. Do not dry seed in sunlight; it decreases germination.
SURINAM CHERRY	Yes.	None.	No.	Yes, under mist late spring.	No.	No.	Commonly propagated by seed.
WHITE SAPOTE	Yes.	None.	No.	No.	No.	No.	Variable from seed. Dry seed out of sunlight for 3 or 4 days and plant in soil high in organic matter.

Genetic dwarf fruit trees, such as 'Southern Sweet' peach above, produce abundant crops of delicious, full-size fruit in a small area.

Growing Fruit in Small Spaces

Growing fruit no longer brings to mind large orchards with trees in long, straight rows. Instead, the modern fruit gardener turns a small back yard, patio or even tiny balcony into a remarkably productive area.

Advances have been made primarily in the areas of growth-controlling rootstocks and compact varieties—*genetic dwarfs*. A better understanding of how tree growth is regulated has also helped fruit growers develop training and pruning practices for small trees.

Summer pruning has been revived as a method of growth control. Growing trees in containers is becoming more popular as a method of controlling tree size. Special training systems such as espalier also keep trees small and use growing space efficiently.

DWARF FRUIT TREES

There are two types of dwarf fruit trees: those in which the fruiting part of the tree, or *scion*, is dwarfed by its rootstock or interstem; and those in which the fruiting part is genetically dwarf. Either way, the advantages are impressive. Controlled size eases pruning, thinning, spraying and harvesting and better adapts the tree to container culture. In general, dwarf trees have versatile use, fit in the smallest landscape and tend to fruit at an earlier age.

DWARFING ROOTSTOCKS

Dwarfing through rootstocks involves budding or grafting a desired variety to the root system of a closely related plant. The rootstock restricts growth of the tree because of one or more characteristics, such as slower nutrient uptake or a smaller root system. These factors are then passed on to dwarf the desired variety.

Vigor of the variety grafted on the dwarfing rootstock influences the eventual size of tree. Even when grown on the same rootstock, a vigorous apple variety such as 'Rhode Island Greening' produces a larger tree than a more restrained variety such as 'Macoun'. A similar comparison could be made between the more vigorous 'Dancy' tangerine and the smaller kumquat.

Dwarfing can also be achieved through use of an *interstem*. A small section of dwarfing rootstock is inserted as an interstem between a standard rootstock and a branchlet (top part) of the desired variety by means of a double graft. This takes advantage of the best qualities of three trees. The result: a dwarf tree with strong roots that produces desirable fruit.

Unfortunately, doing your own grafting is sometimes the only way to be sure which rootstock a variety is grown on. Fruit trees are often labeled and sold simply as "dwarfs" or "semidwarfs." The rootstock is not specified. This gives you no indication of the tree's eventual mature size.

GENETIC DWARFS

The second type of dwarf fruit tree is called a *genetic dwarf*. Here, the actual fruiting part of the tree, the scion, is dwarfed in size. It is grafted onto a standard-size rootstock and special care is taken to remove vigorous suckers. Many genetic dwarfs have tightly spaced fruit buds, resulting in a huskier-looking tree and a spectacular spring bloom. Spur-type apple varieties also have closely spaced fruiting buds, but they are not nearly as tightly packed as those of a genetic dwarf.

Genetic dwarfs require little pruning but need special attention to fruit thinning—many have a tendency to overbear. Most reach a height of 6 to 10 feet, depending on fruit type.

Genetic dwarfs have one distinct disadvantage compared to fruit types that are grafted onto dwarf rootstocks: a limited choice of varieties. You can graft any variety you like onto dwarfing rootstocks. Genetic dwarf varieties are limited to those that have been specially bred that way.

THREE IN ONE?

Many nurseries offer trees with two or more varieties of fruit on one tree. Grafting a twig of another variety onto a tree with the same bloom period is also a good way to provide cross-pollination. In certain cases, several species may be combined into one. See compatibility chart below.

DWARF APPLE ROOTSTOCKS

Percent dwarfing of Malling (M) and Merton Malling (MM) apple rootstocks.

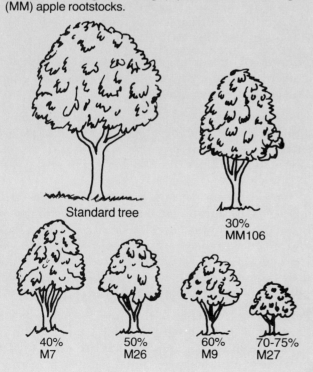

Standard tree

30% MM106

40% M7

50% M26

60% M9

70-75% M27

TREE FRUIT COMPATIBILITY

STOCK	SCION									
	ALMOND	APPLE	APRICOT	CHERRY, SOUR	CHERRY, SWEET	PEACH	PEAR	PLUM, EUROPEAN	PLUM, JAPANESE	QUINCE
ALMOND	X					X				
APPLE		X								
APRICOT			X			*		X	X	
CHERRY, SOUR				X	X					
CHERRY, SWEET				X	X					
PEACH	X		X			X		X	X	
PEAR							X			
PLUM, EUROPEAN	X		X			*		X	X	
PLUM, JAPANESE			X			*		*	X	
QUINCE							*			X

Trees bearing multiple types of fruit can be created by grafting or budding wood from one fruit type, or the scion, on to a tree, or the stock, of another fruit type. The chart above indicates compatibility between fruit types. This symbol * indicates that the combination is possible but may be short-lived or weak.

This 'Jonwin' apple on Malling 9 dwarf rootstock is 27 years old.

Citrus in containers are attractive landscape plants, and produce worthwhile crops as well.

Although this is a good way to grow several types of fruit in a small area, you must match variety vigor carefully. A combination of vigorous-growing 'Rhode Island Greening' apple and the less-vigorous 'Macoun' apple would probably end up with 'Rhode Island Greening' taking over, strangling the 'Macoun'. Careful pruning practices must balance varieties.

Another method that yields good results is to plant several varieties in one hole. Choose varieties of matching vigor and climate adaptation. Each tree is trained as a scaffold limb. They are slanted slightly outward and often tied together to support each other. See the photographs on pages 28 and 29.

DWARFING METHODS

Following is a summary of the methods used to control various fruit and nut trees.

Apples—Any desired tree size can be obtained by choice of rootstock alone. This is fortunate, because some of the highest quality scion varieties are not available as genetic dwarfs. 'Garden Delicious' is the only *widely* available variety. The most-dwarfing rootstock, 'M-27,' (M stands for Malling) produces a tree 3 to 5 feet tall. On 'M-9' rootstock, some varieties may reach a height of 12 feet if supported. They can be held to 5 or 6 feet high by pruning. 'M-26,' 'M-7,' 'M-106' and 'M-111' rootstocks produce trees of increasing size in the order listed. On these rootstocks, trees can be pruned hard for growth control without being forced out of production. With some scion varieties, spur-type *mutants,* explained in the chapter on apples, are also available. When spur-type mutant varieties are grafted on growth-controlling rootstocks, remarkably productive and compact trees are obtained.

Apricots—Dwarfing techniques for apricots are not very advanced. A few scion varieties with genetically dwarfed growth habits such as 'Garden Annie' are available.

Almonds—The variety 'All-in-One' is a semidwarf tree with a dense habit and good productivity that does not require cross-pollination. 'Garden Prince' is a fully dwarf almond that grows to 8 feet tall and is very productive. It also produces good crops without cross-pollination.

Cherries—A few, compact scion varieties of sweet cherry—'Compact Lambert', 'Compact Stella', 'Garden Bing'—are available through some nurseries. Semidwarf trees are obtained by use of 'North Star' sour cherry interstem or 'Stockton Morello' sour cherry rootstock. *Prunus mahaleb* rootstocks are often said to be dwarfing, but are not. Newer dwarfing rootstocks, such as 'Colt' from England and 'MxM 14', may prove to be better than existing rootstocks but have not yet been widely tested.

Figs—Figs are generally grown from cuttings and thus have no rootstock. No compact scion varieties are known. Figs are well adapted to growing in containers and can also be trained as a multitrunk bush. Bush forms can be controlled by heavy pruning.

Filberts—The size of filbert trees can be limited by growing plants as multitrunked bushes and periodically thinning large branches.

Nectarines and peaches—Genetic dwarfs of nectarine and peach have been developed by hybridization with such Chinese dwarf peaches as 'Flory' and 'Swatow'. These trees are very compact and can be grown easily in containers.

Size of standard nectarine and peach varieties can be controlled by central leader training, plus summer and dormant-season pruning. Rootstocks of *Prunus besseyi* and *Prunus tomentosa* are used to dwarf peaches but trees sucker profusely and are often short-lived. No doubt these rootstocks have been the source of disappointment for many home fruit growers.

Pears—Pear varieties with compact growth habits have not yet been developed. No fully dwarfing rootstocks are available. Quince roots are often used to provide semidwarf trees. Trees on quince rootstock

This Oregon State University experiment is visual proof that apples can be trained along wires. Result is a productive, fruiting fence in minimum space.

Many fruit grown in containers have restricted growth, as shown by fig above.

sometime become sick and die in hot climates. Some quince roots provide very little dwarfing. 'Malling Quince A' is the most dwarfing. Provence types, such as 'BA 29,' dwarf the tree very little. Quince roots also lack hardiness. The hybrid 'Old Home' x 'Farmingdale 51' is cold hardy and tolerates heat but trees are only average in productivity. 'Old Home' x 'Farmingdale 333' is semivigorous but stimulates early production. Espalier training is a well-proven way to grow pears in a small space. See page 55.

Plums and prunes—Rootstocks such as *Prunus besseyi* and *Prunus tomentosa* have been used to dwarf plums but the trees usually don't live long. 'St. Julian A' gives some but not much dwarfing. A rootstock from England called 'Pixie' promises to produce a more satisfactory dwarf plum tree. Espalier training can be used very successfully to grow plums in small spaces. Container culture is also used for growth control.

Walnuts—There are no growth-controlling rootstocks for walnuts. Certain varieties such as 'Chico' set so profusely that they cease growth and stop bearing if not pruned heavily every year. Heavy pruning tends to dwarf them. These trees can be grown with multiple trunks to divide and reduce the vigor from a single root system.

GROWING FRUIT IN CONTAINERS

Restricting root growth of a fruit tree by growing it in a container usually results in dwarfing. Successful container growing requires the use of a soil with excellent drainage and a high percentage of air space. The best loam garden soil will rarely work when placed in a container, even if amended. It doesn't have the necessary amount of air space.

Therefore, a *synthetic soil* is recommended. It is frequently sold as a potting mix. In most cases potting soils should be used just as they come from the bag. These soils are lightweight, easy to handle, uniform in texture and free of disease organisms. Standard container mixes are sold under a variety of names, such as Jiffy Mix, Jiffy Mix Plus, Supersoil, Good Earth and Redi-Earth.

Synthetic soils are composed of an organic portion and an inorganic portion. If you mix your own soil, the organic portion may be peat moss, pine bark, hardwood bark or fir bark. The inorganic portion may be vermiculite, perlite or fine sand. Potting soils in the West are often patterned after the University of California soil-less mixes. A typical example follows.

> To make one cubic yard of container mix, combine:
> 1/3 cubic yard peat moss
> 1/3 cubic yard fine sand
> 1/3 cubic yard ground pine or fir bark
> 1-1/2 pounds urea-formaldehyde (38-0-0)
> 3 pounds single superphosphate (0-20-0)
> 1 pound potassium nitrate (13-0-44)
> 8 pounds calcium carbonate lime
> 5 pounds dolomite lime
> 1 pound iron sulfate

The urea formaldehyde (38-0-0) compensates for the nitrogen used as the bark and peat moss decay. Four pounds of blood meal or four pounds of hoof and horn meal serve the same purpose.

The calcium carbonate and dolomite are finely ground limes and their amounts are typical for most areas. In areas of high calcium-magnesium bicarbonate waters, lower rates should be used. Check with your water department to find out the mineral composition of your water.

All of the ingredients of a potting mix need to be thoroughly blended. Mix the components by shoveling them into a cone-shaped pile. Rebuild the pile three times to mix the ingredients thoroughly.

Trees grown in containers dry out faster than those grown in the ground. Water more frequently according to the needs of the tree during warm weather. Watering also leaches many nutrients, especially nitrogen, iron, zinc and manganese from the container soil. Apply nutrients more frequently but in smaller doses than with in-ground trees.

Which Fruit, Berry or Nut?

This chapter explores tree fruit, with subsequent sections on berries, nuts and subtropicals. The following pages include information to help you select and grow the best fruit and nuts for your area. However, this chapter is incomplete without a thorough reading of other sections in this book. Climate, pruning, propagation, pest and disease control and cultural methods should also be examined carefully before planting or caring for your fruit and nut trees.

Climate adaptation is of prime concern. In the charts entitled Where They Will Grow, information on adaptation is given for tree fruit, berries and nuts. These charts are meant only as guidelines. If a type of fruit is shown with a colored block for your zone, this does not necessarily mean all varieties of that fruit can be grown there. Individual varieties have their own specific adaptations that may limit or extend their range.

A fruit type listed with an **X** for your zone means special requirements must be met to grow it successfully. It may mean only a few specially adapted varieties can be grown there. These requirements or varieties are covered in the description of the fruit or in the variety charts.

Even if a fruit is not recommended for your zone, you may still want to read its description. With clever use of *microclimates* you may be able to grow the plant successfully in certain areas around your home. See page 4 for a discussion of microclimates.

The division of plants into tree fruit, berries, nuts and subtropicals is done out of convenience rather than by strict botanical adherence. Avocados are described with tree fruit. They could also be grouped with subtropicals. Kiwifruit is included with subtropicals. This plant could also be listed with berries and vines. If you have difficulty locating a fruit type, see the index.

Fruit in each section are alphabetized by common name. Varieties in the charts are also listed alphabetically. If there are many varieties of a fruit, they are listed in a separate chart in order of ripening dates. By comparing variety charts and ripening dates, you may select from varieties that will extend harvest over a long period. Many connoisseurs of fruit will tell you that midseason varieties will usually have better flavor than either very early or very late-ripening varieties.

Left: Developing 'Mutsu' apple.

Unless otherwise noted, ripening dates were determined from information provided by University of California at Davis field stations. Davis, in California's Sacramento Valley, has a hot, dry climate which ripens fruit early. Fruit growers in cooler locations can expect their fruit to ripen somewhat later. In warmer areas of the Southwest, fruit will probably ripen even earlier.

Each fruit, with the exception of subtropicals and citrus which have a wide range of forms, has a chart termed Vital Statistics. A glance at this chart will give you some of the most important information about the fruit: eventual size of the plant in both standard and dwarf forms, years to bearing, life expectancy of the plant and more. Both text and charts should be read for complete information about any given fruit.

ABOUT THE CHARTS

Most variety descriptions are presented in chart form. Choosing the right variety for your needs and location is important. For this reason the variety charts are very detailed. In many cases, the chart is introduced with a discussion of variety selection entitled, About The Charts. It highlights important characteristics of the fruit and how these characteristics influence variety selection. About The Charts also indicates most frequently recommended varieties as determined by university extension services in the West. These recommendations are not meant as the only guide to variety selection. A variety can be widely recommended in the West but may not be recommended for your specific location. Zone recommendations in the variety charts are your best guide.

Pollination requirements, if any, are also included in the charts. This is one aspect of fruit growing that is often overlooked, sometimes with unfortunate results. If you live in an isolated area, with few fruit trees, providing for pollination is all-important. In areas with many fruit trees, bees and wind bring pollen from neighboring trees.

If cross-pollination is required, you need not always plant a second tree. *Pollinizer branches* can be grafted onto a tree to provide pollination. You can even hang a bucket filled with blooming branches from another variety in the tree. Many people plant more than one tree in a single hole. This saves space and provides for cross-pollination.

Descriptions of fruit and plant are included in the variety charts. Ornamental quality and vigor should be considered before a fruit tree is brought into the garden. Vigor is important if you wish to plant more than one tree in a hole. This is done most successfully with varieties of relatively equal vigor.

The remarks column sums up climate adaptation and uses of the fruit. It also provides additional insights and comments relative to the variety.

Tree Fruit: Where they will grow

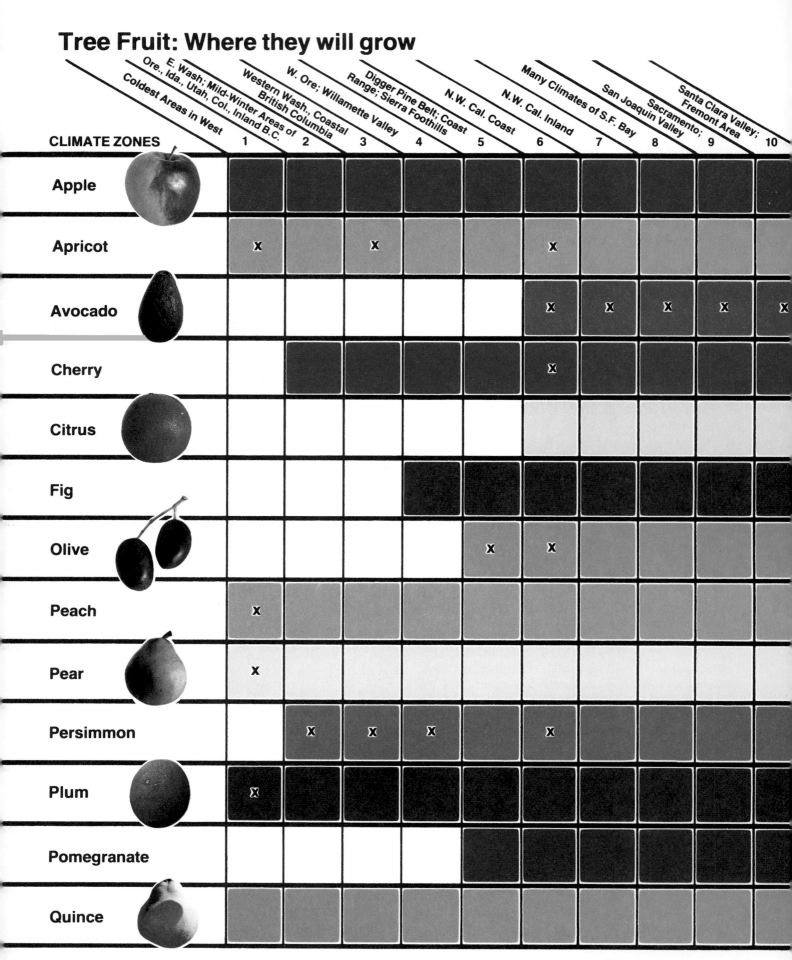

CLIMATE ZONES	Coldest Areas in West; Ore., Ida., Utah, Col., Inland B.C. (1)	E. Wash; Mild-Winter Areas of British Columbia; Western Wash., Coastal (2)	W. Ore; Willamette Valley (3)	Digger Pine Belt; Coast Range; Sierra Foothills (4)	N.W. Cal. Coast (5)	N.W. Cal. Inland (6)	Many Climates of S.F. Bay (7)	San Joaquin Valley (8)	Sacramento; Fremont Area (9)	Santa Clara Valley; Fremont Area (10)
Apple	■	■	■	■	■	■	■	■	■	■
Apricot	X	■	X	■	■	X	■	■	■	■
Avocado						X	X	X	X	X
Cherry		■	■	■	■	X	■	■	■	■
Citrus						■	■	■	■	■
Fig				■	■	■	■	■	■	■
Olive					X	X	■	■	■	■
Peach	X	■	■	■	■	■	■	■	■	■
Pear	X	■	■	■	■	■	■	■	■	■
Persimmon		X	X	X	■	X	■	■	■	■
Plum	X	■	■	■	■	■	■	■	■	■
Pomegranate						■	■	■	■	■
Quince	■	■	■	■	■	■	■	■	■	■

X — See fruit description for special cultural requirements, planting site selection or variety adaptation needed to be successful in this zone.

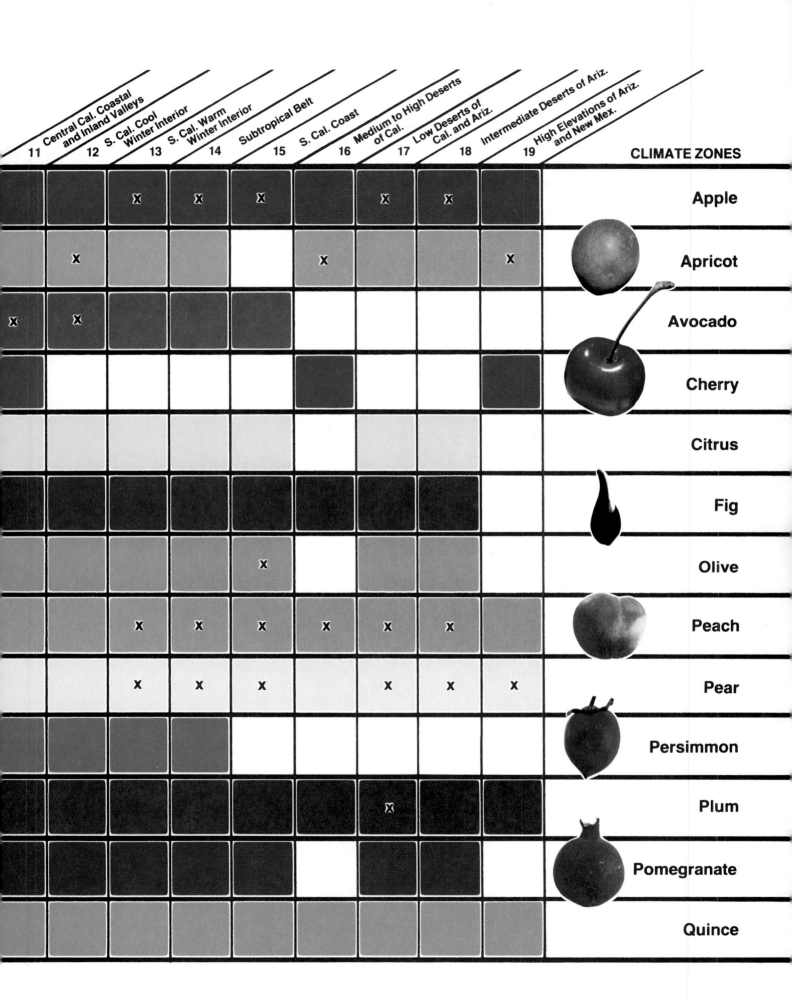

CLIMATE ZONES

Fruit	11 Central Cal. Coastal and Inland Valleys	12 S. Cal. Cool Winter Interior	13 S. Cal. Warm Winter Interior	14 Subtropical Belt	15 S. Cal. Coast	16 Medium to High Deserts of Cal.	17 Low Deserts of Cal. and Ariz.	18 Intermediate Deserts of Ariz.	19 High Elevations of Ariz. and New Mex.
Apple			X	X	X		X	X	
Apricot		X				X			X
Avocado	X	X							
Cherry									
Citrus									
Fig									
Olive					X				
Peach			X	X	X	X	X	X	
Pear			X	X	X		X	X	X
Persimmon									
Plum							X		
Pomegranate									
Quince									

'Jonamac' apple

Apple

Apples are the most widely adapted of all temperate zone deciduous fruit. There are varieties appropriate to almost all the climatic regions of the western states.

Apples do best in climates with considerable winter cold, moderate summer temperatures and, unlike most other tree fruit, rather high humidity. Where adapted they have a long life. See Vital Statistics.

Most apples have a high chilling requirement, some more than 1,000 hours. A few varieties have been developed that need little winter chilling, often less than 600 hours. Standard low-chill varieties include 'Winter Banana', 'Beverly Hills' and 'Dorsett Golden'. More recent introductions include 'Gordon', 'Anna',

'Ein Shemer' and 'Tropical Beauty'. Increasing experience with these varieties in southern California is proving valuable. For instance, 'Dorsett Golden' is replacing 'Ein Shemer' as a pollinizer for 'Anna'.

Chilling requirements are sometimes difficult to predict. Several varieties not normally considered low chilling are being grown successfully in southern California by members of The California Rare Fruit Growers. The address of this association is on page 189.

Relatively low night temperatures and high light intensity during the ripening period favor color development of apples. Regions such as eastern Washington develop highly colored apples to perfection. Too much fog or too many cloudy days during the summer results in poor coloring of red and striped varieties, often with objectionable russeting. Fog or cloudiness may also reduce resistance of trees and fruit to some diseases.

The apple is one of the hardiest deciduous fruit. Its northern and high-elevation range is considerably greater than that of peach and other stone fruit. A general rule for the coldest areas of the West is to plant midseason varieties that will escape spring frosts and ripen before extreme cold in fall.

Montana State University, which has researched apple hardiness, lists the following varieties as being extremely hardy: 'Close', 'Crimson Beauty', 'Goodland', 'Haralson', 'Hibernal', 'Mandan', 'Mantet', 'Patterson' and 'Red Astrachan'.

SIZE CONTROL

The size of apple trees can be controlled by selecting spur-type varieties, genetic dwarfs or dwarfing rootstocks. Size can also be controlled by pruning.

Spur-type apples—Mutations called *sports* sometimes occur in apple varieties. Sports may result in better fruit color or a spur habit of tree growth. Geneticists theorize that mutations are caused by cosmic rays which pierce through the growing tip of a shoot, causing a gene or chromosome change. This growth contains a new type of tissue. Mutations can affect many characteristics, including productivity, fruit shape, flavor and time of ripening. Such mutations have been found most frequently in 'Delicious', partly because it is the most widely grown variety. For reasons unknown mutations frequently occur on heavily pruned or winter-injured trees.

Spur-type apple trees are smaller than the parent variety—usually about two-thirds the size. Fruit-bearing wood is packed closer together and trees grow more slowly.

VITAL STATISTICS—APPLE

	Standard	Dwarf
Height at maturity (feet)		
Unpruned	40	*
Pruned	20	*
Spread at maturity with		
no competition (feet)	30-40	*
Recommended planting		
distance (feet)	20-40	10-16
Years to reach bearing age	4-8	3-4
Life expectancy (years)	60	60
Chilling requirement (hours)	900-1,000	900-1,000
Pollinizer required	See text.	
Good for espalier	Yes	Yes
Good for containers	No	Yes

*Various size trees are available with the use of Malling rootstocks. Spur types, genetic dwarfs and low-chill varieties are also available.

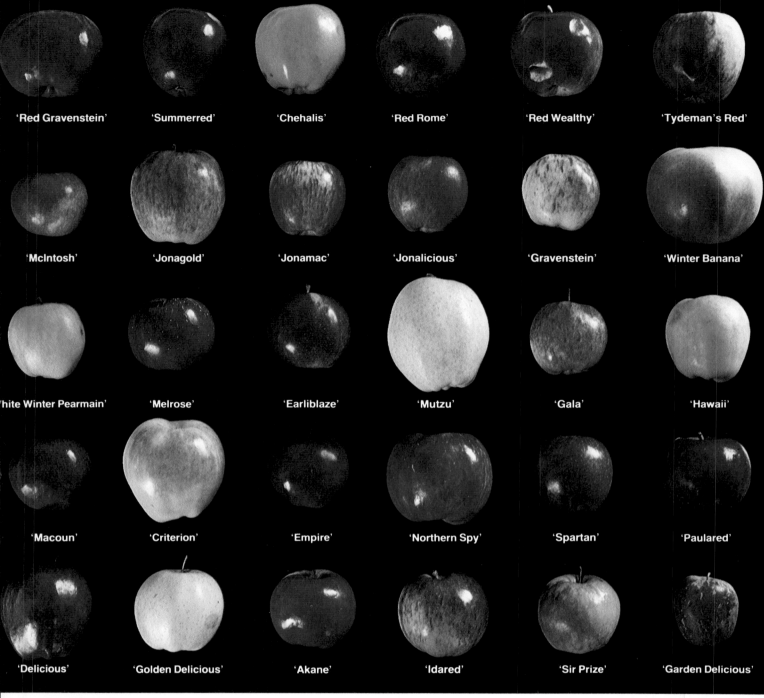

Popular apple varieties are remarkably different in color and form. These differences are surprising to those who think the only good apple is a bright red one.

Although spur-type varieties are valuable, control over tree size differs greatly among these varieties.

Other changes that can take place in spur-type apples include narrower crotch angles, increased hardiness, fewer side branches, thicker twigs and thicker and greener leaves. Greater fruit production and greener fruit flesh may also come from spur-type apples.

Spur varieties generally need less pruning, but they may be a bit more difficult to train into formal shapes. For an espalier they are best pruned in an informal manner.

Dwarfing rootstocks and genetic dwarfs—Dwarfing rootstocks and genetic dwarf apples are discussed in the section Growing Fruit In Small Spaces. See page 68. Dwarf apple trees make perfect garden dividers or hedges. They can easily be trained along a wire or fence and are ideal for growing in containers.

Pruning for size control—Apple trees will bear on the same wood for many years so they can be pruned severely without removing the crop. Proper pruning for size control should be done in summer as well as winter. These pruning methods are discussed in detail on pages 44 to 55.

Apples are easy to espalier, and make an attractive fruiting hedge or fence. Above is 'Pacific Pride'.

POLLINATION

Most apple varieties will set adequate crops without cross-pollination from another variety. Some varieties produce sterile pollen. If completely isolated, these sterile varieties will not bear fruit. Such apple varieties are indicated in the variety chart remarks column. With the exception of other pollen-sterile varieties, any apple variety that blooms about the same time as other apples can be used as a pollinizer. Early-ripening varieties usually bloom with other early varieties, midseason varieties bloom with other midseason varieties, and so forth.

If you live in an area where apples are grown, you probably won't have to provide for cross-pollination even if a variety produces sterile pollen. Apples in the neighborhood will provide pollination via bees and wind. All the various crabapple varieties can be used as pollinizers for apples.

TOPWORKING

Old apple trees or those with undesirable characteristics can easily be regrafted, or topworked, with one or more new varieties. Methods are described in the section on propagating. See page 57.

PRUNING

Training dwarf and semidwarf apple trees to a central leader, as described on page 50, favors good fruit quality and high production in a small space. These trees are fairly easy to establish and maintain. Very vigorous varieties, such as 'Gravenstein' grown on semidwarf rootstock, are best trained to a multileader

system. Otherwise, the central leader can become too tall for easy maintenance. Spur types on seedling roots can be trained to a central leader or a multileader. Long shoots of tip-bearing varieties such as 'Rome Beauty', 'Tydeman's Red' and 'Granny Smith' should be *headed*—cut back—in midsummer or winter to induce branching and reduce the amount of bare wood that will develop.

Apple trees are easily trained into espalier, palmette or cordons. Pinching buds in early summer is sometimes recommended. It does not increase the number of flower buds, but causes branches to become thicker and more substantial. Apple trees can be trained further by spreading and judicious summer pruning.

Pruning bearing trees—With spur types, individual spurs may remain fruitful for ten years or more. Only an occasional large cut close to the trunk is needed for renewal. Standard types bear on spurs that tend to be shorter lived. Therefore, more cuts must be made in smaller branches and shoots to renew fruiting wood farther from the trunk. Tip-bearing varieties bear fruit on the end of last season's growth and on some spurs. Much cutting of fine branches is required to replace fruiting wood.

Prune apple trees with thinning cuts and few if any heading cuts. Excessive pruning easily upsets the equilibrium between fruiting and vigor and leads to poorly colored fruit with *bitter-pit*. These are small sunken spots on lower end of the apple that give the fruit a bitter taste. If this happens, thin out the most vigorous shoots in late summer, leaving the weaker ones.

Espaliered apples save space, make harvesting and spraying easier, and give a dramatic look to the garden.

Pruning old trees—Removing the outer, upper limbs of a tree favors production on the lower, inner wood. Lower branches are then easier to reach for spraying, thinning and picking. A good deal of old wood can be removed without harming an old tree, as long as you use thinning cuts rather than heading cuts.

Much thinning of shoots is required for old trees. Whole scaffold or support limbs can be renewed by sawing them to within 4 or 5 feet of the ground. Train new shoots as you would a young tree.

FRUIT THINNING

Apples are often grown without thinning. But to ensure quality fruit of good size, thinning is helpful, especially following heavy fruit sets. Proper fruit thinning also reduces the tendency of some varieties to *alternate-bear*, or bear a crop every other year.

It is difficult to tell just when to thin apples. A few weeks after fruit has set there may be a noticeable drop of fruit. This is called *June drop* and is a natural occurrence. Trees produce many more blossoms and fruit than are necessary for a full crop. Thinning soon after this drop is usually the most opportune time to regulate and improve the crop.

Apples may be thinned to a distance of 6 to 8 inches apart on the branch. Another method is to remove all fruit on every other spur, or leave fruit on one spur and remove those on the next two as you work outward on a branch. Leave plenty of room for fruit to develop. Unless the set is very light, break up all clusters, leaving only a single fruit. This aids in producing clean fruit. Fruit that touch each other provide a place for insects and disease to attack.

HARVESTING AND STORAGE

Apples approaching maturity may be broken from the spur easily. Do not pull an apple downward or you may damage the spur. Twist it upward with a rotating motion.

When a few, nonwormy apples fall to the ground, this is a sign that fruit is nearly ripe. Softness and flavor are also useful in judging maturity. When an apple becomes slightly soft and juicy and develops characteristic flavor, it is mature.

Color, both outside and under the skin, is a useful indication of maturity.

Where cold-storage facilities are not available, late-ripening apples can be held several weeks in a cool place. They need relatively high humidity to prevent excessive moisture loss and shriveling. Winter varieties such as 'Yellow Newtown' and 'Winesap' can be kept until April or May. Stored apples readily pick up odors, so keep them away from other products or molds that can produce off-flavors. Covering the boxes will help.

Tart varieties of apple are usually preferred for drying.

Apple cider—Making home apple cider is increasing in popularity. It is also a good way to preserve your harvest because cider can be stored frozen for many months.

The best cider is usually made from a blend of varieties. A blend provides an appealing balance of sweetness, tartness, tang and aromatic overtones.

The United States Department of Agriculture, Farmers' Bulletin No. 2125, *Making and Preserving*

Apple Cider, includes a helpful guide for blending varieties. For good cider, select one variety from each group for your blend.

Sweet group—'Baldwin', 'Hubbardston Nonesuch', 'Rome Beauty', 'Stark', 'Red Delicious', 'Grimes' and 'Cortland'.

Mildly acid to slightly tart group—'Winesap', 'Stayman', 'Jonathan', 'Northern Spy', 'York Imperial', 'Wealthy', 'Rhode Island Greening' and 'Newtown Pippin'.

Aromatic group—'Red Delicious', 'Golden Delicious', 'Winter Banana', 'Ribston' and 'McIntosh'.

Astringent group—'Florence Hibernal', 'Red Siberian' (crab), 'Transcendant' (crab) and 'Martha'.

DISEASES AND PESTS

Among the most serious apple diseases are apple scab and powdery mildew.

New scab-resistant varieties have been developed in the eastern United States. 'Liberty' was introduced by the New York Agricultural Experiment Station in Geneva, New York. 'Priscilla', 'Sir Prize' and 'Prima' were developed through cooperative research by the University of Illinois, Purdue University and Rutgers University.

Codling moth is the most serious pest of apples. Their worms are sure to be found almost everywhere apples are grown. For information on other pests that occasionally bother apples, see pages 36 and 37.

CRABAPPLES

As a rule, all apple trees with fruit 2 inches or less in diameter are considered crabapples.

Crabapples are highly regarded for making jelly and pickling. Some varieties are delicious for eating fresh. Beautiful flowers and brightly colored fruit make crabapples one of the most popular groups of ornamental trees in North America.

Crabapples belong to many species of *Malus*. The majority of edible ones, as distinct from the primarily flowering kinds, belong to *M. baccata*, Siberian crabapple, and *M. ioensis*, prairie or western crabapple. All have the same cultural and climate requirements as regular apples except that there are many more very hardy and low-chill varieties.

'Florence', 'Hyslop', 'Transcendent', 'Whitney' and 'Profusion' are just a few of the many edible crabapples.

ABOUT THE CHARTS

• The apple varieties most often recommended and with the widest adaptation are 'Golden Delicious', 'Gravenstein', 'Lodi', 'Delicious', 'Rome Beauty', 'McIntosh', 'Winesap' and 'Jonathan'.

• Washington State University tested many baking varieties for flavor and shape. They found these four varieties tops in both respects: 'Cox Orange Pippin', 'Mutsu', 'Melrose' and 'Jonagold'. On a 1-to-5 scale, the flavor ratings are as follows: 'Cox Orange Pippin', 4.9; 'Mutsu', 4.3; 'Melrose', 4.2; 'Jonagold', 3.9. The shape ratings are 3 for 'Cox Orange Pippin' and 'Mutsu' and 4 for 'Melrose' and 'Jonagold'.

• If you want apples that are good for eating fresh and for pies—the so-called dual-purpose apples—you might choose 'Gravenstein', 'Newtown', 'Melrose', 'Cortland', 'Winesap', 'Stayman Winesap', 'Jonagold', 'Mutsu' and 'Golden Delicious'.

• If you want to plant four varieties in one hole, examples of compatible varieties are 'Vista Bella', 'Akane', 'Jersey Mac' and 'Spartan'. Another suitable combination would be 'Gala', 'Empire', 'Macoun' and 'Melrose'. In choosing combinations, check the apple chart for varieties with compatible growth characteristics.

APPLES
Average picking dates at Corvallis, Oregon.

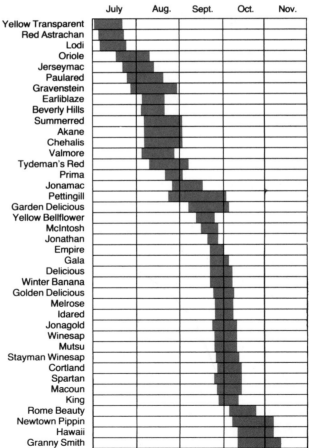

For harvest season of low-chill apples, see variety chart.

'Mutsu' apple

'Summerred' apple

APPLES

VARIETY	ORIGIN	ZONE	HARVEST SEASON	FRUIT AND TREE	REMARKS
'AKANE'	Tohoku, Japan, 1970.	2, 4.	Midseason.	Fruit small to medium, round and flat. Skin bright solid red. Flesh white, firm, crisp, juicy, slightly coarse. Flavor slightly acid. Pronounced crown resembles 'Jonathan'. Tree semidwarf. Weak to moderate vigor. Tendency for weak crotches.	Excellent quality fruit. Very good to excellent dessert quality. Bears annually at an early age. Crops light. No preharvest drop. Does not store well but holds well on tree.
'ANNA'	Israel.	13-15.	Early.	Fruit large, skin checked red, flesh low-acid to sweet, flavor mild. Large, vigorous tree.	Annually productive tree, low chilling requirement. Requires pollinizer such as 'Dorsett Golden'. Fruit stores up to 2 months in a cool place.
'BEVERLY HILLS'	California.	13-15.	Early.	Fruit small to medium. Skin pale yellow splashed with red. Flesh tender, juicy, somewhat tart. Tree is medium size and vigorous.	Good quality, resembles 'McIntosh'. Used for cooking. Moderately well suited to cool, coastal climate of southern California because of low chilling requirement.
'CHEHALIS'	Washington.	3, 4.	Early.	Fruit large. Skin greenish yellow to full yellow with an occasional pink blush. Flesh white to cream, crisp, juicy, slightly acid, not aromatic. Tree has moderate vigor, upright and spreading growth.	Fruit resembles 'Golden Delicious'. Good dessert-quality eating apple. Best picked while firm, greenish yellow. Stores poorly. Bruises easily. Very resistant to scab but not immune. Adapted west of Cascade Mountains.
'CORTLAND'	Geneva, New York, 1915.	1-4, 16, 19.	Late.	Fruit large, roundish to flat. Skin attractive red. Flesh white, crisp, tender, juicy, slightly acid. Tree strong, spreading and drooping.	Fruit hangs well on tree. Good for salads. Resembles 'McIntosh'. Stores well. Tree susceptible to powdery mildew. Bears annually. 'Ben Davis' x 'McIntosh'.
'DELICIOUS' (RED)	Iowa.	2-4.	Midseason.	Fruit medium, long and tapering shape. Skin striped or solid red with yellowing. Flesh juicy, aromatic and sweet tasting. Tree is large, upright and spreading.	Most widely grown apple in the world. Requires pollinizer if isolated. Tree responds well to heavy feeding. Produces a full crop every other year, unless properly thinned. Very susceptible to scab.
'DISCOVERY'	England.	2-4.	Early.	Fruit small, uniform shape and size. Skin bright red striped. Flesh crisp and flavorful. Medium size tree with attractive shape.	Very good quality fruit. Fair storage. Fairly resistant to scab and mildew.
'DORSETT GOLDEN'	Bahamas.	13-15.	Early.	Resembles 'Golden Delicious' but less coloring, often seedless. Large, vigorous tree.	Low chilling requirement. Produces crops in a tropical climate where no temperatures occur below 45° F (7° C). Pollinizer for 'Anna'.
'EARLIBLAZE'	Illinois.	1, 2, 5, 8, 10, 11.	Early.	Fruit medium, roundish to oblong. Skin greenish yellow blushed and striped with red. Flesh white, crisp, firm, juicy, good quality. Medium size tree.	Good for cooking.
'EIN SHEMER'	Israel.	13-15.	Early.	Fruit medium. Skin greenish yellow. Flesh crisp, melting, moderately juicy. Mild flavor. Medium size tree.	Low chilling requirment. Good overall quality. Stores for only 1 to 2 weeks. A 'Golden Delicious' hybrid. Tree needs a pollinizer.
'EMPIRE'	New York, 1966.	2, 4, 5.	Midseason.	Fruit medium, round to somewhat blocky. Skin dark red, distinctly striped, heavy wax bloom. Flesh cream-colored, crisp, juicy, slightly acid, aromatic. 'McIntosh' type. Semisweet flavor. Semispur tree is large, upright and spreading.	Excellent quality fruit, stores well. Good for eating fresh. Fruit stay on tree better than 'McIntosh'. Tree productive annually, requires a pollinizer. Early bloomer with good pollen.

'Gravenstein' apple

APPLES

VARIETY	ORIGIN	ZONE	HARVEST SEASON	FRUIT AND TREE	REMARKS
'GALA'	New Zealand.	2-7.	Midseason.	Skin bright scarlet striped over yellow. Dense aromatic flesh with semisweet flavor. Large, upright tree with somewhat drooping branches.	Dessert apple. Excellent quality. Keeps very well.
'GARDEN DELICIOUS'	California.	1-11, 13, 16.	Midseason.	Fruit small to medium. Skin yellow-green to golden yellow, no striping. Light pink blush in warmer climates; bright red in colder areas. Tree a genetic dwarf 6 feet high with a 5 to 6-foot spread at maturity.	Very good to excellent dessert quality. Often russeted.
'GOLDEN DELICIOUS'	West Virginia by Stark Bros., 1916.	1-15.	Late.	Fruit medium to large, resembles 'Delicious' in shape. Skin yellow, occasionally with pink blush. Flesh crisp, firm, juicy, sweet and aromatic. Tree medium height, moderately vigorous, upright and roundheaded. Bears young.	Fruit has both good eating and cooking qualities. Does not store well, shrivels. Bears annually if thinned. Blossoms frost resistant in California conditions. Spur-type 'Golden Delicious' same except for rougher fruit and compact growth habit.
'GORDON'	California.	12-15.	Midseason.	Fruit medium to large, nearly globe shaped. Skin green, blushed red, striped. Flesh crisp, juicy, firm texture, color near white. Tree vigorous, upright and productive.	Good fresh or cooked. Regular bearer. Low chilling requirement, suitable for growing in mild, coastal regions of southern California. Prolonged season of flowering and fruiting.
'GRANNY SMITH'	Australia.	4, 5, 7-11, 16.	Late.	Fruit large, round, slightly elongated. Skin bright green with white dots, tart and very juicy. Tree very vigorous, upright and spreading with much bare wood.	Fruit good for eating, cooking and sauces. Becomes sweeter in storage, a good keeper. Tree bears annually on ends of shoots. Very susceptible to mildew. Blooms very early in California. 'Summerred' is good pollinizer in California's central valleys.
'GRAVENSTEIN'	Germany.	2-11, 13-15, 19.	Early.	Fruit medium to large, roundish, irregular shape. Skin red striped over light green. Flesh creamy white, fine-textured, crisp, firm and juicy. Tree extremely vigorous with an upright, spreading growth habit. Slow to begin bearing.	Outstanding flavor. Good for cooking and eating. Tree bears alternate years unless thinned. Requires a pollinizer. Pollen sterile. 'Red Gravenstein' is similar, more highly colored red, but original is generally preferred.
'HAWAII'	California.	2-11.	Late.	Fruit is 'Golden Delicious' type. Sweet, juicy flavor. Tree is tall, vigorous and productive.	Keeps well. Highly susceptible to scab. Somewhat susceptible to bitter pit.
'IDARED'	Idaho, 1942.	4-8, 10, 11, 16.	Late.	Fruit medium to large, uniform in shape, nearly round. Skin nearly solid red over faint yellow. Flesh white, crisp, juicy, fine grained, aromatic. Tree medium to small with moderately vigorous, upright growth. Blooms early.	Good for cooking and desserts. Excellent keeping qualities. Flavor improves with storage. Prolonged period of ripening. Susceptible to powdery mildew. Bears annually and heavily. Subject to stem cracking. 'Wagener' x 'Jonathan'.

'Hysop' crabapple

Crabapple blossom

APPLES

VARIETY	ORIGIN	ZONE	HARVEST SEASON	FRUIT AND TREE	REMARKS
'JERSEYMAC'	Rutgers, New Jersey, 1971.	2, 4-9.	Early.	Fruit medium to large, regular and cone shape. Skin blushed red over yellow. Flesh yellow-white, slightly acid with good quality. Tree strong, upright, spreading.	A 'McIntosh' type. Blooms with 'Gravenstein', which it pollinizes. Annual, heavy producer at an early age.
'JONAGOLD'	Geneva, New York, 1968.	2, 4-8, 16.	Late.	Fruit large, red stripes over lively yellow-green. Round to oblong. Cream-colored flesh, moderately firm, crisp, juicy, slightly coarse in texture. Good flavor. Tree sturdy, productive, with wide, strong crotches. Not too vigorous.	One of the best, dual-purpose apples. Very good for dessert and excellent for cooking. Stores very well. Requires pollinizer if isolated. Pollen sterile. 'Golden Delicious' x 'Jonathan'.
'JONAMAC'	Geneva, New York, 1968.	2, 4, 5.	Midseason.	Fruit medium size. 'McIntosh'-type apple. Skin red. Flavor tart and refreshing. Tree medium size, productive.	Dessert apple. Excellent quality when allowed to ripen on tree. Stores well. Susceptible to scab and especially mildew. Superior to both parents. 'Jonathan' x 'McIntosh'.
'JONATHAN'	New York.	2, 4, 5.	Midseason.	Fruit small to medium, uniform round to oblong. Skin red striped over yellow. Flesh firm, crisp, juicy, white. Tart with a characteristic flavor. Tree is small with low vigor.	Tree very susceptible to mildew. Budsports: 'Blackjon', 'Jonee', 'Jon-A-Red', 'Jona'.
'KING' ('TOMPKINS KING')	New Jersey.	4.	Late.	Fruit very large. Skin red or red striped. Flesh pure white, coarse, firm, crisp, juicy, richly flavored and sweet. Tree weak, slow growing and semidwarf. Lacks hardiness.	Good for baking and fair for eating. Bears annually. Old-timer in western Washington. Stores well.
'LODI'	Geneva, New York.	1-4, 9, 16, 19.	Early.	Fruit larger than 'Yellow Transparent'. Skin greenish yellow and thick. Flesh is moderately soft and crisp with a tart, acid flavor. Tree large, hardy.	Fruit keeps longer than 'Yellow Transparent'. Good for cooking, sauce and pies. Bears alternate years. 'Montgomery' x 'Yellow Transparent'.
'MACOUN'	Geneva, New York.	1-5, 7, 8, 10, 11, 16, 19.	Late.	Fruit smaller than 'McIntosh', similar in appearance. Skin very dark red. Flesh white, richly flavored and aromatic. Tree upright with long, lanky branches.	Very good dessert-quality fruit. Tree may need extra thinning to develop a spreading top. Bears biennially unless thinned. Fruit drop as they ripen. Good storage life.
'McINTOSH'	Dundas County, Ontario, Canada, about 1800.	1, 2, 4.	Midseason.	Fruit medium, nearly round. Skin yellow with bright red blush. Flesh white, sweet, tender, moderately soft and juicy. Tree has vigorous growth habit. Cold hardy.	Good dessert quality fruit when grown in cool climates. This famous apple from Canada needs special care in thinning in the West. Requires pollinizer if isolated. Severe preharvest fruit drop. Spur-type 'McIntosh' also available.
'MELROSE'	Ohio.	1-5, 16.	Late.	Fruit medium to large, uniform, roundish in shape. Skin yellow with bright red blush. Flesh white, firm, juicy, crisp, slightly acid. Tree very productive, medium height, moderately vigorous, upright and spreading.	Fruit resembles 'Jonathan' in color and shape. Excellent dessert and cooking qualities. Good for storage. Highly susceptible to scab and mildew. 'Jonathan' x 'Delicious'.

The beautiful spring bloom of apples and crabapples rivals that of any ornamental tree.

APPLES

VARIETY	ORIGIN	ZONE	HARVEST SEASON	FRUIT AND TREE	REMARKS
'MUTSU'	Japan.	3-5, 9.	Late.	Fruit large to very large, somewhat oval. Skin green, developing yellow color at maturity, with an occasional orange blush. Flesh is yellow-white, firm, juicy, crisp but coarse. Slightly acid. Tree large, vigorous, with strong crotches.	Good for cooking and baking. Bears annually and heavily. Large fruit tend to have bitter pit. Pollen sterile. Needs pollinizer if isolated. 'Golden Delicious' x 'Indo'.
'NEWTOWN PIPPIN' (YELLOW)	New York.	6-8, 10, 11, 13, 16.	Late.	Fruit large, roundish to slightly flat. Skin solid green. Flesh cream colored, crisp and tart. Tree large and vigorous.	Skin is yellow-green or full yellow at maturity, with low amounts of nitrogen in the soil. Fruit ideal for eating fresh, baking and cooking. Very good for cider. A good keeper.
'ORIOLE'	Minnesota.	1, 2, 4, 5, 16.	Early.	Fruit large to very large. Yellow-orange skin. Tree is medium to tall and upright.	Very good culinary apple. Dessert quality fair. Poor keeper. Very susceptible to mildew.
'PAULARED'	Sparta, Michigan, 1967.	2, 4-8.	Early.	Fruit medium size, round to flat. Skin solid red blush. Flesh white to cream, very firm. Nonbrowning, flavor slightly tart. Tree strong, upright, good branch structure.	Dual-purpose market apple with good eye appeal. Fair for cooking, good for dessert. Fair storage quality.
'PETTINGILL'	California.	14, 15.	Midseason.	Fruit large and round. Skin deep red overlaying green. Flesh nearly white, firm, crisp, juicy, slightly acid. Tree large, upright, vigorous, very productive.	Good for baking, cooking and sauces. Tree has low chilling requirement and bears early.
'PRIMA'	Northeast United States, 1945.	3, 4, 6.	Midseason.	Fruit almost round, medium to large. Skin glossy, medium dark red washed on bright yellow. Flesh greenish white to yellow, fine grained texture, moderately firm, crisp and juicy. Tree vigorous and spreading.	Fair to good for dessert and cooking use. Juicy, not highly flavored. Fruit tend to have bitter pit in early years. Completely resistant to apple scab. Bears annually.
'RED ASTRACHAN'	Russia.	1, 5-11, 13, 19.	Early.	Fruit medium to large. Skin whitish green with crimson stripes, thin and smooth. Flesh white, crisp, soft, juicy and tart. Tree medium size, upright with spreading growth habit.	Good for eating, excellent for cooking, very short storage life. Sometimes bears annually. Grows well in hot areas. University of California recommends 'Red Astrachan' for Sacramento and San Joaquin valleys.
'ROME BEAUTY'	Ohio.	2, 4, 5.	Late.	Fruit large and round. Skin red. Flesh greenish white, medium texture, crisp, very firm. Tree moderately vigorous, small to medium.	Good for baking with subtle flavor. Bears annually at an early age on the tips of shoots. Budsports are numerous. Late bloom, good for frost areas. Also matures late. Not suited to high altitudes.
'SPARTAN'	Summerland, B.C., Canada, 1936.	3-5, 8, 10, 11.	Late.	Fruit medium, almost round. Skin mahogany-red. Flesh white, crisp, firm, juicy. Highly aromatic. Tree strong, moderately vigorous, heavy producer.	Excellent for eating fresh and for desserts. Bears annually if thinned. Some preharvest drop. Good keeper. 'McIntosh' x 'Newtown'.
'STAYMAN WINESAP'	Kansas.	1-5, 19.	Late.	Fruit large, roundish to cone shape. Skin is greenish yellow with red blush speckled with dots. Flesh fine textured, crisp and tangy. Tree medium size, moderately vigorous.	Flavor better than 'Winesap'. A good keeper. Bears annually. Budsports: 'Improved Black Stayman', 'Scarlet Stayman', 'Blaxstayman', 'Acme' and others. 'Winesap' has smaller fruit. Requires pollinizer if isolated. Pollen sterile.

'Akane' apple

Wooden slats protect this ancient 'Shirley' apple.

APPLES

VARIETY	ORIGIN	ZONE	HARVEST SEASON	FRUIT AND TREE	REMARKS
'SUMMERRED'	Summerland, B.C., Canada.	3-5, 8, 10, 11.	Early.	Fruit medium to large, oblong. Skin is solid red speckled with dots. Flesh cream colored, firm, fine textured, tender with a rich flavor. Tart until fully ripe. Tree has strong, upright growth habit.	Good for cooking and desserts. Holds well on tree. Stores well. Bears annually if thinned. Good pollinizer for 'Granny Smith' in California's central valleys. 'McIntosh' x 'Golden Delicious'.
'TROPIC BEAUTY'	South Africa.	13-15.	Early.	Fruit medium-large. Smooth mild flavor. Skin rich carmine red. Tree is moderately vigorous and small to medium size.	Bears at an early age. Tree has low chilling requirement. Self-fruitful, production may be enhanced with pollination by 'Anna' or 'Ein Shemer'.
'TYDEMAN'S RED'	England, 1964.	3-5, 8, 10, 11.	Early.	Fruit large, roundish to flat. Skin solid bright red, resembles 'McIntosh'. Flesh white, fine textured, moderately firm. Tree tends to have long, lanky branches with much bare wood in need of regular pruning. Can grow as espalier.	Good for eating and cooking. Bears annually on the tips of shoots. Prone to pre-harvest drop. Poor pollinizer. 'McIntosh' x 'Worcester Pearmain'.
'VALMORE'	California.	9, 13-15.	Early.	Fruit large, cone shape. Skin bright red, occasional yellow blush, medium thick, waxy. Flesh yellow-white, fine texture, juicy, sweet and aromatic, slightly acid. Tree vigorous, upright and productive.	Good for eating and cooking. Fruit and tree resemble 'Stayman Winesap'. Tree has low chilling requirement.
'WINESAP'	New York.	1-5, 16, 19.	Late.	Fruit medium, round or oblong. Skin striped red over yellow at maturity. Flesh yellow, coarse, crisp, juicy, firm. Flavor sprightly, slightly acid. Tree vigorous, slow to begin bearing.	Good for desserts or canning. Keeps well. Budsports: 'Stayman Winesap', 'Starkspur Winesap' and others. Fruit slightly smaller than 'Winesap'. Requires pollinizer if isolated. Pollen sterile.
'WINTER BANANA'	Europe.	3-15.	Late.	Fruit medium to large. Skin pale yellow to pink blush, waxy texture. Flesh tender, juicy, tangy and aromatic. Tree vigorous.	Tree accepts mild winters. Will support a graft of 'Bartlett' pear. Requires pollinizer if isolated. Spur-type 'Winter Banana' is same but with compact growth habit.
'YELLOW BELLFLOWER'	New Jersey.	7, 8, 10, 11, 13.	Midseason.	Fruit medium to large, oblong to cone shape, prominent ridges at the apex. Skin greenish to yellow often with a pink blush. Flesh semifirm, juicy, crisp, slightly acid. Tree vigorous grower with a spreading form. Good shade tree.	Tree very sensitive to scab. Suited to southern California because of low chilling requirement.
'YELLOW TRANSPARENT'	Russia, nearly 100 years ago.	1-5, 7-15, 19.	Early.	Fruit medium. Skin clear yellow, thin, smooth and tender. Flesh is white, very tender, acid and tart. Tree is tall, upright and vigorous.	Good for cooking if harvested when greenish yellow. Bruises easily; drops when ripe. Extremely short life when ripe.

OLD VARIETIES

Old apple varieties hold a special place in the hearts of many people. The tree they climbed when they were young or the apples that produced Grandma's pies may have been an old variety. In fact, old varieties are still an important resource. While some may be impossible to enjoy unless you grow them yourself, others such as 'Granny Smith', 'Newtown Pippin and 'Gravenstein' are important commercially. Still others such as 'Bellflower' and 'Winter Banana' have low chilling requirements and can grow where other apples can't.

The accompanying table lists old apple varieties that are still widely available. Most are also available on dwarfing rootstocks.

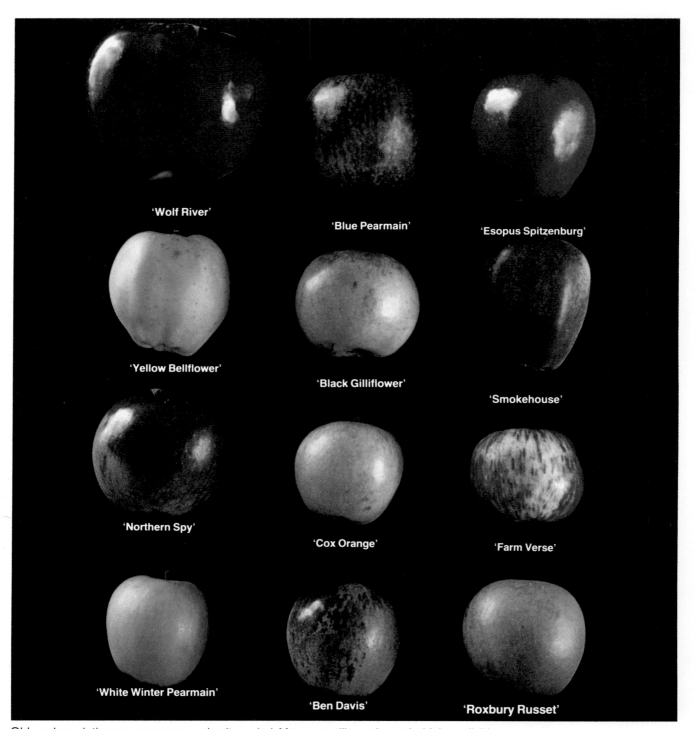

'Wolf River' 'Blue Pearmain' 'Esopus Spitzenburg'

'Yellow Bellflower' 'Black Gilliflower' 'Smokehouse'

'Northern Spy' 'Cox Orange' 'Farm Verse'

'White Winter Pearmain' 'Ben Davis' 'Roxbury Russet'

Old apple varieties are numerous and quite varied. Many are still popular and widely available.

OLD APPLES

VARIETY	ORIGIN	SEASON	FRUIT DESCRIPTION	REMARKS
'AMERICAN BEAUTY STERLING'	Sterling, Massachusetts.	Late.	Very dark color, aromatic, slightly acid.	Very good quality; good for desserts.
'ARKANSAS BLACK'	Benton County, Arkansas.	Late.	Yellow covered with purplish red. Flesh hard and crisp, tinged yellow.	Good for applesauce.
'BALDWIN WOODPECKER'	Wilmington, Massachusetts, About 1740.	Late.	Yellow or greenish, striped red. Flesh yellow juicy, hard and crisp.	Good for freezing, sauce, jam or jelly.
'BEN DAVIS'	Tennessee, Kentucky or Virginia, Early 1800.	Late.	Bright red or red striped. Flesh firm, crisp, slightly acid.	Good for drying, fair for cooking, poor for eating.
'BLACK GILLIFLOWER' (SHEEPNOSE)	Connecticut, Early 1800.	Mid to late.	Red to dark purple. Flesh whitish or slightly tinged with yellow.	Sometimes used for baking. Considered too dry and not sour enough for cooking. Good fresh.
'BLUE PEARMAIN'	United States, About 1800.	Mid to late.	Red with blue bloom. Mild, aromatic flavor.	Good for cider.
'CHENANGO STRAWBERRY'	New York, About 1850.	Midseason.	Yellow and white skin, striped red. Flesh white, firm, tender and aromatic. Juicy.	Four to six years to first crop. Good for cooking and eating fresh. Not a keeper.
'COX ORANGE'	Bucks, England, About 1830.	Mid to late.	Red and yellow. Flesh juicy, firm, aromatic.	Good for dessert and processing.
'DUCHESS OF OLDENBURG'	Russia, Early 1800.	Early.	Stripes of red shaded with crimson. Sprightly flavor, acid, aromatic.	Good for cooking. Too much acid for dessert.
'EARLY HARVEST'	Unknown, Before 1800.	Early.	Pale yellow, smooth waxen skin. White flesh, soft, fine, tender to crisp. Aromatic.	Four to six years to first crop. Not a good keeper but good cooked or fresh, for salads and desserts.
'ESOPUS SPITZENBURG'	Ulster County, New York, 1800 or before.	Late.	Large bright red with yellow dots. Firm, crisp, tender. Very good, slightly acid flavor.	Good all-around apple. Choice for dessert.
'FAMEUSE' (SNOW APPLE)	France, Before 1730.	Mid to late.	Bright red skin, pure white flesh, sometimes streaked red. Crisp, aromatic, juicy.	One of the oldest varieties. Excellent for eating and desserts, not for cooking. Grows best at high elevations.
'GOLDEN RUSSET'	Unknown, Before 1870.	Mid to late.	Round, golden russet with a bronze cheek. Flesh crisp and tender. Sugary juice.	Good eaten fresh or for desserts. Excellent keeper.
'GRIMES GOLDEN'	West Virginia, Before 1800.	Late.	Rich golden yellow. Flesh tender, crisp, juicy, aromatic.	Good for eating and freezing. Poor for baking.
'HUBBARDSTON NONESUCH'	Massachusetts, Early 1800.	Mid to late.	Large, rugged, mostly red skin. Flesh hard, crisp, fine grained.	Small, highly colored fruit are good keepers. Eating apple, does not cook well.
'HUNT RUSSET' (RUSSET PEARMAIN)	Massachusetts.	Late.	Golden russet with red-russet cheeks.	Good fresh or for sauces, pies, jams, jellies, cider or juice.
'LADY'	France, Before 1628.	Late.	Beautiful, small, red flattish apple. Flesh tender, white, crisp, juicy, aromatic.	Used at Christmas for decoration and dessert. Dwarfish tree.
'MAIDEN'S BLUSH'	Unknown, Early 1800.	Mid to late.	Pale lemon-yellow with crimson cheeks. Slightly acid flavor, fine to moderately crisp.	Very juicy with a sprightly flavor. Excellent drying apple; not a good keeper. Four to six years to first crop.
'MOTHER'	Boston, Massachusetts, Early 1800.	Midseason.	Bright deep red over golden. Flesh creamy yellow, sweet, juicy, aromatic.	Excellent dessert apple.
'NORTHERN SPY'	East Bloomfield, New York, About 1800.	Late.	Large roundish, bright red, striped fruit. Flesh firm, tender and juicy.	Use for cooking and dessert. Grown on Oregon coast.
'PALMER GREENING' (WASHINGTON ROYAL)	Sterling, Massachusetts.	Midseason.	Waxy, green-yellow skin shaded red. White flesh with yellow cast. Crisp, firm, tender, juicy.	Excellent for eating fresh.
'PORTER'	Sherburne, Massachusetts, 1800.	Mid to late.	Yellow, marked with red. Agreeably aromatic.	Good for cooking and dessert.
'POUND SWEET' (PUMPKIN SWEET)	Manchester, Connecticut.	Late.	Large size. Light and dark green with whitish cast. Peculiar, sweet flavor.	Good for baking and canning.
'RED JUNE'	North Carolina.	Midseason.	Deep red over yellow or greenish skin. Flavor brisk. Texture fine and tender.	Excellent eaten fresh or in desserts.

Apricots ready to harvest.

Apricot

The apricot is a tree of superlatives. Certainly there is no more beautiful orchard tree. In fact, it is sometimes planted primarily for its ornamental value. You can fully appreciate its beauty if you see the apricot orchards of Stanislaus, San Joaquin, San Benito and Fresno Counties in California, where commercial apricot production is greatest.

The early-blooming habit of the apricot limits its range to areas where late spring frosts do not occur. In St. Helena, California, for example, fruiting of apricots is unpredictable at best. Last spring frosts occur on April 2 50 percent of the time, but occur as late as April 28 10 percent of the time. In Santa Clara, California, last spring frosts occur on February 18 50 percent of the time and as late as March 28 10 percent of the time. Santa Clara County and San Benito County to the south are considered prime apricot country. But even in these regions, site selection is important and crops may be light some years.

Apricots are not as well adapted to areas with high summer temperatures as peaches. Apricots are subject to heat damage at temperatures most other fruit endure. But limitations imposed by high summer temperatures do not exclude apricots from home gardens, except in low desert regions. In most of the West, apricot is one of the healthiest, strongest and most vigorous fruit trees. Its vigor and strength are such that it can be planted at close intervals as a windbreak to protect other trees.

Apricot has a chilling requirement of 600 to 900 hours, lower than peach. In areas with mild winters only a few varieties do well. 'Earligold', 'Gold Kist', 'Royal', 'Katy' and 'Newcastle' are considered low-chill apricots.

In cool, humid coastal districts, apricots usually set poor crops that do not reach high quality.

VITAL STATISTICS—APRICOT

	Standard	Dwarf
Height at maturity (feet)		
Unpruned	30	8-10
Pruned	15	6-8
Spread at maturity with		
no competition (feet)	30	6-8
Recommended planting		
distance (feet)	24-30	8-12
Years to reach bearing age	3-4	3-4
Life expectancy (years)	75	75
Chilling requirement (hours)	350-900	350-900
Pollinizer required	See chart, pages 90-91	
Good for espalier	Informal Only	
Good for containers	No	Yes

Comments: Genetic dwarfs and low-chill varieties are available.

Apricots are one of the most attractive deciduous fruit trees.

Apricots are one of the most popular dried fruit. Drying is an easy way to extend your fruit harvest.

NEW VARIETIES AND INTERSPECIFIC HYBRIDS

A great deal of apricot breeding is being done in the California Central Valley by renowned fruit breeder Floyd Zaiger. Besides developing quality genetic dwarf apricots such as 'Garden Annie', he has introduced low-chill 'Gold Kist', a standard-size apricot. Others include 'Flora Gold', which is much more tolerant of warm days and cold nights during bloom. He has also developed *interspecific hybrids*, hybrids between two different fruit species, such as the plum-cot (plum x apricot) 'Plum Parfait'. 'Plum Parfait' is described in the apricot variety chart, page 91.

POLLINATION

Requirements for cross-pollination, if any, are included in the variety chart. Any other variety will serve as a pollinizer.

PRUNING

Trees should be trained to a vase shape as described on page 49. Apricots are pruned in the formative years and also when mature. Do not be afraid to cut out 2-year or older branches that gradually bend downward as the tree develops. Cut them to an upward-growing branch or remove entirely.

If a tree starts to lose fruiting spurs in its lower branches and no new shoots form there, heavier pruning through the top is needed. Remove branches entirely. Do not head branches.

FRUIT THINNING

Because trees usually set too heavily, fruit must be thinned severely when about an inch in diameter.

Trees that overbear may set little or no fruit the following year. Unless trees are vigorous and watered regularly, fruit will be very small.

HARVESTING AND STORAGE

Apricots develop delectable flavor when allowed to ripen fully on the tree. A single tree will ripen its fruit over a period of about three weeks. If you plan to can or store fruit, pick when firm-ripe, before fruit skin has developed its typical apricot color. When stored in a cool place, fruit will keep fairly well for another three or four weeks. But stored fruit will not have the sprightly flavor of a tree-ripened apricot.

INSECTS AND DISEASES

Brown rot is almost certain to develop in humid weather. Shot-hole fungus sometimes mars fruit and causes numerous small holes in leaves.

Few insects are harmful to apricots. Codling moth and twig borers may infest fruit in considerable numbers in a few areas, but they are relatively uncommon.

Apricots are subject to damage from wet soils. Roots are well-liked by gophers. Trees are susceptible to oak root fungus unless they are grown on plum rootstocks.

Other diseases and pests sometimes attack apricots but occur sporadically and rarely require control measures.

DRYING APRICOTS AND OTHER FRUIT

The most frequently dried fruit are prunes and apricots. The most popular apricot varieties for drying are 'Royal', 'Blenheim' and 'Tilton'.

Sulfuring is recommended as part of the drying process today, as it was more than 50 years ago.

The sulfuring step is discussed in detail in the HPBook *How To Dry Foods:* "The sulfuring process is simple and relatively inexpensive. Fruits are first prepared for drying. The pieces are placed on trays and covered with an adjustable vented chamber, a cardboard or wooden box and exposed to sulfur dioxide (SO_2) fumes created by burning sulfur.

"Use only *sublimed sulfur,* U.S.P. standard, for burning. It is also called *flowers of sulfur.* It is free of impurities, burns readily and may be purchased at most pharmacies. You can also buy it in large quantities at a reasonable price from chemical supply companies. It can be stored indefinitely or you can share the purchase with neighbors or friends. Garden-dusting sulfur has more impurities and is not recommended."

This caution is included in *How To Dry Foods:* "During the sulfuring process, sulfur dioxide fumes *must not be inhaled.* They can cause damage to the delicate membranes of the lung. Sulfur fruit outside where there is a good flow of fresh air. Do not breath the fumes and be certain that children or animals are not close by.

"Natural food advocates maintain that sulfured fruit is harmful and that sulfuring is done mainly for cosmetic reasons. There is currently no evidence to substantiate this claim. It has been proven that sulfuring retards spoilage and darkening of fruit, lessons the contamination by insects during sun drying and reduces the loss of vitamins A and C.

"If sulfured fruit is dried in the oven there is also danger of inhaling the fumes. Dry sulfured fruit in the sun or in a dehydrator."

ABOUT THE CHART

● Of all fruit trees, apricot is the most versatile for grafting. You can graft apricot varieties or graft plum and peach to apricot, although only plum will form a lasting union. The following plum varieties, when grafted onto an apricot tree, extend harvests from the end of May to the second week in August: 'Redheart', 'Santa Rosa', 'Elephant Heart' and 'Casselman'. If you want prunes with apricots, try 'French Prune', 'Sugar' and 'Italian'.

● A new genetic dwarf variety of apricot, 'Garden Annie', is now available. Here's what the Dave Wilson Nursery catalog says about this variety: "Regarded by many as the most beautiful of the genetic dwarfs, this new compact-growing tree is sure to gain a reputation as a landscape specimen as well as a reliable provider of fresh fruit."

APRICOTS
Average picking dates at Davis, California.

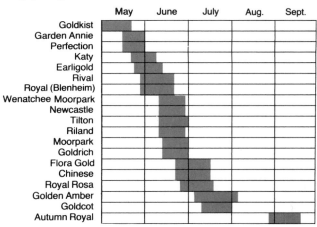

APRICOTS

VARIETY	ORIGIN	ZONE	HARVEST SEASON	FRUIT AND TREE	REMARKS
'AUTUMN ROYAL'	California.	2, 7-14, 17, 18.	Late.	Medium fruit is somewhat flattened. Skin is yellow with slight orange blush. Flesh is yellow, slightly acid. Large, vigorous tree produces regularly.	A sport of 'Royal' with the same quality. Use fresh, canned or dried.
'CHINESE' ('MORMON')	Utah.	1, 2.	Midseason to late.	Fruit is small. Skin is orange with red blush, smooth in texture. Flesh is sweet, juicy and firm with fair quality. Medium, spreading tree is a heavy cropper.	Good selection for late-frost areas. Tree is frost resistant and bears young. Ripens unevenly.
'EARLIGOLD'	California.	6-14, 16, 18.	Early.	Medium fruit is similar to 'Newcastle'. Skin is golden yellow, fuzzless. Flesh is fair quality, rich and juicy. Tree is hardy and a heavy cropper.	Use fruit for canning and for eating fresh. Tree has a low chilling requirement. Needs a pollinizer.
'FLORA GOLD'	Modesto, California (F. Zaiger).	2, 7-13, 16.	Midseason to late.	Fruit is small to medium. Skin is yellow. Flesh is very good quality. Tree is relatively small but a heavy cropper.	Consistent producer of fruit. Resistant to temperature fluctuations during bloom.
'GARDEN ANNIE'	Modesto, California (F. Zaiger).	2, 7-13, 16.	Early.	Medium to large fruit. Skin is bright yellow. Clingstone flesh is juicy and firm. Genetic dwarf tree grows 7 to 8 feet high.	Tree is self-fruitful. Lower chilling requirement than 'Royal'.

APRICOTS

VARIETY	ORIGIN	ZONE	HARVEST SEASON	FRUIT AND TREE	REMARKS
'GOLD KIST'	Modesto, California (F. Zaiger).	2, 7-14, 16-18.	Early.	Fruit is medium to large. Yellow skin with red blush has slight tendency to crack. Colors 2 to 4 weeks before ripening. Orange flesh is firm, with mild flavor. Very good quality. Large, upright tree is vigorous and a regular, heavy bearer.	Use fruit for canning, freezing, drying and for eating fresh. Low chilling requirement.
'GOLDCOT'	Michigan.	1, 2, 5, 9, 16, 19.	Late.	Medium to large fruit is nearly round. Bright gold skin is thick and tough. Flesh is orange, firm and sprightly flavored. Tree is exceptionally strong, blooms late.	Use fruit for processing or eating fresh. Tree is very productive and a good, consistent cropper. Resistant to cold.
'GOLDEN AMBER'	California.	2, 7-14, 17, 18.	Late.	Fruit is large, uniform and symmetrical. Skin is yellow. Yellow flesh is firm, slightly acid. Large, upright tree is vigorous, hardy and very productive.	Excellent quality for eating fresh, canning or drying. Tree is resistant to pit burn.
'GOLDRICH'	Prosser, Washington (H.W. Fogle, 1971).	2, 19.	Midseason.	Fruit is large and oval. Skin develops waxy, orange color when still firm. Allow color to develop fully before harvest for maximum quality. Deep orange flesh is firm and fine textured. Vigorous, productive tree.	Tree hardy. Needs a pollinizer.
'KATY'	Modesto, California (F. Zaiger).	2, 7-14, 16-18.	Early.	Fruit is large, uniform and slightly flattened on sides. Deep yellow flesh has red-blushed skin. Fruit colors on side exposed to sun. Yellow, freestone flesh is firm. Strong, vigorous, upright tree.	Low chilling requirement. Withstands varying temperatures during blooming season without dropping blossoms.
'MOORPARK'	England.	2, 7-11, 16.	Midseason.	Large fruit is the best quality of any apricot. Sweet, rich, plum-like taste. Brownish red skin has numerous specks and dots. Yellow to orange flesh is sweet, juicy and aromatic. Tree is hardy but light bearing.	Fruit ripen unevenly. Best for home gardener who can wait until each fruit is fully ripe before use.
'NEWCASTLE'	California.	13, 14, 16, 18.	Midseason.	Small to medium, round, well-shaped fruit. Skin is lemon-yellow. Flesh texture is coarse and soft. Tree is large and vigorous. A regular, heavy cropper.	Tree needs relatively little winter chill. Very subject to brown rot and bacterial gummosis.
'PERFECTION'	Washington.	2, 7-14, 17, 18, 19.	Early.	Fruit is large, oval to oblong. Light yellow-orange skin has "pebbly" appearance with no blush. Yellow to yellow-orange flesh is good quality, firm with large pit. Vigorous, hardy tree is a heavy cropper.	Tree needs a pollinizer. Low chilling requirement.
'PLUM PARFAIT'	Modesto, California (F. Zaiger).	2, 7-14, 16-18.	Early.	Medium fruit. Skin is red blushed over dark yellow. Flesh is dark yellow marbled red at pit, similar to apricot. Very good to excellent flavor, slightly tart, firm. Tree is semidwarf, 10 to 12 feet high, spreading and densely foliated. Attractive ornamental. Resembles a plum in form.	Tree bears light when young. Very early bloom. Hybrid of Japanese plum and apricot.
'RILAND'	Washington.	2.	Midseason.	Nearly round, medium fruit is covered with fine velvety hairs. Light yellow skin has deep red blush over half of fruit. Flesh is firm and meaty, somewhat acid, slightly coarse. Tends to ripen from pit out. Keeps well. Vigorous, upright tree branches sparingly, breaks easily.	Fruit has rich, plum-like flavor.
'RIVAL'	Prosser, Washington (H.W. Fogle).	2.	Early to midseason.	Very large, oval fruit. Light orange skin develops pronounced blush on exposed cheeks. Very firm, deep orange flesh is low in acid, mild flavor. Productive, very vigorous and leggy tree.	Fruit is good for canning but skin turns brown. Remains firm when peeled with good flavor. Tree is more resistant to cold than 'Wenatchee Moorpark'. Requires early-blooming pollinizer.
'ROYAL' ('BLENHEIM')	'Royal' France 'Blenheim', England.	2, 7-14, 16-18.	Early to midseason.	When well thinned, fruit is large. Thick, aromatic, yellow to yellowish orange flesh is firm, sweet and sprightly. Tree is very productive.	Principal commercial variety. Low chilling requirement. Excellent quality for all uses—fresh, canned or dried.
'ROYAL ROSA'	Modesto, California (F. Zaiger).	2, 7-11, 16, 18.	Midseason to late.	Medium fruit. Skin is bright yellow. Firm flesh has pronounced, pleasant aroma. Flavor has good balance between sugar and acid. Tree is moderate grower with heavy production.	Outstanding eating quality fruit.
'TILTON'	California.	1, 2, 9, 16, 19.	Midseason.	Large to very large fruit. Skin is orange. Flesh is yellow-orange. Tree is a heavy bearer.	High chilling requirement. Fair flavor when eaten fresh. Canned flavor is bland. Poor when dried.
'WENATCHEE MOORPARK'	Wenatchee, Washington.	2, 19.	Midseason.	Large, oval, flattened fruit. Skin and flesh are orange-yellow. Suffers from unequal halves, uneven ripening. Fair texture and quality. Tree is a heavy, annual bearer.	Quality is inferior to 'Royal'. Adapted to Northwest climate conditions.

Four varieties of avocado. Top row from left to right: 'Mexicola' and Fuerte'. Bottom row: 'Uvaldi' and 'Reed'.

Avocado

Two types of avocados are grown in the West, each with its own varieties. *Guatemalan avocados* have larger fruit but are more sensitive to climate variations. *Mexican avocados* bear smaller fruit but are hardier and extend the range in which avocados can be grown.

Guatemalan varieties are generally restricted to Zones 13 to 15 in southern California. 'Hass', the most widely adapted Guatemalan avocado, can be grown along the central coast of California and north into relatively frost-free areas around the San Francisco Bay.

Mexican varieties are more widely adapted and extend avocado culture to Zones 6 to 11 and warm parts of Zone 12. 'Mexicola', 'Bacon' and 'Zutano' are the hardiest varieties, in that order. In Zones 6 to 12, protected sites or those with good air drainage are most successful. The University of California claims a foliage cold hardiness of 24° F (−4° C) for the hardiest Mexican varieties. However, fruit and blossoms are more susceptible to cold than the foliage and will be killed at higher temperatures. Despite this, large avocado trees can be seen in the cities of Napa, Palo Alto, Berkeley, San Jose, Watsonville, Salinas, Santa Cruz and San Luis Obispo.

Mild frost damage may partially blacken fruit flesh but does not impair flavor. Severe damage will cause the flesh to brown and to lose flavor. Sometimes fruit is killed outright. Leaves and shoot ends will turn black. If the injury is not too severe, young growth may start before old leaves have fallen. Trees that are given regular care will be more cold resistant.

Cool weather during bloom period can reduce or cause complete failure of fruit set. After fruit set, sudden hot spells can cause serious drop of young fruit.

VARIETIES

Avocado fruit varieties range from very small to very large. Skin may be smooth or very rough, colored green, purple or brown. Oil content varies considerably. Generally, the higher the oil content, the better the fruit quality. The time of fruit maturity also varies with variety. By planting several varieties with staggered maturity dates, you can have fruit the entire year. Also realize that fruit grown in warmer climates will ripen earlier in the season than the same variety grown in cooler climates.

'Bacon'—Mexican. Medium tree with upright branches. Medium fruit with smooth, thin, green skin.

VITAL STATISTICS—AVOCADO		
	Standard	**Dwarf**
Height at maturity (feet)		
Unpruned	25-40	N/A
Pruned	15-20	
Spread at maturity with		
no competition (feet)	20-40	
Recommended planting		
distance (feet)	20-40	
Years to reach bearing age	3	
Life expectancy (years)	25	
Chilling requirement (hours)	None	
Pollinizer required	No	
Good for espalier	No	
Good for containers	No	

Comments: 'Wurtz', a slow-growing variety, is often sold as a dwarf. Adapted to containers.

N/A = Not Available

Avocados are attractive, evergreen landscape trees.

Yellow-green flesh. Good frost tolerance. Produces at a young age. Ripens November to March.

'Duke'—Mexican. Large, vigorous and productive tree. Medium fruit of good quality. Skin yellowish green, smooth, thin and glossy. Used mostly as a rootstock because of its resistance to *Phytophthora* root rot. Hardy and resistant to wind damage. Ripens September to November.

'Fuerte'—Mexican-Guatemalan hybrid. Tree large and spreading. High-quality fruit with thin, smooth, green skin. Very sensitive to climate changes. Flowers early and thus susceptible to frost. Popular commercial variety. Ripens November to June.

'Hass'—Guatemalan. Large, vigorous tree—more upright than 'Fuerte'. Medium fruit very dark with thick, pebbled, leathery skin. Flesh is creamy with excellent flavor. Sensitive to climate changes. Most popular supermarket avocado. Ripens April to October.

'Mexicola'—Mexican. Small, attractive tree. Small fruit with black skin. Large seed. Hardy. One of the best avocados for flavor. Ripens August to October.

'Reed'—Guatemalan. Very narrow, upright tree. Medium to large, round fruit with smooth, buttery flesh. Ripens July to September.

'Rincon'—Guatemalan. Small but productive tree. Small fruit with thick skin and rich flavor. Ripens January to April.

'Thille'—Guatemalan. Vigorous, upright tree. Medium to large, green fruit with thick skin and excellent flavor. Ripens July to November.

'Wurtz'—Guatemalan. Less than half the height of most other varieties. Weeping habit. Medium-size, green fruit of good quality. Large seed. Sold as dwarf avocado. 'Littlecado' may be a different variety but is also very slow growing. Good in containers or small yards. Ripens June to August.

'Zutano'—Mexican. Vigorous, upright tree with consistent productivity. Medium fruit with thin, green skin and fair quality. Ripens October to February.

SOIL, NUTRIENT AND WATER REQUIREMENTS

Because avocados are very susceptible to root rot, good soil drainage is absolutely essential. Water deeply and infrequently but don't let young trees dry out. Before watering older trees, allow them to draw on existing soil moisture for as long as possible without wilting.

Avocados require very little fertilizer. As long as young trees make adequate annual growth, there is no need to apply nitrogen. If it becomes necessary to apply nitrogen to older trees, 1-1/2 pounds actual nitrogen per tree annually is sufficient. If *chlorosis*—yellowing—occurs, it is probably due to iron deficiency.

PRUNING

Avocados require little pruning. Because the trees do become quite large and branch to the ground, pruning is usually done periodically to shape trees and control size.

FRUIT THINNING

Fruit thinning is not required unless set is so heavy that it might break the branch.

HARVESTING AND STORAGE

Avocados do not soften on the tree, so it is difficult to tell when they are ripe. When picked, fruit should soften without shriveling. The skin of dark-colored varieties will be fairly well colored when fruit is ready for harvesting. Green-skinned fruit are usually picked when skin brightness begins to lessen and changes to a slight yellowish tint. Seeds harden and seedcoats become dry and papery as maturity approaches.

Fruit should be clipped from tree. Do not pull off because loss of the button, *pedicel,* will almost certainly result in decay. Because fruit is very tender it must be handled carefully. Allow to soften at room temperature. Refrigeration will slow ripening.

DISEASES AND PESTS

Avocados are susceptible to a number of diseases. The most serious and common is root rot caused by the fungus *Phytophthora cinnamomi*. This disease is encouraged by poor drainage and excessive soil moisture. Initial symptoms include smaller-than-normal new leaves and yellow, wilting foliage. Often there will be no new growth. As the disease progresses some branches die back and fruit will often be small. After initial infection a tree may survive many years or decline rapidly. The best prevention is to follow good cultural practices and be sure soil drainage is adequate when trees are planted. Avoid planting in infected areas. Do not bring infected soil into your garden. If you think your trees have root rot consult your county extension agent.

Warm weather during blossom stage is critical for avocados. Cool weather at this time reduces fruit set.

'Royal Ann' cherries

Cherry

Sweet cherries are best suited to an intermediate climate. High summer temperatures cause doubling and spurring of fruit. In foggy, humid, coastal sites diseases are almost impossible to control.

Sweet cherries withstand considerable winter cold but are not as hardy as other stone fruit. They have a uniformly high chilling requirement. Flowers are late blooming so tend to suffer less from spring frosts. Leaf buds that have started growth in late winter or early spring are often injured when those of other fruit trees escape damage.

Sour cherry, also known as *pie* or *red cherry,* is an ideal garden tree. It is not as large as the sweet cherry and is easy to grow. Sour cherries are better adapted to more rigorous climates in every respect.

Duke cherries are hybrids between sweet and sour cherries. Tree growth and climate requirements are more similar to that of sweet cherry. Fruit flavor is more like that of sour cherry. Varieties are difficult to find in nurseries, but they are worth the search.

Cherry-plums are recently developed interspecific hybrids between cherries and plums. They are discussed with Plums, page 126.

SIZE CONTROL

Genetic dwarf varieties such as 'Compact Lambert', 'Compact Stella' and 'Garden Bing' not only save space in the garden but help win the battle against an age-old enemy—birds. Smaller trees are much more easily protected with netting.

Lack of production of 'Garden Bing' is a common complaint. However, it often produces vigorous branches that are not dwarf. If you allow these branches to remain, the tree will bear more fruit than normal.

'Meteor' and 'North Star' are genetic dwarf sour cherries.

POLLINATION

Most sweet cherries are *self-unfruitful,* meaning two varieties have to be planted close to each other to produce fruit. Bees are also necessary to distribute pollen from tree to tree.

Sour cherries and Duke cherries are *self-fruitful,* meaning that a single tree can pollinate itself. Sour cherries are also suitable pollinizers for sweet cherries.

VITAL STATISTICS—SWEET CHERRY

	Standard	Dwarf
Height at maturity (feet)		
Unpruned	40	6-12
Pruned	25	6-8
Spread at maturity with		
no competition (feet)	30	4-8
Recommended planting		
distance (feet)	35-45	4-8
Years to reach bearing age	4-6	3-4
Life expectancy (years)	30-35	30-35
Chilling requirement (hours)	800-1,200	800-1,200
Pollinizer required	Yes	No
Good for espalier	No	Yes
Good for containers	No	Yes

VITAL STATISTICS—SOUR CHERRY

	Standard	Dwarf
Height at maturity (feet)		
Unpruned	20	10
Pruned	15	6-8
Spread at maturity with		
no competition (feet)	30	8-10
Recommended planting		
distance (feet)	18-24	8-10
Years to reach bearing age	5	3
Life expectancy (years)	30-35	30-35
Chilling requirement (hours)	800-1,200	800-1,200
Pollinizer required	No	No
Good for espalier	Yes	Yes
Good for containers	No	Yes

Comments: Height varies by variety.

Pollinizers for other varieties are included in the variety chart.

SOIL AND WATER REQUIREMENTS

Watering practices may well be the deciding factor in the success of your sweet cherries. Trees suffer more from drought than most deciduous trees. They must also have a well-drained soil because standing water promotes root rots. Duke cherries have a similar watering requirement. Sour cherries are somewhat more tolerant of poor watering, but like other fruit trees, they respond to regular watering by producing heavier crops of quality fruit.

PRUNING

Sweet cherry trees grow upright and do not produce side branches during early life. Each branch should be *headed*—cut back—rather severely in early years to force branch development. Make cuts at points where you want future branches. Head new growth moderately for the first three or four years and thin out undesirable branches. If possible, always cut to an outward-growing branch to force tree to spread.

The purpose of pruning fruit-bearing trees is to remove dead and interfering branches and to renew fruiting wood. Sweet cherries are borne mostly on long-lived spurs that are productive for 10 to 12 years. Cherries therefore need less renewal wood than nearly any other deciduous fruit tree. When trees first begin to bear, they require little pruning. Thin out new shoots lightly each year and cut out weak or interfering branches. Keep tops from growing too high by occasionally cutting back to strong lateral branches. Once trees have become thoroughly established, they require little pruning.

Duke cherry trees can be pruned the same as sweet cherries.

Sour cherry trees are best adapted to vase-type training, described on page 49. They spread much more than young sweet cherries, so there is no difficulty in creating proper distance between main branches. On older bearing trees, merely thin out excess shoots so that light can enter tree. Cut back weaker branches to strong laterals. Sour cherry bears fruit on 2 to 5-year-old spurs.

HARVESTING AND STORAGE

Cherries are picked when fully ripe, usually with stems on fruit. They keep much better that way. If you plan to use fruit for canning or other processing, strip cherries from trees without the stems. This method is much easier and faster but messy.

Sour cherries are usually served cooked in some manner. Another name, *pie cherry*, indicates their most popular use. Although some individuals relish them as fresh fruit, they are too acid for most palates. Sour cherries are mostly prepared fresh from the tree, but may be canned or frozen for later use.

DISEASES AND PESTS

Cherries are subject to a long list of diseases and pests. A few are almost certain to develop to troublesome proportions. This is especially true in the more humid regions of the Northwest. Possibly the most serious disease is bacterial gummosis. Brown rot of blossoms and especially brown rot of fruit will prove troublesome in humid regions. See the section on pests and diseases, page 34. Fruit cracking is caused by late spring rains.

Genetic dwarf cherries such as 'Compact Stella' can easily be protected from birds with netting.

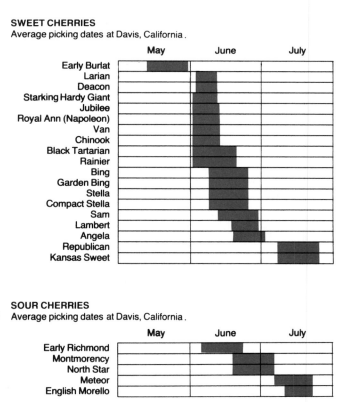

SWEET CHERRIES
Average picking dates at Davis, California.

	May	June	July
Early Burlat			
Larian			
Deacon			
Starking Hardy Giant			
Jubilee			
Royal Ann (Napoleon)			
Van			
Chinook			
Black Tartarian			
Rainier			
Bing			
Garden Bing			
Stella			
Compact Stella			
Sam			
Lambert			
Angela			
Republican			
Kansas Sweet			

SOUR CHERRIES
Average picking dates at Davis, California.

	May	June	July
Early Richmond			
Montmorency			
North Star			
Meteor			
English Morello			

ABOUT THE CHARTS

• Climate adaptation is most important in choosing cherry varieties. One important clue is the origin of the variety. Note the wide variation in places of origin: Russia, Europe, Utah, Washington, Oregon, British Columbia, Wisconsin, Kansas and California.

• The most popular sweet cherry varieties are 'Bing', 'Van', 'Royal Ann', 'Black Tartarian' and 'Lambert'. However, note that no combination of 'Bing', 'Royal Ann' and 'Lambert' will cross-pollinate.

• Some cherries have strange names like 'Van', 'Sam' and 'Burlat'. The variety 'Sam' received its name from the 'S' of Summerland, B.C., where it originated, and the first and last initials of A. J. Mann, its originator. 'Van', also originating in Summerland, was named in honor of J. R. Van Haarlem. 'Burlat' gets its name from Bigarreau Hatif de Burlat of Morocco.

• When planting sour cherries, you should know the difference between the two types. Sour cherries of the *amarelle* group have yellow flesh and clear juice. Amarelle sour cherries are the commercial cherries of the coldest northern climates. Sour cherries of the *morello* group, including the variety of that name, have red flesh and juice.

• When considering varieties for your garden, pay particular attention to those that can be planted singly and those that require pollizers. All sour cherries are self-fruitful and can be planted singly. However, the only self-fruitful, standard-size sweet variety is 'Stella'. Study the chart for sweet cherries to see which varieties pollinate each other. A pollinizer must be planted with or grafted onto a chosen variety. Note that 'Stella', 'Starking Hardy Giant' and 'Deacon' are very effective pollinizers for many varieties.

SWEET CHERRIES

VARIETY	ORIGIN	ZONE	HARVEST SEASON	POLLINIZER	FRUIT AND TREE	REMARKS
'ANGELA'	Utah State University.	2, 5, 7-11.	Late (with 'Lambert').	'Lambert' 'Early Burlat'	Medium to large fruit. Almost as firm as 'Bing'. Good flavor. Medium, upright, vigorous and very productive tree—hardier than 'Lambert'.	Resistant to buckskin disease. Blooms late, approximately the same time as 'Lambert'.
'BING'	Oregon, 1875.	2, 3, 5, 7-11, 16, 19.	Midseason.	'Republican' 'Black Tartarian' 'Sam' 'Van' 'Chinook' 'Early Burlat' 'Larian'	Consistently large, mahogany-red fruit is firm, meaty, sweet and juicy. Vigorous and spreading tree. Produces heavy crops.	One of the best cherries. Excellent for canning. Hot climate often produces doubling of fruit. Rain causes cracking. Check for bacterial attack in humid climates.
'BLACK TARTARIAN'	Russia.	2, 5, 7-11, 16.	Early.	Any sweet cherry	Fruit is smaller than 'Bing', bright purplish black, thick and sweet. Softens quickly when picked. Tree is vigorous grower and heavy bearer.	Used as a pollinizer in California. One of the earliest cherries. Cracks, spurs and doubles badly.
'CHINOOK'	Prosser, Washington, 1960.	2, 5, 7-11.	Early.	'Bing' 'Sam' 'Van'	Fruit is similar to 'Bing'. Mahogany-colored skin. Vigorous and spreading tree.	Tree is more hardy than 'Bing'. Same rain-cracking problem as 'Bing'. Good production. Resistant to buckskin disease.
'COMPACT STELLA'	Summerland, B.C., 1973.	2, 3, 5, 7-11.	Slightly later than 'Stella'.	Self-fertile. Universal pollinizer.	Large to medium-large black fruit is heart shaped to oval. Medium-firm flesh has good to fair texture and flavor. Semidwarf tree is half the size of 'Stella'. Older growth is heavily spurred.	Fruits early with heavy crops. Flesh cracks moderately in rain.
'DEACON'	Olympia, Washington.	2, 5, 7-11, 16.	Early.	'Lambert' 'Black Tartarian' 'Sam' 'Van' 'Republican'	Medium-large black fruit is firm with sweet flavor. Smaller than 'Bing'. Vigorous tree.	Available only in the Northwest. Used as a pollinizer for other sweet cherries.
'EARLY BURLAT'	USDA, California.	8-11.	Early.	'Bing' 'Van' 'Chinook' 'Black Tartarian' 'Larian'	Fruit is large with moderately firm texture. Similar to 'Bing'. Tree slightly less vigorous than 'Bing'.	Normal cracking and doubling of fruit. Resistant to buckskin disease.
'GARDEN BING'	Dave Wilson Nursery, California.	Not fully tested.	Midseason.	Self-fertile.	Dark red fruit is similar to 'Bing'. Tree is approximately 6 feet tall at maturity with spread of 4 feet.	Highly ornamental, genetic dwarf tree. Excellent for patio containers. Light bearing.
'JUBILEE'	Davis, California, 1964.	2, 5, 7-11.	Early.	'Lambert' 'Larian'	Fruit is similar to 'Bing' but larger with glossy, dark red skin. Firm, dark red, sweet flesh. Tree very similar to 'Bing'.	Fewer spurs and double fruit than 'Bing'. Resists cracking. Does not ship well. Flat flavor in years of heavy set.

SWEET CHERRIES

VARIETY	ORIGIN	ZONE	HARVEST SEASON	POLLINIZER	FRUIT AND TREE	REMARKS
'KANSAS SWEET'	Wichita, Kansas.	2, 5, 7-11.	Late.	'Black Tartarian' 'Deacon' 'Republican' 'Sam' 'Van'	Fruit is similar to 'Bing', but larger. Skin is glossy and dark red. Tree vigorous and hardy.	Fruit is sweet and juicy.
'LAMBERT'	Summerland, B.C., 1964.	2-5, 7-11, 16, 19.	Late.	'Van' 'Sam' 'Rainier' 'Angela'	Large, dark reddish purple fruit is firm and sweet. Vigorous, large tree is less spreading than 'Bing'. Upright growth produces weak crotches if left untrained.	Connoisseur's cherry. Hardy. Often difficult to train and prune. Subject to cracking but resistant to doubling in hot climates. Blooms late.
'LARIAN'	Davis, California.	2, 5, 7-11, 16.	Early.	'Bing' 'Early Burlat' 'Rainier'	Medium-large fruit is firm and ships well. Low vigor on Mahaleb rootstock. Productive.	Drops part of crop midseason in some years. Resistant to cracking, spurs and doubles.
'RAINIER'	Prosser, Washington, 1960.	2, 3, 5, 7-11, 16, 19.	Early.	'Bing' 'Sam' 'Van'	Attractive yellow with red blushed fruit. Similar to 'Royal Ann' with firm and juicy flesh. Fruit resembles 'Bing' in shape. Vigorous, upright, spreading tree tends to overbear.	Very productive. Resists cracking, spurs and doubles.
'REPUBLICAN' ('BLACK REPUBLICAN', 'BLACK OREGON')	Oregon, 1850.	2, 5, 7-11, 16.	Late.	Any sweet cherry.	Small, round fruit, very dark purple. Firm, tender and tart. Large, spreading tree tends to overbear.	Good flavor and a long keeper. Excellent, late-ripening variety.
'ROYAL ANN' ('NAPOLEON')	Europe.	2-5, 7-11, 16.	Early.	'Van'	Fruit is very large. Skin is yellowish amber and blushed red. Firm and juicy flesh has a sprightly flavor. Tree is large, vigorous and productive. Grows upright and spreads with age.	Fruit is used for maraschino cherries. Good for canning. Commercial cherry for California. In hot climates, tends to double as much as 'Bing'. Cracks and spurs badly.
'SAM'	Summerland, B.C., 1953.	2-5, 7-11, 16.	Midseason.	'Lambert' 'Bing'	Medium-large, black-skinned fruit. Firm and juicy. Tree grows vigorously and produces heavily. Somewhat slow to bear initially.	Tree is hardy. Fruit is high quality and resists cracking.
'STARKING HARDY GIANT'	Cedarburg, Wisconsin, 1948.	8-11.	Early to midseason.	'Black Tartarian' 'Republican' 'Sam' 'Van'	Dark red fruit is large, similar to 'Bing'. Good flavor. Stem is short and thin. Large, upright tree.	Effective pollinizer for sweet cherries, especially 'Lambert'. Tree very hardy.
'STELLA'	Summerland, B.C., 1968.	2-5, 7-11, 16.	Midseason.	Self-fertile.	Large, 'Lambert'-type fruit. Dark red, firm and sweet. Hardy, vigorous tree bears early.	Suitable pollinizer for all other sweet cherries. Resistant to cracking after rains.
'VAN'	Summerland, B.C., 1944.	2, 3, 5, 7-11,	Midseason.	'Bing' 'Lambert' 'Royal Ann' 'Rainier'	Dark, shiny fruit is slightly smaller than 'Bing'. Tree is hardy, bears 1 to 3 years earlier than 'Bing'.	Fruit doubles in some years. Some resistance to cracking. Excellent quality but subject to bacterial canker in western Washington. Tendency to overset crop—fruit is small in those years.

SOUR CHERRIES

VARIETY	ORIGIN	ZONE	HARVEST SEASON	POLLINIZER	FRUIT AND TREE	REMARKS
'EARLY RICHMOND'	Unknown.	2-5, 16, 19.	Early.	Self-fertile.	Small fruit is round with bright red skin. Tart flavor. Tree is medium size—10 to 15 feet tall.	Amarelle-type fruit. Especially hardy. Fruit is used for jams, pies, jellies and preserves.
'ENGLISH MORELLO'	Unknown.	2-5, 16, 19.	Late.	Self-fertile.	Deep red fruit is nearly black. Large, tender and juicy. Slightly tart. Very productive tree.	Excellent for pies. Good pollinizer.
'METEOR'	Minnesota.	2-5, 16, 19.	Late.	Self-fertile.	Large, bright red fruit with yellow flesh, mildly acidic. Tree is hardy and vigorous.	Amarelle-type fruit. Tree is genetic dwarf, grows to 10 feet tall. Does well in mild climates. Fine tree for home garden.
'MONTMORENCY'	France.	2-5, 16, 19.	Varies, depending on strain.	Self-fertile.	Large, roundish, bright red fruit with yellow flesh. Mildly acidic. Hardy, vigorous tree produces heavily. Medium to large and spreading.	Amarelle-type fruit with clear juice and yellow flesh. Tree is disease resistant. One of the most popular for canning and pies. Leading cherry for commercial canneries.
'NORTH STAR'	Minnesota.	2-5, 16, 19.	Early, but fruit holds for 2 weeks on tree.	Self-fertile.	Bright red to mahogany fruit has tart, juicy, yellow flesh. Smaller fruit and tree than 'Montmorency'. Tree is genetic dwarf and grows less than 10 feet tall.	Morello-type fruit with red juice and flesh. Hardiest of sour cherries. Resistant to cracking and brown rot.

'Page' mandarin

Citrus

The citrus family is a large one. It includes familar supermarket fruit such as oranges, grapefruit, lemons, limes and tangerines. However, many types of citrus are never seen in American supermarkets. Uniquely flavorful blood oranges, huge pummelos and hardy kumquat hybrids are but a few.

Citrus are evergreen plants with bright green foliage, fragrant flowers and colorful fruit. They are valuable as ornamental landscape plants. They can be used as hedges, espaliers and specimen trees and make excellent container plants.

For a complete discussion of citrus, refer to the HPBook, *Citrus: How to Select, Grow and Enjoy.*

CITRUS CLIMATE

Citrus trees are not difficult to grow but do have climatic requirements and restrictions. Once their cultural needs are understood, you will be able to grow the highest-quality fruit. In addition, you may be able to make use of microclimates around your home and be successful with types of citrus not normally grown in your area.

The two climatic factors that influence citrus most are winter cold and accumulated heat.

Cold hardiness—Different types of citrus show varying degrees of cold hardiness, but exact temperatures are difficult to predict. Variables such as duration of cold, position of the tree in the garden and even position of fruit on the tree determine how badly a tree or its fruit will be damaged.

The following citrus species are listed in order of increasing foliage hardiness from most tender to most hardy: citron, lime, lemon, grapefruit and pummelo, sweet orange, mandarin and kumquat. Tangelo and tangor hybrids rank about equal to sweet orange in hardiness. 'Meyer' lemon, 'Rangpur' lime, calamondin, Satsuma mandarin and kumquat hybrids rank between mandarin and kumquat.

Foliage of citron and 'Mexican' lime is usually damaged at 32° F (0° C). Foliage of kumquat will usually tolerate temperatures down to 18° F (−8° C) or slightly lower.

Citrus fruit is usually less hardy than the foliage. Most fruit will be damaged between 26° to 28° F (−3° to −2° C). Grapefruit is slightly more cold resistant. Mandarin fruit is more frost sensitive.

Growing citrus in the western United States means living with the threat of frost. This is true even in the mildest areas of the commercial citrus belt. Every ten years or so, your citrus will probably experience some frost damage. But citrus trees are surprisingly resilient. A tree that loses all its leaves can come back and produce fruit the following year.

Beating the cold—Here are a number of ways you can avoid cold damage or at least keep it to a minimum.
• Plant the hardiest citrus. Even within citrus types, some varieties are hardier than others.
• Choose early ripening varieties such as Satsuma mandarin or 'Skaggs Bonanza' navel orange, which can often be harvested before damaging frosts.
• Protect plants with covers or heating devices. See illustrations on pages 6 and 9.
• The rootstock on which a variety is grafted can have a profound influence on its hardiness. Trifoliate orange used as a rootstock increases hardiness. The same is true of citrange rootstock, but to a lesser degree.
• Follow a properly timed fertilization program.
• Make the most of the microclimates around your home. See page 4.
• Plant in containers and move trees indoors or to a protected site in winter.

Heat requirements—Accumulating enough heat is as important to citrus as cold tolerance, because only heat can produce truly ripe fruit. Ripeness means sweetness.

Lemons are an acid fruit and don't need to "sweeten up." Consequently, they are ideally suited to cool, coastal conditons.

Grapefruit, on the other hand, have a high heat requirement and only reach peak quality in hot inland and desert regions.

There are a number of ways you can ripen citrus in areas without adequate heat. Most citrus will hold their fruit on the tree in good edible condition over long periods of time. In fact, many citrus fruit increase in quality as they remain on the tree.

You can also accumulate more heat by planting trees in the sunniest spots around your home, such as against a south wall.

RIPENING PERIODS

Ripening periods vary greatly due to climate. Even seasonal weather changes can influence when a particular variety will ripen. In general, the hotter the climate, the earlier a variety will be ready to harvest. Fruit of a given variety will ripen first in desert zones 17 and 18, next in warm interior zones 13 and 9. Citrus grown in other zones ripen according to how hot it gets in summer, fall and winter. Fruit grown close to the coast ripen last. Some types of citrus, such as lemons and limes, are nearly everbearing in cool climates. In hotter areas their ripening period may be concentrated into one or two seasons.

Under each citrus type—orange, mandarin, grapefruit and others—we have listed overall ripening periods. If there are many varieties within a type that ripen over a long period, we have listed them as *early*, *midseason* or *late* in the remarks column of the variety charts. Everbearing varieties produce fruit the entire year.

DWARF CITRUS

Dwarf citrus are usually 40 to 50 percent of the size of standard orchard trees, yet produce 50 to 60 percent of the fruit of standard trees. This is an obvious advantage to the gardener with limited space.

Some varieties such as 'Meyer' and 'Ponderosa' lemons are naturally dwarf. They are often propagated and sold as rooted cuttings. Otherwise, dwarf citrus should be budded or grafted on a specific rootstock.

Some dwarfing is caused by an interaction between the variety and the rootstock it is grafted to. Common rootstocks used by dwarf citrus growers include trifoliate orange, 'Cunningham' citrange and Cuban shaddock.

Because standard citrus trees vary in size depending on the variety, dwarf citrus vary proportionately. 'Valencia' orange or 'Marsh' grapefruit becomes 18 to 20 feet high on standard roots. Dwarf forms reach 8 to 12 feet. Kumquat grows only 8 to 12 feet high. Dwarf varieties will be 3 to 6 feet.

Dwarf citrus are ideally suited to containers. The restricted root space will further limit growth and trees will be fruitful for years.

CITRUS CARE

Growing citrus is relatively easy compared to growing deciduous fruit trees. Dormant sprays are rarely needed and pruning is kept to a minimum.

Citrus does demand that the soil be well drained. Citrus plants are very sensitive to soggy soil but need a constant supply of moisture. If you live in an area with poor soil, you might consider planting citrus in containers or raised beds in light, commercial potting soil. Or, you can make your own planting mix. More information on container soils can be found on page 71.

FERTILIZING

Most western soils contain ample amounts of all the nutrients required by citrus except nitrogen. If leaves remain yellow with dark green veins after nitrogen has been applied, applications of minor nutrients such as iron, zinc and manganese are needed. See photos, page 33.

Mature citrus trees should be fertilized at a rate of 1 to 1-1/2 pounds of actual nitrogen per year (# act/N). Trees younger than 5 years should receive nitrogen at the following rate: 1 year—0.1 # act/N; 2 years—0.2 # act/N; 3 years—0.35 # act/N; and 4 years—0.5 # act/N. Commercially available citrus and avocado foods prescribe this rate.

Nitrogen should be applied three or four times a year with the first and most important application in January or February. Make additional applications every 6 to 8 weeks until the end of summer. Nitrogen applied in fall encourages frost-sensitive growth.

Citrus grown in containers require more frequent applications of nitrogen. Repeated waterings, necessary for plants in containers, *leach* (wash) nutrients from the soil. Micronutrient deficiencies are also more common in container-grown citrus for the same reason. Fertilizing once a month is usually recommended. Pounds of actual nitrogen applied are divided up accordingly.

PRUNING

Citrus trees need little pruning. When a tree is mature, pruning should be confined almost entirely to removing dead, diseased or broken branches. Young trees may occasionally require removal of vigorous shoots and suckers.

PESTS AND DISEASES

Relatively few pests or diseases cause serious problems in home gardens, so a preventive spray program is usually unnecessary. By growing healthy trees through proper watering and fertilization, pest and disease damage will be minimized.

Occasional problems may develop from aphids, mealy bugs, scale, citrus red mite, snails or thrips.

HARVESTING AND HANDLING

The best way to tell if a citrus fruit is ripe is to pick one and taste it. With sweet types, color alone is a poor way to judge ripeness. The best way to pick citrus is with pruning shears, leaving a little of the stem attached to the fruit.

Ideally, citrus should be stored on the tree, but fruit will keep in a refrigerator for two to three weeks. Tree

From left to right: blood oranges 'Tarocco', 'Moro' and 'Sanguinelli'.

storage time differs by variety and is included in the variety chart, pages 103 to 105. If fruit has been held on tree too long, it will begin to dry out, become puffy and lose flavor.

SWEET ORANGES

There are two types of sweet oranges: navel and common.

Navel oranges—The navel itself is the development of a secondary fruit at the end of the main fruit. This secondary fruit is the odd, top-shaped portion that is so evident when a navel orange is peeled and separated.

As a group, navel oranges are known for their crisp, rich flavor and ease of peeling and separation. They grow best and develop top flavor under a narrower range of climatic conditions than other oranges. Generally, they are not recommended in hot desert climates or cool coastal areas. Some varieties such as 'Skaggs Bonanza' may ripen early enough to be picked before damaging frost occurs.

Common oranges—This group is characterized by sweet, juicy oranges. Some, such as 'Valencia', are normally relegated to juicing because fruit are difficult to peel. There are over one hundred common orange varieties. We have described several that perform best in the western United States.

ARIZONA SWEETS

Several varieties of oranges are sold in Arizona under the name Arizona Sweets. They include 'Marrs', 'Pineapple', 'Diller', 'Hamlin' and 'Trovita'. Most of these varieties are also popular in Texas and the Gulf Coast states. They are the most dependable bearers and avoid the tendency to bear fruit in alternate years, as 'Valencia' does. To find out which variety you are buying under this label, ask your nurseryman.

Earliest-ripening oranges are harvested in late November to early December in the warmest climates. Late varieties can be harvested into May in cool climates. 'Valencia' oranges can hang on the tree into September in cool areas.

BLOOD ORANGES

The name *blood orange* describes one aspect of the fruit's uniqueness—its deep red internal color.

Blood oranges are also called the connoisseur's or gourmet's citrus. Their flavor is distinctive and rich with overtones of raspberries or strawberries. Fruit is a bit hard to peel but excellent for juicing. Flavor is outstanding in all areas regardless of coloration, but sweetest in warmer climates.

The flesh color of blood oranges is generally deepest in hot regions. Varieties differ: 'Tarocco' may develop deep color in California's interior valleys, but none at all in the desert. Rind coloration will be the most dramatic on fruit located on the inside or northern side of the tree, where they are somewhat protected from the sun.

One-third of all oranges consumed in Mediterranean Europe are blood oranges. The unpredictability of their color probably accounts for their failure to gain popular acceptance in the United States.

Blood oranges are harvested from December to May.

SOUR ORANGES

Sour oranges include many ornamental varieties. In general, they have distinctive foliage, compact growth habits and beautiful, fragrant flowers.

Sour orange fruit begin to color in November or December. Fruit will hang on the tree 9 or 10 months, greatly adding to the tree's ornamental quality.

MANDARINS AND MANDARIN HYBRIDS

Mandarins easily make up the largest and most varied group of edible citrus. As landscape plants they provide an array of textures and tree forms. As edible fruit, they are distinctive and delicious. With careful variety selection, as few as three or four mandarin trees can yield fresh fruit for up to eight months each year.

Mandarins are adapted to a wider range of climates than any other citrus group. Climate also has a great deal of influence on fruit quality. High heat in the latter part of the ripening period generally results in the best flavor. In the desert, fruit is usually sweeter, juicier and larger than fruit of the same variety grown in cooler climates.

Mexican' Lime Lemon Grapefruit Pummelo Tangelo Orange Mandarin 'Meyer' Lemon Kumquat

From left to right, citrus fruit are lined up in order of increasing foliage hardiness.

Some mandarins are called *tangerines*. The word tangerine seems to have developed with the variety 'Dancy', which has a more brightly colored, orange-red peel than most mandarins. Now most varieties with a deep red coloration are called tangerines.

The description of mandarins as "slip-skin oranges" or "kid glove" fruit refers to their ease of peeling and separation. However, if the rind is puffy and extremely easy to peel, the fruit may be overripe.

Tangors—mandarin and sweet orange hybrids—and tangelos—mandarin and grapefruit hybrids—are often grouped with mandarins because of their parentage. These three groups appear separately in the variety chart.

Alternate bearing, the appearance of a heavy crop of fruit every other year, is often a problem with mandarins. Fruit thinning during heavy years may help.

Some mandarin and mandarin hybrid varieties produce larger crops when cross-pollinated with another mandarin or other citrus type. 'Dancy' and 'Kinnow' mandarins and 'Valencia' orange are good pollinizers. See variety chart for specifics.

Mandarins and their hybrids ripen from November to May.

LEMONS

Acid content of lemons is maximum just prior to fruit maturity. Commercially, they are picked by size rather than ripeness. The earlier they are picked after they reach sufficient size and juiciness, the longer they can be stored.

The home lemon grower has the advantage of picking a lemon at the optimum time. For best flavor, a lemon should be picked as soon as it becomes fully yellow. Left too long on the tree, it becomes pithy and loses flavor and acidity.

Lemons are everbearing in cool climates. In warmer areas crops are concentrated in fall and spring.

LIMES

Two species of acid limes are classified as *large fruited* and *small fruited*. In the western United States, the small-fruited variety is called 'Mexican' lime or bartender's lime. In Florida, 'Mexican' lime is known as 'Key' lime.

'Bearss' is the variety of large-fruited lime commonly available in the West. It is identical or very similar to 'Tahitian' or 'Persian' lime of Florida.

Limes are sensitive to cold and should only be grown in areas protected from frost.

In areas where they are adapted, limes are usually everbearing. Most of the ripe fruit is harvested in spring and fall.

GRAPEFRUIT

Grapefruit are divided into two natural groups: common and pigmented (pink). Trees grow vigorously and are among the largest citrus trees.

Grapefruit need extremely high heat in order to reach maximum eating quality. In the long, hot, growing season of the low deserts of California, Arizona and Texas, they reach their prime in about 12 to 14 months. Grapefruit grown in cooler regions closer to the coast take as long as 18 months to ripen. Coastal fruit will also be more tart and have a thicker rind.

Because of the different ripening periods in the major growing areas, grapefruit are available at the supermarket almost year-round.

PUMMELOS

Pummelos are the largest citrus. Varieties range from round to pear shaped, with thick skin, firm flesh and less juice content than grapefruit.

Because of their mildly sweet juice and firm flesh, pummelos are not eaten in the same manner as grapefruit. Instead, you peel the fruit, segment it and shell the edible pulp vesicles out of their membranes. You can do this without rupturing the vesicle walls. The

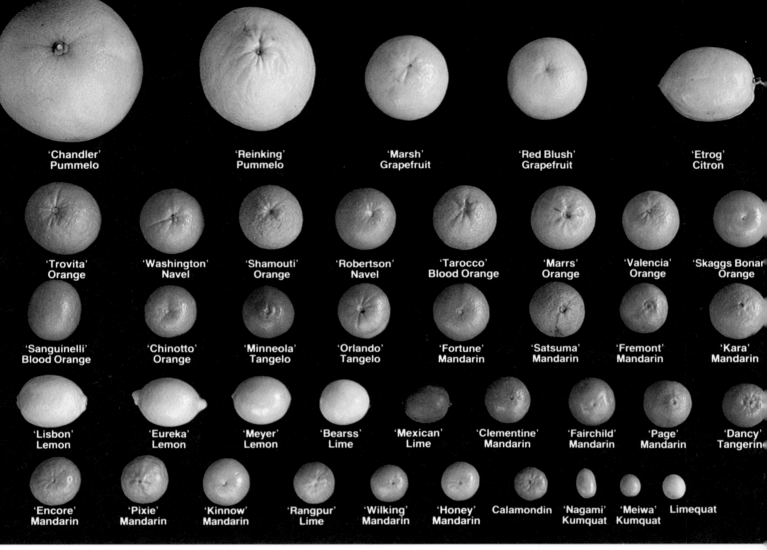

The citrus family offers a variety of shapes and sizes, from pummelo to kumquat.

shelled segments of fruit can be white or pigmented. They are eaten with or without sugar.

'Reinking' and 'Chandler' are two varieties developed for western climates. They ripen on the same schedule as grapefruit.

KUMQUATS

Kumquats are small, orange-colored fruit. Their rind is thick, tender and sweet and fruit flesh is moderately acid. Thus the whole fruit, rind and all, is edible—a unique feature among citrus.

Kumquat trees need relatively high heat to grow well. During the summer they grow, bloom and set fruit. High heat yields bigger fruit. High humidity yields the best-flavored fruit.

The extended period of dormancy for kumquats probably contributes to their being the most cold hardy of all citrus species.

Kumquats begin ripening in early November in desert areas and continue into March in coastal climates. Fruit can hang on the tree for months after ripening without deterioration.

KUMQUAT HYBRIDS

Limequat, orangequat, citrangequat and calamondin make up an interesting group of ornamental kumquat hybrids. Calamondin is a natural hybrid, generally considered a cross between kumquat and sour mandarin. It is probably the citrus best suited to indoor culture.

Kumquat hybrids begin ripening in September and continue into March. The fruit hangs on the tree for long periods without deterioration.

CITRON

The citron was the first citrus to reach the western world. Like lemon and lime, citron is a sour fruit. However, unlike lemon and lime, flesh or pulp of citron is scanty, firm and lacking in juice. Citron rind can be eaten fresh or used to make marmalade.

Citrons are generally everbearing, but most fruit are harvested in the fall.

CITRUS

NAME	ZONE	ABILITY TO HOLD ON TREE	TREE CHARACTERISTICS	REMARKS
SWEET ORANGES				
'DILLER'	17, 18.	Good.	Moderately vigorous, somewhat upright.	An excellent juice orange adapted to desert conditions and sold as an 'Arizona Sweet'. Early to midseason harvest period.
'HAMLIN'	9, 13, 14, 17, 18.	Good.	Moderately vigorous, productive. Slightly more hardy than other sweet oranges.	One of the earliest-maturing 'Arizona Sweet'. Excellent juice orange. Small but tasty fruit.
'MARRS'	9, 17, 18.	Good.	Bears heavy crop of fruit, usually in clusters near the outside of the tree.	Earliest-maturing 'Arizona Sweet'. Naturally dwarf tree produces heavy crops of small but juicy fruit.
'PINEAPPLE'	9, 17, 18.	Fair.	Moderately vigorous. Few thorns. Productive but less tolerant of cold than most oranges.	Popular Florida juice orange occasionally sold in the Southwest as an 'Arizona Sweet'. Name comes from the delicate fragrance of the fruit. Early to midseason.
'ROBERTSON' NAVEL	6-11, 13, 14, 17, 18.	Good.	Slow growing. Fruit borne in clusters near outside of tree.	Similar to 'Washington' navel but slightly earlier and more heat resistant. Bears at an early age. Early.
'SHAMOUTI'	6-11, 13, 14, 17, 18.	Good.	Upright, moderately vigorous. Few thorns. Highly productive in favorable locations.	Very popular European orange grown primarily in Israel. Very attractive tree with dense foliage and large leaves and fruit. Midseason.
'SKAGGS BONANZA'	6-11, 13, 14.	Fair to good.	Similar to 'Washington' but with a smaller, denser round head.	Bud sport of 'Washington' navel. Bears 2 weeks earlier in season than 'Washington'. Trees bear at an earlier age. Won't hold on tree as long as parent. Early.
'SUMMERNAVEL'	6-11, 13, 14.	Good.	More vigorous and spreading than 'Washington' with an open growth habit. Large leaves and russet bark.	Late-ripening bud sport of the 'Washington' navel. Easy to espalier.
'TROVITA'	6-11, 13-15, 17, 18.	Good.	Rather vigorous, upright. Very attractive, dense, dark green foliage.	'Washington' navel seedling without a navel but with a wider range of adaptation. Good in the desert and near the coast. Very juicy. Tends to bear alternate years. Often sold as 'Arizona Sweet'. Midseason.
'VALENCIA'	6-11, 13-15, 17, 18.	Excellent.	One of the most vigorous orange trees. Globe-shaped. Dense habit.	Standard juice orange. Wide range of adaptation. Excellent holding quality—up to 5 months near the coast. Late.
'WASHINGTON' NAVEL	6-11, 13, 14.	Fair to good.	Round topped, slightly drooping habit with dense, dark green foliage.	Eating orange. Excellent flavor, easy to peel and separate. Poor in desert heat and very near the coast. Often ripens before threatening frosts. Early.
SOUR ORANGES				
'BOUQUET'	6-11, 13-15, 17, 18.	Excellent.	Spreading tree produces thornless branchlets and rounded, ruffled leaves.	Prized ornamental with brightly colored fruit and ruffled deep green leaves. Profuse bloom of heavenly scented flowers. Excellent hedge or container plant. Fruit can be used to make marmalade.
'CHINOTTO'	6-11, 13-15, 17, 18.	Excellent.	Grows with thornless branchlets into rounded, very symmetrical tree. Leaves are very small, closely spaced and dark green.	Uniquely handsome, small, compact tree. Profuse bloom and heavy set of clustered fruit that will hold for nearly 12 months. Excellent ornamental for container. Fruit can be used to make marmalade.
'SEVILLE'	6-11, 13-15, 17, 18.	Excellent.	Vigorous, upright growth habit. Thorny. Long, dark green leaves taper to a point.	Historic orange of ancient mosques and European courtyards. Fruit used to make marmalade. Widely planted in Arizona as street tree, specimen and hedge. Fine ornamental.
BLOOD ORANGES				
'MORO'	6-11, 13-15, 17, 18.	Good.	Vigorous, spreading and roundheaded. Very productive.	Deepest red flesh color in most climates. Ornamental fruit held in clusters near outside of tree. Excellent flavor. Earliest of the blood oranges.
'SANGUINELLI'	6-11, 13-15, 17, 18.	Good.	Almost thornless. Long, narrow, light green foliage. Fruit held on outside of tree.	Dense foliage and abundant, oval-shaped fruit with high external blush make it a good ornamental. Good holding quality and wide range of adaptation. Excellent flavor.
'TAROCCO'	6-11, 13-15, 17, 18.	Poor.	Moderately vigorous, somewhat irregular in form. Fruit held toward inside of tree.	Very distinctive flavor. Less productive than other blood oranges but bigger fruit with high juice content. Colors best in warm interior valleys. Open growth habit needs shaping. Good espalier.

CITRUS

NAME	ZONE	ABILITY TO HOLD ON TREE	TREE CHARACTERISTICS	REMARKS
MANDARINS				
'CLEMENTINE'	6-11, 13, 14, 17, 18.	Excellent.	Grows at moderate rate. Very attractive with weeping form and dense, dark green foliage.	Excellent-tasting, early-season mandarin. Best adapted to high-heat areas. Beautiful ornamental. Requires pollinizer. Important commercial variety in California. Early.
'DANCY'	6-11, 13, 14, 17, 18.	Fair.	Most vigorous growth habit of any mandarin. Few thorns. Fruit held toward outside of tree.	Traditional Christmas tangerine and major commercial variety in Florida. Produces best fruit in desert regions. Tends to alternate-bear. Early.
'ENCORE'	6-11, 13, 14, 17, 18.	Good.	Moderate growth rate. Upright, spreading habit, rather open. Few or no thorns.	Produces heavy crop of delicious late-season fruit with speckled rinds. Tends to alternate-bear. Late.
'FAIRCHILD'	6-11, 13, 17, 18.	Fair to good.	Grows at a fairly vigorous rate. Roundheaded, dense and nearly thornless.	Richly flavored variety developed for high-heat areas. Dense foliage and abundant fruit. Gaining in commercial importance. Needs pollinizer. Early.
'HONEY'	6-11, 13, 14, 17, 18.	Good.	Grows vigorously into spreading tree.	Small but wonderfully sweet fruit produced abundantly. Excellent choice for the home garden. Midseason.
'KARA'	6-11, 13, 14.	Good.	Moderate growth rate. Open tree similar to but larger than Satsuma. Large, dark green leaves with a drooping habit. Nearly thornless.	Rich, sprightly, distinctive flavor. Produces best fruit in interior regions. Poor in the desert, tart near the coast. Tends to alternate-bear. Late.
'KINNOW'	6-11, 13, 14, 17, 18.	Good to excellent.	Vigorous, upright tree. Foliage is dense and willow-like.	Beautiful tree with delicious fruit. A bit seedy and hard to peel. Midseason to late.
'MEDITERRANEAN'	6-11, 13, 14, 17, 18.	Fair.	Moderately vigorous, broad, spreading tree. Few or no thorns. Tree hardy to cold and resistant to unfavorable conditions.	Beautiful tree. Produces best fruit in high heat. Important commercial variety outside the United States. Tends to alternate-bear. Midseason.
'PAGE'	6-11, 13, 14, 17, 18.	Good.	Moderately vigorous, attractive, roundheaded tree. Dense foliage. Few or no thorns.	Possibly the best mandarin for juice lovers. Heavy producer of small but very juicy, flavorful fruit. Needs pollinizer. Midseason.
'PIXIE'	6-11, 13, 14.	Fair to good.	Vigorous growth with an erect, open habit. Dark green foliage.	Late-maturing variety best adapted to coastal and intermediate areas. Tends to alternate-bear.
SATSUMA	6-11, 13, 14.	Poor.	Slow, spreading growth. Open, dark green foliage. Tree resistant to unfavorable conditions and very cold hardy.	Earliest-ripening mandarin. Ripens with low summer heat. Performs poorly in the desert. Very important variety in cold areas. Fruit hold poorly; pick as soon as fruit develop good color.
'WILKING'	6-11, 13, 14, 17, 18.	Good.	Dense, moderately vigorous. Willow-like foliage. Few or no thorns.	One of the most ornamental mandarins. Good cold tolerance. Tends to bear heavily in alternate years. Midseason.
TANGELOS				
'MINNEOLA'	6-11, 13, 14, 17, 18.	Good.	Vigorous, roundheaded tree. Large, deep green, pointed leaves.	Distinctively necked, bright orange-red fruit. Best flavor in hot climates. Attractive tree with very visible fruit. Midseason.
'ORLANDO'	6-11, 13, 17, 18.	Fair.	Moderately vigorous. Distinctively cupped, deep green leaves. Fruit held toward outside of tree.	Slightly hardier and earlier-ripening than 'Minneola'. Best adapted to hot desert areas. Fruit small but juicy. Needs pollinizer. Midseason.
'SAMPSON'	9, 13, 17, 18.	Good.	Tree grows vigorously, resembles grapefruit tree. Glossy, cupped leaves.	Grapefruit-like flavor. Attractive tree with shiny foliage and golden fruit. Needs pollinizer. Midseason to late.
TANGORS				
'DWEET'	6-11, 13.	Poor.	Moderately vigorous, rather open growth habit.	Rich-flavored variety best adapted to coastal and intermediate areas. Reddish orange color. Very juicy. Late.
'TEMPLE'	17, 18.	Fair.	Moderately vigorous, spreading, rather shrubby plant. Many thorns.	Popular in Florida but only reaches its distinctive, rich, spicy flavor in western desert climates. Sensitive to cold. Midseason.
LEMONS				
'EUREKA'	6-11, 13-15, 17, 18.	Good.	Moderately vigorous, somewhat open growth habit. Nearly thornless. Flowers and new growth tinged with purple.	Handsome tree with strong, everbearing tendency. Ever-present flowers, fruit and attractive foliage. Ripens year-round in coastal areas. Produces two crops inland.
'LISBON'	6-11, 13-15, 17, 18.	Good.	Vigorous growth, dense foliage, thorny. Most productive and cold hardy of the true lemons. Flowers and new growth tinged with purple.	Fruit identical to 'Eureka' but tree more tolerant of heat, cold, wind and neglect. Dense, light green foliage and heavy production make it an attractive tree.

CITRUS

NAME	ZONE	ABILITY TO HOLD ON TREE	TREE CHARACTERISTICS	REMARKS
'MEYER'	6-11, 13-15, 17, 18.	Good.	Moderately vigorous and spreading. Almost thornless. nearly everblooming.	Not a true lemon—has sweeter flavor. Tree very hardy and ornamental. Fruit thin-skinned and juicy. The 'Improved Meyer' is a virus-resistant plant. Excellent container or hedge plant.
'PONDEROSA'	6-11, 13-15, 17, 18.	Good.	Vigorous, roundheaded, thorny and productive. Large leaves. Flowers and new growth tinged with purple. Sensitive to frost.	Actually a lemon-citron hybrid. Thick rind around large fruit. Excellent in containers, as a hedge or espalier.

GRAPEFRUIT

NAME	ZONE	ABILITY TO HOLD ON TREE	TREE CHARACTERISTICS	REMARKS
'MARSH SEEDLESS'	6-11, 13, 14, 17, 18.	Excellent.	Vigorous growth. Productive, spreading tree. Glossy, deep green foliage. Fruit visible. Many borne in clusters.	Premier white-fleshed grapefruit because of its excellent flavor and lack of seeds. Fruit will hang on tree for months. Like all grapefruit it needs heat to ripen. Fruit quality increases as it hangs on tree.
'REDBLUSH'	6-11, 13, 14, 17, 18.	Excellent.	Same as 'Marsh' but pink-blushed fruit can add a different ornamental quality.	Standard pigmented variety similar to 'Marsh Seedless', except ample heat is needed to develop pink flesh and rind color.

LIMES

NAME	ZONE	ABILITY TO HOLD ON TREE	TREE CHARACTERISTICS	REMARKS
'BEARSS'	6-11, 13-15, 17.	Fair to good.	Vigorous with dense green foliage, round-headed. Some thorns.	Most valuable lime for western gardeners. Hardier and much more ornamental than 'Mexican'. Fruit picked green or yellow. Fruit juicy and pale yellow at maturity.
'MEXICAN'	Frost-free areas only.	Poor.	Grows at a moderate rate into twiggy tree. Leaves small but dense.	Aromatic bartender's lime normally grown in tropical and semitropical climates. Requires hot summers and frost-free winters.
'RANGPUR'	6-11, 13-15, 17, 18.	Good.	Vigorous and very productive. Slender twigs and comparatively few or small thorns. Leaves dull green. New growth tinged with purple.	Not a true lime. Sometimes grouped with mandarins because of its bright orange color, ease of peeling and hardiness. Good lime substitute with similar flavor. Attractive tree. Everbearing in most areas.

PUMMELOS

NAME	ZONE	ABILITY TO HOLD ON TREE	TREE CHARACTERISTICS	REMARKS
'CHANDLER'	6-11, 13, 14, 17, 18.	Fair.	Vigorous. Open growth habit. Leaves large and broadly winged. Flowers large and woody.	Large, pink-fleshed fruit with excellent flavor. A beautiful, open tree with dark green leaves. Needs considerable heat for best flavor.
'REINKING'	6-11, 13, 14, 17, 18.	Poor.	Vigorous tree with denser foliage than 'Chandler'. Fruit is positioned toward inside of tree.	White-fleshed variety with excellent flavor.

KUMQUATS

NAME	ZONE	ABILITY TO HOLD ON TREE	TREE CHARACTERISTICS	REMARKS
'MEIWA'	6-11, 13-15, 17, 18.	Excellent.	Virtually indistinguishable from 'Nagami'.	Round fruit. Best kumquat for eating fresh. Juicy. Prized ornamental. Highly productive.
'NAGAMI'	6-11, 13-15, 17, 18.	Excellent.	Fine stems, few or no thorns, dense foliage. Small, dark green, pointed leaves.	Oval fruit. Most popular variety. Best used for preserving, candying and marmalade. Highly productive. Excellent ornamental.

KUMQUAT HYBRIDS

NAME	ZONE	ABILITY TO HOLD ON TREE	TREE CHARACTERISTICS	REMARKS
CALAMONDIN	6-11, 13-15, 17, 18.	Excellent.	Very shapely, almost thornless. Finely textured branchlets. Leaves small, broadly oval. Highly productive and very cold hardy.	Spectacular ornamental, bearing hundreds of bright orange fruit larger than kumquats. Juicy but acid in flavor. Can be planted in containers or used as a hedge.
CITRANGEQUAT	6-11, 13-15, 17, 18.	Excellent.	Moderately vigorous, nearly thornless and highly productive. Cold hardy.	Very attractive tree. Hardier than a kumquat. 'Macciaroli' and 'Sinton' are named varieties. Fruit can be used for acid juice or to make marmalade.
LIMEQUAT	6-11, 13-15, 17, 18.	Good.	Angular, open growth habit. Leaves small and round tipped. Highly productive, very cold hardy compared to lime parent.	Mexican lime-kumquat hybrid. Very hardy. Small, yellow, kumquat-size fruit are excellent lime substitutes. 'Eustis', 'Lakeland' and 'Tavares' are recommended varieties.
ORANGEQUAT	6-11, 13-15, 17, 18.	Excellent.	Dense, spreading tree. Dark green foliage. Highly productive.	Larger and sweeter than a kumquat. Eaten the same way. Lower heat requirement. Very cold hardy. Excellent ornamental. 'Nippon' is a named variety.

CITRON

NAME	ZONE	ABILITY TO HOLD ON TREE	TREE CHARACTERISTICS	REMARKS
'ETROG'	6-11, 13-15, 17.	Good.	Scanty foliage. New growth and flower buds tinged with purple. Short life cycle compared to other citrus.	Ceremonial fruit of the Jewish Feast of the Tabernacles. Very cold sensitive. Large fruit with thick rind. Rind can be candied or used fresh in salads. Tree easily espaliered.
FINGERED CITRON	6-11, 13-15, 17.	Good.	Large, round, leathery leaves. Very frost sensitive.	Also called 'Buddha's Hand'. Well-known and highly esteemed for its fragrance in China and Japan. Everblooming shrub. Valued in the Orient as an ornamental.

'Mission' fig

Fig

Large, tropical-looking leaves and a gnarled branching pattern make the fig an attractive addition to the garden. And plants are easy to grow.

Figs are unique in that they provide two crops of fruit a year: the first in early summer, the second midsummer to fall. If a tree is allowed to develop, it attains a tremendous spread—up to 90 feet or more. With large trees, permanent propping of the lower branches is necessary to keep them off the ground.

Figs can be pruned severely and kept small—as low as 5 feet high. When trees are pruned this way, the first crop is often sacrificed. Figs planted in containers are also restricted in growth.

Because of a fig's appearance, some think it is purely subtropical. But most commercial orchards are in the interior valleys of northern California. Figs can be grown wherever temperatures do not drop below 15° F (−10° C), although varieties differ in adaptation. Very young trees may be injured by early or late frosts, but can be easily protected.

VARIETIES

'Brown Turkey'—Sometimes sold as 'Black Spanish' in the Northwest. Widely adapted to Zones 4-18. Medium-size fruit with mahogany-brown skin tinged purple. Few seeds. Rich flavor. Best eaten fresh. Not good for canning or drying. Tree cold hardy.

'Conadria'—Best adapted to warmer climates, Zones 5, 7-13, 16-18. Medium-size, firm fruit with greenish yellow to white skin often blushed purple. Very sweet. Best fig for drying. Tree vigorous.

'Desert King'—Also known as 'King'. Widely adapted to Zones 4-18 but best in cooler climates. Large fruit with dark green skin. Excellent quality. Drops second crop in warm areas.

'Genoa' ('White Genoa')—Best adapted to cooler, coastal areas, Zones 6-8, 10, 11, 14, 15. Medium-size fruit with whitish skin. Good quality and flavor. Excellent for fresh eating.

'Kadota'—Best in hot climates, Zones 5, 7-13, 16-18. Medium to large fruit with yellowish green, tough skin. Flavor rich and sweet. Used for canning commercially. Tree vigorous.

'Mission' ('Black Mission')—Widely adapted to Zones 4-18. Large fruit with purplish black skin. Most

VITAL STATISTICS—FIG

	Standard	Dwarf
Height at maturity (feet)		
Unpruned	40	N/A
Pruned	6-25	
Spread at maturity with		
no competition (feet)	25-60	
Recommended planting		
distance (feet)	20-40	
Years to reach bearing age	2-3	
Life expectancy (years)	100	
Chilling requirement (hours)	100-350	
Pollinizer required	For some types	
Good for espalier	Yes	
Good for containers	Yes	

Comments: Can be pruned to fit small space.

N/A = Not Available

Fig leaf   Young developing fig

dependable back yard fig. Can be eaten fresh, dried or canned. Excellent flavor.

'Osborn Prolific'—Best in cooler areas, Zones 6-8, 10, 11, 14, 15. Medium-size, purplish brown fruit. Strong flavor. Fair quality.

'Texas Everbearing'—Best in the Southwest, Zones 16-18, especially higher elevation areas that have a short growing season. Medium to large fruit with purplish skin. Good quality.

Several more varieties are being tested at the University of California at Riverside. Perhaps superbly flavored figs such as 'Panachee', 'Excell', 'Flanders' and 'Tena' will soon be widely available.

SOIL, NUTRIENT AND WATER REQUIREMENTS

Fig trees do well in a wide range of soils. They will show tip burn and reduction of yield in alkaline or salty soils.

If shoot growth averages less than 6 inches a year, nitrogen should be applied in the winter months at a rate of 1 to 1-1/2 pounds of actual nitrogen per tree per year. If tree begins to shed leaves fairly early in the season, the cause may be lack of nitrogen, insufficient water or both. As with other deciduous trees, figs will produce higher-quality fruit with regular irrigation.

PRUNING

Trees can be pruned in a variety of ways—from no pruning to heavy pruning that results in a dwarf. Figs are readily trained into an informal espalier. The gardener's wishes determine the style.

To prune a standard tree, follow the advice given for the vase-type tree. See page 49. As the tree gets older, pruning should be much less severe than for other deciduous fruit. It may consist of occasional thinning of relatively large branches. Heavy annual thinning or cutting back can be done if desired.

POLLINATION

Only the 'Calimyrna' variety requires cross-pollination, involving a complicated but interesting process known as *caprification*. It includes introduction of blastophaga wasps and a male fig (caprifig) tree. Undoubtedly, this requirement has caused this excellent-tasting fig to be unpopular.

HARVESTING AND STORAGE

For maximum richness and flavor, figs should not be picked until individual fruit wilt at the neck and bend over on the stem from their own weight. If any milky latex develops at the stem end when fruit is picked, it has not reached full ripeness. Figs are excellent for eating fresh and for freezing and drying. They should be soft for maximum flavor and eating quality. For pickling, figs should be picked when firm-ripe. Fresh-frozen figs retain their natural color, flavor and texture remarkably well.

The best way to dry figs is to let them dry partially on the tree and drop naturally to the ground. They can then be gathered and dried further on drying trays. Figs left to mature completely on the tree have a high sugar content and quality that can never be obtained by drying firm-ripe fruit. Pick up figs that have fallen to the ground as soon as possible—within at least one or two days. This avoids insect and disease infestations.

DISEASES AND PESTS

Only a few diseases or insects attack the tree's trunk, branches or foliage. Regular garden care normally prevents problems from occurring. Roots are quite susceptible to at least two kinds of nematodes. Figs, however, are not susceptible to oak root fungus.

Fruit may be infected by a variety of bacterial rots and molds and infested with several insects. Such problems are more severe in cooler climates. Pick fruit immediately after the problem is discovered to lessen damage. See page 34 for more on insects and diseases.

Fig trees are tropical in appearance but are hardy to 15°F (−10°C).

Green olives ready for harvest.

Olive

Many people admire the graceful, billowing appearance of a large olive tree. Its grayish foliage offers a welcome accent to an all-green garden. The attractive, gnarled branching pattern is also quite distinctive.

Olives are easy to care for. They are drought resistant, require little pruning and have few serious pests.

Olives are evergreen and can be grown satisfactorily except where winter temperatures drop below 12° F (−10° C). Green fruit is damaged at about 28° F (0° C). Ripe fruit withstand somewhat lower temperatures. Trees are best adapted to hot, interior valleys of California and desert regions. Olives will grow near the coast, but are not likely to bear fruit regularly.

VARIETIES

'Ascolano'—Fruit are large with relatively small pit. Good oil content for a large olive but less than 'Mission' and 'Manzanillo'. Fruit is tender and must be handled carefully when harvested. Of the four varieties described here, it is best for processing.

'Manzanillo'—Spreading tree with larger fruit than 'Mission'. Fruit ripens earlier, which can help avoid damage from early fall frosts. Average oil content.

'Mission'—Medium-size fruit, blue-black when ripe. Average oil content. Grows much taller than either 'Manzanillo' or 'Sevillano'. More cold resistant than other varieties.

'Sevillano'—Largest fruit but with the least oil. Flesh has a woody texture. Poor choice for processing unless size is the only concern.

POLLINATION

Olives are self-fruitful. Occasionally there are difficulties in securing adequate crops. This is related to climate and to their biennial bearing habits, not to failure of pollination.

SOIL, NUTRIENT AND WATER REQUIREMENTS

Olives will grow in a wide range of soils as long as soil is well drained. Trees are more resistant to mild salinity than any other fruit tree. Trees survive and fruit well even with considerable neglect.

FRUIT THINNING

Olives are usually not thinned. But if crops are exceptionally heavy, fruit will be quite small. For the largest olives possible, you can increase fruit size by thinning. This should be done as soon as possible after fruit set. Thin until remaining fruit average about two or three per foot of twig.

Fruit drop is a problem if olives are grown only for ornamental purposes. Sprays are available to prevent fruit set. 'Swan Hill' is said to be fruitless. Hosing off blossoms with water is one way to reduce fruit set.

HARVESTING AND STORAGE

Harvest time depends on how you plan to process the olives. They can be pickled green, made into green olives, ripe olives or Greek olives. They can also be used to make olive oil.

All olives must be cured before they can be eaten. Consult your local county extension agent for instructions.

VITAL STATISTICS—OLIVE	Standard	Dwarf
Height at maturity (feet)		
Unpruned	50	N/A
Pruned	20	
Spread at maturity with		
no competition (feet)	30	
Recommended planting		
distance (feet)	30	
Years to reach bearing age	4	
Life expectancy (years)	500	
Chilling requirement (hours)	None	
Pollinizer required	No	
Good for espalier	Yes	
Good for containers	Yes	

Comments: Can be pruned to fit any size space.

N/A = Not Available

Genetic dwarf peach 'Bonanza II'.

Peach and Nectarine

Queen of the temperate-zone fruit, the peach is a fitting partner to "King Apple." Peaches are easy to grow and many varieties are attractive, especially in bloom.

Nectarine is simply a smooth-skinned peach. Besides having a smooth skin, it is usually smaller and sweeter and often has a more distinctive aroma. It has other peach characteristics, but its climate adaptation is slightly more limited. See the zone adaptations in the variety chart. Nectarines are less hardy and more susceptible to brown rot and peach leaf curl in humid areas than peaches.

Because peach trees are less hardy, their range is somewhat farther south or lower in elevation than that of the apple. Apple requires about 900 hours of chilling, while the standard peach requires 600 to 900 hours. Some varieties of nectarine are adapted to mild winter climates.

Peaches like clear, hot weather during their growth period. For this reason peaches do best in hot, inland areas. In cooler climates choose early ripening varieties.

Insufficient chilling results in delayed foliation, which can be serious enough to cause injury and eventual death of tree. Low-chill varieties are indicated in the variety chart.

SPACE SAVING

Peaches and nectarines are available in more genetic dwarf forms than any other fruit tree. Genetic dwarf varieties of each are listed separately in the variety charts. More than one variety of standard peach or nectarine can be grafted on the same tree. Or, more than one tree can be planted in one hole. Additional space-saving ideas can be found in the section Growing Fruit in Small Spaces, page 68.

POLLINATION

Nearly all peaches and nectarines are self-fruitful and do not need pollinizers. Exceptions are 'J.H. Hale', 'Indian Free' and 'Indian Blood Cling', which produce sterile pollen and need another peach or nectarine variety nearby.

VITAL STATISTICS—PEACH & NECTARINE

	Standard	Dwarf
Height at maturity (feet)		
Unpruned	25	6
Pruned	15	5-6
Spread at maturity with no competition (feet)	25	4-6
Recommended planting distance (feet)	18-22	5-8
Years to reach bearing age	3	1-2
Life expectancy (years)	20	20
Chilling requirement (hours)	600-900	600-900
Pollinizer required	See chart, pages 112-117	
Good for espalier	Informal	Yes
Good for containers	No	Yes

Comments: Wide selection of genetic dwarfs available, also a few low-chill varieties. Can be pruned to a hedge row.

Low, wide angle of branches makes it easy to spray and harvest this peach tree. It also serves as a seat for weary pruner.

NUTRIENT REQUIREMENTS

Peaches and nectarines respond remarkably well to nitrogen fertilizers. Few soils can support vigorous tree growth for very long without needing additional nitrogen. As with most deciduous fruit trees, 1 to 1-1/2 pounds of actual nitrogen per year is usually recommended.

PRUNING

Peaches and nectarines are usually pruned to a vase shape, described on page 49. Peach trees can be trained to a central leader, but have a tendency to overgrow in the tops. Where sunburn of fruit and bark is a problem, as in the low elevation deserts of California and Arizona, the central leader or modified central leader system is recommended. Central-leader peach trees with nondwarf growth habits can be planted as close as five feet apart. They can be contained with late-summer and dormant-season pruning.

For central leader training, instead of heading a newly planted peach tree, remove all side limbs entirely. Use the highest new shoot to continue the central leader. As the trunk develops, continue to remove all side branches over two years old.

Peaches and nectarines are pruned more heavily than other deciduous fruit trees. They produce fruit on shoots of the past season's growth. It is necessary to replace nearly all fruiting wood each season. Unpruned trees will set tremendous crops of very small fruit the season after pruning is omitted. However, they will make such poor growth that little fruit will be set the following years.

Mature trees should produce 15 to 30 inches growth at the top and around sides of tree each season. If growth is less and is not caused by heavy cropping or insufficient nitrogen, prune more heavily. Too much growth through top and center of tree tends to shade out shoot growth. To remedy, thin out upper branches so the sun can reach the tree's interior.

FRUIT THINNING

Peaches and nectarines tend to set too heavily nearly every year. Fruit need to be hand thinned or they will be small and poor in quality. Growth will also be reduced and the chance of limb breakage will be higher. Thinning increases sugar content and improves flavor.

The time to thin depends on the growth stage of the fruit. After set, fruit enlarge to about 1 to 1-1/4 inches in diameter, then go through a resting period during which there is little or no growth. This period may last a week to a month, depending on the variety. The best time to thin is during this rest period. Fruit should be spaced about 6 to 10 inches apart, depending on amount of fruit set. With heavy sets, fruit should be spaced farther. Fruit of extra-early varieties should be spaced 10 inches or more because they have less time to reach full size between thinning and harvest. Thinning may be repeated later if too many fruit still remain for normal growth.

HARVESTING AND STORAGE

Generally, the best peach or nectarine is tree ripened. Pick fruit when they are firm-ripe, not soft-ripe. Sugar content and flavor are best when fruit are allowed to come almost to maturity on the tree. Soft-ripe fruit are sweeter but they lose some of their aroma and quickly become overripe. A few varieties, especially late-maturing ones, are better if harvested earlier and allowed to ripen indoors at a moderate temperature.

If peaches or nectarines are to be stored, pick them when firm-ripe. Keep in the refrigerator or other cool place.

Harvest clingstone varieties for canning when fruit breaks away from the stem when picked. To can freestone peaches, pick fruit when hard-ripe. Allow to soften a day or two. Fruit will peel much easier after it has softened slightly, and will be more attractive when canned.

DISEASES AND PESTS

Peaches and nectarines are subject to many problems. Diseases most likely to be troublesome are peach-leaf

Spring flowers of a peach tree are highlighted dramatically by evergreens.

curl—the usual problem with garden peaches and nectarines—and mildew, rust and blight.

Insect pests most likely to cause damage are those that attack ripening fruit. This is especially true of codling moth. See section on pests and diseases, page 34.

ABOUT THE CHARTS

• Peaches most often recommended and with the widest adaptation are 'Redhaven', Rio Oso Gem', 'July Elberta', 'Early Elberta', Elberta' and 'Fay Elberta'.

• Many gardeners are fascinated by the word *Elberta*. These are the Elberta varieties: 'Early Elberta', ripening mid-June to early August; 'July Elberta', ripening late June to late July; 'Elberta' and 'Fay Elberta', ripening late July to mid-August. According to connoisseurs, 'Fay Elberta' is *the* peach for flavor and texture.

• Here are some further tips from peach experts. 'Nectar' is the best-flavored, white-fleshed peach. 'Flavortop' is the best nectarine. 'Rio Oso Gem' is a paradox. It is on the list of most recommended and most adaptable peaches. It is also one of the most flavorful peaches. But, as the chart shows, the tree has its weaknesses.

• Some guidelines for choosing varieties by ripening date: Choose 'Springtime' for May, 'Redhaven' for June, 'Golden Jubilee' for July, 'Fay Elberta' for August and 'Fairtime' for September.

• A tip about canning: 'Redhaven', one of the most widely recommended varieties, is a good canner. So are 'Elberta', 'July Elberta', 'Early Elberta', 'Fay Elberta' and 'Veteran'.

• To plant four compatible peach varieties in one hole try 'Gold Dust', 'Redhaven', 'Nectar' and 'Fay Elberta'. Harvest dates begin in early June and end in late August. Studying the chart will reveal other compatible varieties.

• Don't forget the genetic dwarf peaches and nectarines. See genetic dwarf variety charts following the standard variety charts.

PEACHES
Average picking dates at Davis, California

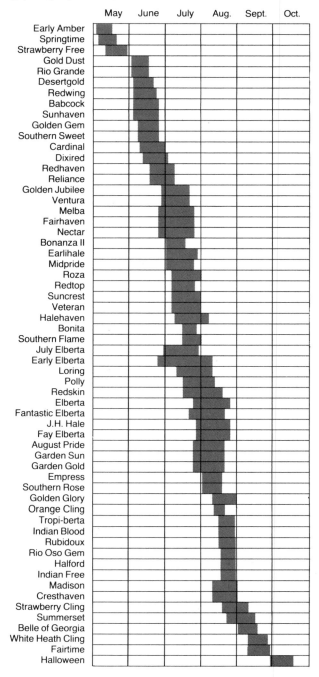

NECTARINES
Average picking dates at Davis, California.

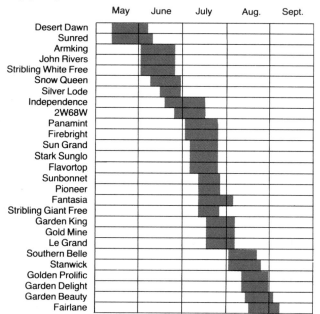

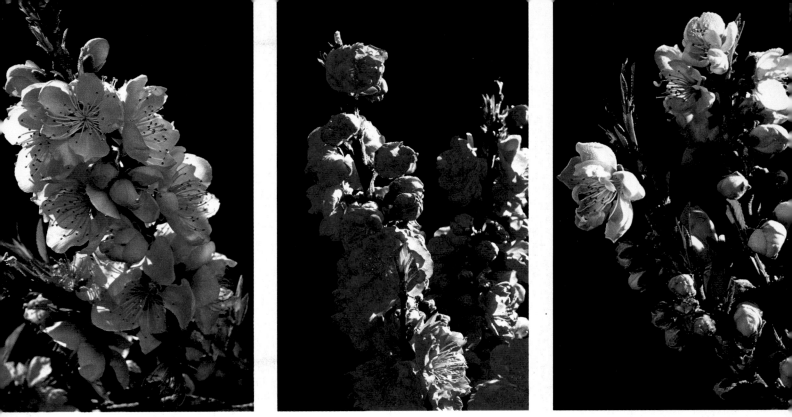

Compact habit of genetic dwarf peaches and nectarines results in spectacular spring bloom. Above, from left to right, are 'Honey Babe' peach, 'Garden Beauty' nectarine and 'Garden Delight' nectarine.

PEACHES

VARIETY	ORIGIN	ZONE	HARVEST SEASON	FRUIT AND TREE	REMARKS
'AUGUST PRIDE'	California.	7-11, 13-15, 17.	Midseason.	Large, round fruit. Skin is yellow with red blush. Yellow, freestone flesh has good texture and flavor. Tree is vigorous, upright and an early bloomer.	Low chilling requirement. One of the best low-chill varieties.
'BABCOCK'	California.	8, 10-15.	Early.	Small to medium fruit. Skin has high blush, little fuzz. White, semifreestone flesh is tender, juicy and sweet with some tang. Tree is spreading and vigorous.	Requires little winter chill. Needs much thinning.
'BELLE OF GEORGIA'	Georgia.	2, 7, 9-12, 16, 18, 19.	Late.	Large fruit. Red over creamy white skin. White flesh is freestone, firm. Tree is vigorous, hardy, frost tolerant and productive.	Very susceptible to brown rot. Fruit is excellent fresh; fair if frozen.
'BONITA'	California.	6, 8, 10-15.	Midseason.	Medium to large fruit. Skin is light yellow with a deep red blush. Yellow flesh is freestone with some fiber. Attractive, firm, fine flavor. Tree is vigorous, upright. Produces well.	Lower chilling requirement than 'Babcock'. Good near the coast.
'CARDINAL'	Georgia.	3-5, 7-11.	Early midseason.	Medium fruit. Bright red over yellow skin, colors long before mature. Average fuzz. Flesh is yellow, freestone, with firm, melting texture. Tree moderately vigorous and productive.	Will set fruit in cool, rainy, spring weather. One of the best early varieties.
'COMPACT REDHAVEN'	Michigan.	2, 3, 5, 7, 8, 10, 11, 18.	Early midseason.	Fruit is same as 'Redhaven'. Tree has semidwarf growth habit.	Bud mutation of 'Redhaven'.
'CRESTHAVEN'	Michigan.	2, 4, 5, 7-11, 16, 19.	Late.	Fruit is medium to large, nearly round. Skin is golden overlaid with red. Firm, yellow, clear, freestone flesh is juicy and resists browning. Holds well on tree. Self-fertile tree of above-average hardiness.	Fruit cans well. Freezes exceptionally well.
'DESERTGOLD'	California.	8-11, 13-15, 17, 18.	Early midseason.	Fruit is medium, round. Skin is yellow with red blush. Yellow, semiclingstone flesh is good quality. Tree is fairly vigorous and productive. Blooms very early.	Low chilling requirement. Excellent for warmer regions.
'DIXIRED'	Georgia.	2, 4, 5, 7, 9, 11.	Early midseason.	Medium fruit. Attractive red skin with light fuzz. Colors two weeks before mature. Yellow, semifreestone flesh is firm with moderately good flavor. Tree is vigorous, highly productive. Resists frost, tolerant of leaf curl.	Fruit mature over a long period.

PEACHES

VARIETY	ORIGIN	ZONE	HARVEST SEASON	FRUIT AND TREE	REMARKS
'EARLIHALE'	Maryland.	2, 5, 7-11.	Midseason.	Medium to large fruit. Skin is dark red over most of surface. Firm, yellow freestone flesh has good flavor. Tree requires a pollinizer. Hardy to low winter temperatures.	Susceptible to bacterial blight.
'EARLY AMBER'	Florida.	12-15.	Early.	Medium fruit. Skin is yellow with dark red blush. Flesh is orange-yellow, freestone, medium-firm. Tree is a good producer, vigorous.	Low chilling requirement. Fruit is mediocre quality.
'EARLY ELBERTA' ('GLEASON')	Utah.	2, 4, 5, 7-11, 16, 17, 19.	Midseason.	Fruit resembles 'Elberta'. Yellow skin has a slight, red blush. Yellow flesh is freestone. Quality is better than 'Elberta'. Tree is relatively cold hardy. Less subject to fruit drop.	Thin well. Use for canning or freezing. Needs less heat in summer and less chill in winter than 'Elberta'.
'ELBERTA'	Georgia.	2, 4, 5, 7, 9, 11, 16, 19.	Midseason.	Large fruit. Skin is deep golden blushed red. Yellow, freestone flesh has slight bitterness around pit. Tree is spreading with large, pink flowers.	Resistant to brown rot. Needs good winter chill and summer heat for full flavor. Old variety that is still popular.
'FAIRHAVEN'	Michigan.	1-5, 7-11, 19.	Midseason.	Medium fruit. Bright yellow skin with bright red cheek and red dots. Yellow, freestone flesh is firm, juicy, with fine texture and very good flavor. Resists browning. Tree is vigorous and hardy, with strong scaffold limbs. Bears annually, sets heavily. Buds relatively hardy.	Use for freezing or canning.
'FAIRTIME'	California.	12-15, 19.	Late.	Large fruit. Skin is blushed red. Yellow, freestone flesh is firm but has smooth, melting texture and good flavor. Tree is vigorous, crops heavily. Needs heavy pruning to control vigor. Flowers are large.	Low chilling requirement. Best used fresh.
'FANTASTIC ELBERTA'	California.	2, 4, 5, 7, 9, 11-13, 19.	Midseason.	Fruit resembles 'Elberta', though more colorful. Tree has showy flowers.	Same variety as 'Fay Elberta' except it has showy flowers.
'FAY ELBERTA'	California.	2, 4, 5, 7, 9, 11-13, 16, 19.	Midseason to late.	Fruit resembles 'Elberta' but more colorful. Yellow, freestone flesh. Tree has showy flowers.	Most popular freestone peach for all uses. Thin heavily for large fruit. Good for freezing.
'FLAVORCREST'	California.	2, 4, 5, 7-12, 18, 19.	Midseason.	Fruit is large and round. Skin is red blushed over yellow. Firm, yellow flesh has excellent flavor and smooth texture. Tree is moderately vigorous. Flowers are large.	Excellent for eating fresh.
'GOLD DUST'	California.	4, 5, 7-13, 16.	Early.	Small to medium fruit. Skin is mottled and streaked red. Yellow, freestone flesh is excellent quality. Large, upright tree is vigorous, productive, hardy.	Adapted to southern California. Low chilling requirement.
'GOLDEN JUBILEE'	California.	2, 4.	Midseason.	Fruit is medium to large, oblong and flattened. Skin is mottled bright red. Yellow, freestone flesh is coarse and soft with melting texture, good quality. Tree sets heavily but thins itself. Flowers are small, not very showy.	Average quality for canning and freezing. Fruit drops early from tree.
'HALEHAVEN'	Michigan.	1, 2, 4, 5, 7-11, 16, 19.	Midseason.	Medium to large fruit. Skin is 25 to 50 percent red over greenish red, changing to yellow only at maturity. Yellow, freestone flesh is juicy and flavorful. Very sweet skin. Tree is vigorous and productive. Medium, nonshowy flowers.	Fruit and leaf buds are winter hardy. Excellent home garden variety.
'HALFORD'	California.	1, 2, 5, 7-11, 16, 18, 19.	Late.	Fruit is large with yellow skin. Yellow, clingstone flesh has nonmelting texture. Tree is a heavy producer.	The major cling variety for commercial canning.
'HALLOWEEN'	California.	2, 4, 5, 7-11, 19.	Late.	Large fruit. Skin is yellow with a red blush. Firm, yellow, freestone flesh. Tree is medium size, productive.	Valued as a very late-maturing peach. 'Halloween' I and II are very similar.
'INDIAN BLOOD CLING'	California.	1, 2, 4, 5, 7-11, 16, 19.	Late.	Medium fruit. Skin is red. Yellow, clingstone flesh is streaked red with firm texture—good for preserves. Tree requires a pollinizer.	An old variety with low chilling requirement. Good for home gardens.
'INDIAN FREE'	California.	5-12, 16, 19.	Late.	Fruit is large, with red skin. Yellow, freestone flesh is deep red near the pit. Tart until ripe. Tree requires a pollinizer—any peach except 'J.H. Hale'. Resistant to leaf curl.	Fine home garden variety.
'J.H. HALE'	Connecticut.	2, 5, 7-11, 16, 19.	Midseason to late.	Very large fruit. Skin is yellow blushed with red, little fuzz. Yellow, freestone flesh is not stringy. A fine keeper with good flavor and aroma. Juicy. Tree not very vigorous. Needs a pollinizer—any peach except 'Indian Blood Cling'.	Prized for its large, high-quality fruit. Matures too late for colder regions.

PEACHES

VARIETY	ORIGIN	ZONE	HARVEST SEASON	FRUIT AND TREE	REMARKS
'JULY ELBERTA' ('KIM ELBERTA')	California.	2, 4, 5, 7-13, 16, 19.	Midseason.	Fruit is medium and round. Skin has regular, dull red streaks over greenish yellow. Yellow, freestone flesh is firm and fine grained. Very good flavor. Small pit. Tree is a prolific bearer. May need extra thinning. Medium-size, non-showy flowers.	Developed by Luther Burbank. Good fresh or canned.
'LORING'	Missouri.	2, 4, 5, 7-11.	Midseason.	Fruit is large, round and fairly attractive. Red blushed skin. Yellow, freestone flesh is firm and melting, with medium texture. Moderately juicy with excellent flavor. Tree is vigorous, bears well when spring weather is unpredictable. Flowers are showy.	Tolerant to adverse spring weather. Main disadvantage is fruit that does not color well. Soft when canned or frozen.
'MADISON'	Virginia.	1, 2, 5, 7-11, 19.	Late.	Medium fruit. Skin is bright red over orange. Flesh is orange-yellow and bright red near pit. Freestone, very firm, fine textured with rich flavor. Nonstringy, nonbrowning flesh. Tree is a heavy producer.	Use fresh, frozen or canned. Adapted to areas with frequent spring frosts.
'MELBA'	Texas.	2, 16, 19.	Midseason.	Large fruit. Pale yellow skin. White, freestone flesh is sweet, juicy, with honey flavor. Tree sets fruit well in cold, unsettled spring weather.	Long ripening season.
'MIDPRIDE'	California.	7-15, 17.	Midseason.	Medium to large fruit. Skin is yellow with red blush. Firm, yellow, freestone flesh has distinctive "orange" flavor. Tree is early blooming and very vigorous.	Low chilling requirement. Good for canning.
'NECTAR'	California.	5, 7-11, 16, 19.	Midseason.	Medium-large fruit. Skin is blushed pink to red. White, freestone flesh is sweet, juicy and aromatic. Excellent flavor. Tree is vigorous, with heavy foliage. Susceptible to brown rot. Nonshowy flowers.	Originated as a seedling of 'Stanwick' nectarine. A fine, white peach. Too soft for shipping.
'ORANGE CLING'	California.	1, 2, 5, 7-11, 16, 18, 19.	Midseason to late.	Large fruit. Skin is blushed red. Deep yellow, clingstone flesh has firm texture. Tree is vigorous and productive.	Favorite for home canning. Ripens late.
'POLLY'	Iowa.	1, 2, 19.	Midseason.	Medium fruit. Skin is white with a red blush. White, freestone flesh is juicy, aromatic and high quality. Tree is very cold hardy.	Home orchard variety for cold areas.
'REDHAVEN'	Michigan.	2, 3, 7, 8, 10, 11, 19.	Early to midseason.	Medium fruit. Skin is brilliant red over yellow. Flesh is yellow, semifreestone. Juicy, sweet and fine grained. Vigorous and spreading tree. Medium size, nonshowy flowers have red petals.	Adapted to cold climates. Often requires heavy thinning. Superior quality for fresh use; very good canned.
'REDSKIN'	Maryland.	1, 2, 4, 5, 9, 16, 18, 19.	Midseason.	Medium fruit. Yellow skin has abundant, deep red blush. Firm, slightly fibrous flesh is yellow, freestone. Nonbrowning. Excellent quality. Tree is spreading, vigorous, very productive. Early-blooming large flowers have showy pink petals.	Fruit keep well. Tree resistant to bacterial spot. Use fresh, canned or frozen.
'REDTOP'	California.	2, 4, 5, 7-13, 19.	Midseason.	Large fruit. Skin is almost completely blushed red over yellow. Flesh is yellow, freestone, firm and fine grained. High quality. Tree has showy petals. Moderately susceptible to bacterial spot. Productive and moderately vigorous.	Low chilling requirement. Good fresh, canned or frozen.
'REDWING'	California.	12-15.	Early.	Medium fruit. Skin is 75 to 100 percent red over greenish yellow. Colors long before mature. White, freestone flesh is firm and very juicy. Sweet, lightly perfumed flavor with no acid. Tree is medium to large, vigorous and productive. Small flowers have deep pink petals.	Low chilling requirement. Resembles 'Babcock' but requires slightly more chilling.
'RELIANCE'	New Hampshire.	1, 19.	Early to midseason.	Medium fruit. Skin is dark red over yellow. Flesh is firm, yellow, freestone. Flavor is good. Tree is very hardy. Productive and self-fertile. Showy bloom.	Adapted to home gardens in cold climates.
'RIO GRANDE'	Florida.	8-13, 19.	Early.	Medium to large fruit. Skin has red blush over yellow. Freestone flesh is yellow and firm, with medium-fine texture. Juicy, delicate flavor. Tree is medium, productive. Flowers are showy.	Low chilling requirement.
'RIO OSO GEM'	California.	2, 5, 7-11, 19.	Midseason to late.	Large fruit. Skin is bright red. Firm, yellow, freestone flesh is fine textured. Tree is small and not vigorous. Often used as a pollinizer for 'J.H. Hale'. Self-fruitful. Flowers are showy.	One of the best peaches for freezing. Superior quality for eating fresh.

PEACHES

VARIETY	ORIGIN	ZONE	HARVEST SEASON	FRUIT AND TREE	REMARKS
'ROZA'	Washington.	2, 4.	Midseason.	Fruit is large and round. Skin has medium red blush. Very firm, yellow flesh is slightly coarse. Excellent flavor. Tree is vigorous and productive. Small blossoms are susceptible to bacterial spot.	Use fresh or canned.
'RUBIDOUX'	California.	12, 13.	Midseason to late.	Large fruit. Skin is blushed dull red over yellow-red stripes. Firm, yellow, freestone flesh is moderately juicy, with only fair flavor. Tree is vigorous and prolific. Moderately spreading. Slow to defoliate.	Fruit keep well. Low chilling requirement. Good in upper elevations of southern California.
'SPRINGTIME'	California.	9-14, 17, 18.	Early.	Fruit is small to medium with a distinct point. Skin is highly blushed, with abundance of short fuzz. Colors bright red at maturity. White, semifreestone flesh. Characteristic fresh white peach flavor — soft and watery. Tree has pink flowers that are medium to small and nonshowy.	Low chilling requirement. Good for southern regions.
'STRAWBERRY CLING'	California.	5, 7-13.	Late.	Large fruit. Skin is creamy white, mottled red. Clingstone flesh is white, juicy, richly flavored. Tree is vigorous and spreading.	Good for canning. Low chilling requirement. Flesh has strawberry marbling.
'STRAWBERRY FREE'	California.	5, 7-13.	Early.	Medium fruit. Skin is light with pink blush. Firm, white, freestone flesh. Tree is vigorous and spreading.	Low chilling requirement. Excellent flavor.
'SUMMERSET'	California.	5, 7-13.	Late.	Large, round fruit. Attractive red blush over yellow skin. Firm, yellow, freestone flesh is high quality. Tree is vigorous and productive. Flower petals are large.	One of the best late-maturing peaches. Fair for eating fresh. Best for canning or freezing.
'SUNCREST'	California.	2, 4, 5, 7-11, 19.	Midseason.	Fruit is large and round. Skin is bright red over yellow. Yellow, firm, melting flavor is freestone with good texture. Tree is vigorous and productive. Flowers are large.	Good flavor for fresh use or canning.
'SUNHAVEN'	Michigan.	2, 4, 5, 19.	Early to midseason.	Medium fruit. Skin is bright red over gold. Yellow, juicy, fine-grained flesh is semiclingstone. Rich, sweet flavor. Tree is large, vigorous and productive. Flowers are nonshowy.	Medium chilling requirement.
'TROPI-BERTA'	California.	7-15.	Midseason to late.	Fruit is large, with red-blushed skin. Flesh is firm, yellow, freestone. Juicy and good flavored. Tree is vigorous with large, pink flowers.	Adapted to warm coastal and mild-winter areas. Very low chilling requirement.
'VENTURA'	California.	12-15.	Midseason.	Fruit is small and oblong. Skin is attractive yellow with wine-red blush. Firm, yellow, freestone flesh is slightly acid. Fair quality. Tree is vigorous and upright. Bears well.	Very low chilling requirement.
'VETERAN'	Canada.	1-4.	Midseason.	Medium fruit. Skin is yellow with slight red blush. Flesh is yellow, freestone, firm and juicy. Fairly coarse grain but easy to peel. Tree is vigorous and highly productive.	Grown in western Washington and Oregon. Slightly soft when canned. Low acid. Sets fruit in adverse conditions.
'WHITE HEATH CLING'	Maryland.	5, 7-11, 16, 19.	Late.	Medium to large fruit. Creamy white skin is blushed red. White, juicy, clingstone flesh has distinctive flavor. Tree is hardy and healthy. Vigorous, somewhat unproductive. Faded pink flowers have white centers.	Satisfactory for coastal California. Low chilling requirement. A favorite for home canning.

GENETIC DWARF PEACHES

VARIETY	ORIGIN	ZONE	HARVEST SEASON	FRUIT AND TREE	REMARKS
'BONANZA II'	California.	2, 5-18.	Midseason.	Large fruit. Skin is orange with red blush. Flesh is firm with melting texture. Compact tree grows 5 to 6 feet high.	Highly aromatic. Better flavor than 'Bonanza'. Large, pink flowers.
'EMPRESS'	California.	2, 5-18.	Late.	Large fruit. Highly colored pink to red skin. Flesh is delicious, with juicy, sweet flavor. Mature tree grows 4 to 5 feet high.	Highly colored fruit actually seems to glow.
'GARDEN GOLD'	California.	2, 5-18.	Late.	Large fruit, up to 3 inches in diameter. Skin is yellow with slight red blush. Flesh is yellow with red near pit. Mature tree grows 5 to 6 feet high.	Bears fruit heavily.

GENETIC DWARF PEACHES

VARIETY	ORIGIN	ZONE	HARVEST SEASON	FRUIT AND TREE	REMARKS
'GOLDEN GEM'	California.	2, 5-18.	Early.	Large fruit with yellow skin. Flesh is yellow resembling 'Rio Oso Gem', with red pit cavity. Very firm, good texture and excellent flavor. Tree low and compact. Grows 5 to 6 feet high.	Beautiful, pink flowers and low, spreading habit make this a versatile landscape plant.
'GOLDEN GLORY'	California.	2, 5-18.	Late.	Very large fruit. Skin is golden with red blush. Flesh is yellow with good, juicy flavor. Mature tree grows 5 feet high.	Recommended for cold climates.
'HONEY BABE'	California.	2, 5-18.	Early.	Large fruit to 3 inches in diameter. Skin is deep red over yellow. Firm orange flesh is flecked red with excellent flavor. Tree is productive and densely foliated.	Best flavored genetic dwarf peach. Attractive habit. Beautiful spring bloom.
'SOUTHERN FLAME'	California.	2, 5-18.	Midseason.	Large fruit. Skin is yellow blushed with red. Yellow flesh is firm, crisp and melting. Pleasing aroma. Mature tree grows 5 feet high.	High-quality fruit for eating fresh.
'SOUTHERN ROSE'	California.	2, 5-18.	Late.	Large fruit. Skin is yellow blushed with red. Firm, yellow flesh is good eating quality. Mature tree grows 5 feet high.	Compares favorably with commercial peaches. Blooms early. Requires little chilling.
'SOUTHERN SWEET'	California.	2, 5-18.	Early.	Medium fruit with nicely colored yellow and red skin. Yellow flesh has good flavor. Mature tree grows 5 feet high.	Bears fruit heavily.

NECTARINES

VARIETY	ORIGIN	ZONE	HARVEST SEASON	FRUIT AND TREE	REMARKS
'ARMKING'	California.	8-15, 17.	Early.	Large fruit. Olive-green skin with attractive reddish cast. Flesh is yellow, semifreestone, with pronounced aroma. Tree is medium size with good vigor.	Flowers are not very showy.
'DESERT DAWN'	California.	8-15, 17.	Early.	Fruit small to medium. Skin is red. Semifreestone flesh is yellow, firm, juicy, sweet and aromatic. Medium size tree.	Low chilling requirement. Requires heavy thinning.
'FAIRLANE'	Fresno, California.	5, 7-9.	Late.	Large fruit. Skin is red over yellow. Flesh is yellow, clingstone. Tree is vigorous and productive.	Flowers are large and showy.
'FANTASIA'	California.	2, 5, 7-13.	Midseason.	Fruit large and oval. Surface is one-third to two-thirds bright red over yellow. Yellow, freestone flesh is firm and smooth. Vigorous and productive tree.	Short chilling requirement. Good, slightly tart flavor. Showy flowers.
'FIREBRIGHT'	Fresno, California.	2, 5, 7-12.	Midseason.	Large fruit. Skin is red over yellow. Yellow flesh is semifreestone, firm with smooth texture and excellent flavor. Tree is vigorous and productive.	Medium chilling requirement. Flowers are large.
'FLAVORTOP'	California.	2, 5, 7-13.	Midseason.	Large fruit. Skin is red with yellow speckles. Flesh is golden yellow streaked with red. Freestone, firm, juicy with excellent flavor. Vigorous and productive tree.	Showy flowers.
'GOLD MINE'	New Zealand.	5, 7-13.	Late.	Large fruit. Skin is red blushed over white. White, freestone flesh has good flavor. Tree is vigorous and productive.	Low chilling requirement.
'INDEPENDENCE'	California.	5, 7-13.	Midseason.	Fruit medium to large. Cherry-red skin. Yellow, freestone flesh is firm, never softens. Good flavor. Moderately vigorous and productive tree.	Showy flowers. Tolerates warm winters.
'JOHN RIVERS'	England.	5, 7-11.	Early.	Fruit medium to large. Skin is white with crimson on cheek. Greenish white flesh is semifreestone, tender and juicy. Medium size tree, vigorous.	The earliest variety with typical nectarine flavor. Showy blossoms. Severely affected by insufficient winter chilling.
'LE GRAND'	California.	5, 7-11.	Late.	Fruit very large. Bright red and yellow skin. Yellow, clingstone flesh has rubbery texture. Delicate, semiacid flavor. Large, spreading and productive tree has showy flowers.	Fruit holds well on tree.

NECTARINES

VARIETY	ORIGIN	ZONE	HARVEST SEASON	FRUIT AND TREE	REMARKS
'PANAMINT'	California.	5, 7-15.	Midseason.	Fruit medium to large. Skin is bright red. Freestone flesh is yellow. Tree is vigorous and productive.	Low chilling requirement.
'PIONEER'	California.	5, 7-14.	Midseason.	Fruit small to medium. Thin, yellow skin is overlaid with red. Yellow, freestone flesh is touched with red. Tree has large, pink flowers.	Requires little winter chill. Good eating quality. Rich, distinctive flavor.
'SILVER LODE'	California.	5, 7-13.	Early to midseason.	Fruit medium. Skin is 75 percent red over creamy yellow with numerous red dots. White freestone flesh is juicy, fine grained with little fiber and good, sweet flavor. Tree is vigorous.	Fruit ripens over a long period. Low chilling requirement. Low cold hardiness.
'SNOW QUEEN'	California.	5, 7-11.	Early.	Fruit very large. Fair-skinned peach lightly blushed with russet. White, freestone flesh is melting, juicy with fine texture. Medium tree.	Flowers are small.
'STANWICK'	Unknown.	5, 7-11.	Late.	Fruit medium. Skin is greenish white shaded purple-red. Flesh is white, semifreestone, juicy with fair flavor. Tree has large flowers.	Use fruit for freezing, canning or drying. Tree tends to drop fruit before fully ripe. An old variety.
'STARK SUNGLO'	Le Grand, California.	2, 5, 7-13.	Midseason.	Large fruit. Yellow skin is partially overspread with red. Yellow, freestone flesh shades to red near pit. Firm, melting, slightly acid. Dwarf tree 8 to 10 feet high.	Ripens mid-July.
'STRIBLING GIANT FREE'	California.	5, 9.	Midseason.	Large fruit. Highly colored skin is yellow blushed with red. Yellow, freestone flesh is high quality. Medium, spreading tree.	Flowers large and pink.
'STRIBLING WHITE FREE'	California.	5, 7-11.	Early.	Large fruit. White skin is blushed with red. White, freestone flesh is sweet and juicy with creamy texture. Tree is vigorous and productive.	A good home orchard tree.
'SUN GRAND'	California.	2, 5, 7-13.	Midseason.	Large fruit. Skin is yellow with red blush. Yellow, freestone flesh is firm. Tree is large, spreading and productive.	Flowers are large.
'SUNRED'	Florida.	12-14.	Early.	Fruit small to medium. Skin is bright red. Flesh is yellow and semifreestone. Firm good flavor. Medium size tree.	Low chilling requirement.
'2W68W'	California.	2, 5, 7-13, 18.	Early to midseason.	Large fruit. Skin is red over yellow. Firm, freestone flesh has outstanding flavor. Medium size tree.	Tree and buds have great cold tolerance, estimated to be better than 'Redhaven' peach. See peaches chart, page 114.

GENETIC DWARF NECTARINES

VARIETY	ORIGIN	ZONE	HARVEST SEASON	FRUIT AND TREE	REMARKS
'GARDEN BEAUTY'	California.	2, 5-18.	Late.	Large clingstone fruit grows to 3 inches in diameter. Skin is yellow with bright, red blush. Tree grows 5 to 6 feet high.	Low chilling requirement. Showy pink blossoms.
'GARDEN DELIGHT'	California.	2, 5-18.	Late.	Large fruit grows to 3 inches in diameter. Skin is yellow with bright red blush. Tree grows 5 to 6 feet high.	Low chilling requirement. Unusually dense foliage.
'GARDEN KING'	California.	2, 5-18.	Midseason.	Large clingstone fruit grows to 3 inches in diameter. Skin is light yellow with bright red blush. Tree grows to 6 feet high.	Low chilling requirement. Unusually dense foliage.
'GOLDEN PROLIFIC'	California.	2, 5-18.	Late.	Large fruit with yellow skin. Flesh is yellow mottled orange. Flavor is rich and sweet. Tree grows to 6 feet high.	High chilling requirement. Recommended for cold areas. Produces heavily. One of the tastiest nectarines.
'NECTARINA'	California.	2, 5-18.	Midseason.	Medium fruit with red skin. Flesh is golden with zesty flavor. Attractive, ruffled pink flowers. Tree grows to 6 feet high.	Original, true dwarf nectarine. Medium chilling requirement.
'SOUTHERN BELLE'	California.	2, 5-18.	Midseason to late.	Large fruit. Skin is yellow with red blush. Freestone flesh is yellow. Tree grows to 5 feet high.	Very productive. Blooms early. Low chilling requirement.
'SUNBONNET'	California.	2, 5-18.	Midseason.	Medium fruit. Skin is yellow overspread with red. Clingstone flesh is yellow with red specks. Flesh is firm, crisp, slightly acid to mild. Tree grows to 5 feet high.	Very productive. Blooms early. Low chilling requirement.

'Clapp Favorite' pear

Pear

There are three classes of pear. *European pears* are the common winter pears but also include the popular summer pear 'Bartlett'. The new *Asian pears*, introduced to the United States by the University of California, are described on page 122. *Hybrid pears* are crosses between European and Asiatic varieties. They generally have a lower chilling requirement than European varieties, as witnessed by their popularity in the Gulf coast regions of the southern United States. Hybrid pears are more similar to European pears than Asian pears.

If you consider all three pear types, there is a variety adapted to almost every climate in the West. Exceptions are very cold high elevation areas. In low elevation desert areas there are reports of success with 'Bartlett' pears planted in low spots where cold air settles. Fruit have thick skins and are only fair in quality.

'Comice', a European type, is a western favorite. It is grown commercially in a wide range of climates from western Washington to the central valleys of California. It has an unusually low chilling requirement and is at home in the mildest areas of southern California. Most varieties of European pear have chilling requirements of at least 600 hours, which excludes them from most areas of southern California.

In addition to tasty fruit, pears bring beauty to the garden. Shiny green, leathery leaves and bright, white spring flowers are very attractive. Pears extend the fruit season. Most pears come into full flavor in fall and winter, after summer fruit are gone.

SIZE CONTROL

The limitations of dwarf pears on quince rootstocks are discussed in Growing Fruit in Small Spaces, page 68. Pears can be trained in many of the same ways as apples. Try them as an espalier, hedge or garden divider trained on wires. They are perfectly suited to containers.

POLLINATION

Pollination requirements for pears differ, depending on where they are grown. In most cases you will get a better crop with another variety nearby, although some are self-fruitful in California. 'Bartlett' and 'Seckel' are a poor combination for cross-pollination.

VITAL STATISTICS—PEAR

	Standard	Dwarf
Height at maturity (feet)		
Unpruned	40	25
Pruned	15	12-15
Spread at maturity with no competition (feet)	25	15
Recommended planting distance (feet)	18-25	12-15
Years to reach bearing age	4-8	3-5
Life expectancy (years)	75	60
Chilling requirement (hours)	600-900	600-900
Pollinizer required	Yes	Yes
Good for espalier	Yes	Yes
Good for containers	No	Yes

Comments: Some low-chill varieties are available. Can be pruned to size. Also consider the many excellent forms of Asian pears, which have similar statistics.

'Comice' pear: free-standing and espaliered on a wire.

If you live in the Pacific Northwest, always provide for cross-pollination. Any variety will serve as a cross-pollinizer if it blooms at the same time as the variety to be pollinized. Specific pollination requirements can be found in the variety charts.

SOIL AND WATER REQUIREMENTS

Pears respond to a regular watering program like most deciduous fruit trees. They are generally more tolerant of heavy, wet soil, common to the Northwest.

PRUNING

Pear trees can be trained to a central or multiple leader as described on page 50. Multiple-leader training is preferred. It spreads the risk of fireblight among three or four leaders, and makes it easier to set a ladder in the tree. Head or cut the leaders annually to stiffen them and to ensure branching. Don't head secondaries.

Young-bearing 'Bartlett' and 'Bosc' trees are especially prone to limb breakage. To prevent branches from splitting due to heavy crops, tie up the main scaffold limbs with a strap or rope. After the limbs set fruit, thin ends of all secondary branches to an upright shoot or bud. The fruit will then be borne on heavier wood rather than on fragile branch ends.

When thinning shoots, leave enough to provide ample fruiting wood. Head shoots only if they grow over 18 inches long. With 'Anjou' and 'Comice', do not head shoots until they have set flower buds. Head to a flower bud just before bloom—this will stimulate fruit set. Pinching the shoot tips in early summer before "June drop" will increase final crop of some slow-to-bear young trees.

FRUIT THINNING

Pear fruit seldom require thinning except when the crop is heavy. Even then thinning is not often done. If a very heavy crop sets, remove small and blemished fruit a few weeks before picking.

HARVESTING AND STORAGE

With the exception of Asian varieties, pears are best when ripened off the tree. Fruit left on the tree will not develop peak flavor or texture. Pick fruit when it is green and hard, but at the mature size for the particular variety. Allow fruit to ripen in a cool place. Summer varieties, which are not stored, should be placed where temperatures will not exceed 75° F (25° C). Lower temperatures will prolong shelf life. Fruit stored at temperatures below 40° F (5° C)—down to as low as 32° F (0° C)—can be kept for several weeks, then brought out to ripen at room temperature.

Winter varieties usually need about six weeks of cold storage before ripening to highest quality. This is particularly true for 'Comice' and 'Anjou'. 'Winter Nelis' and 'Seckel' will ripen if stored in a cool place such as a basement or cellar.

To harvest pears, lift up fruit until the stem separates from the spur; do not pull or twist. If the stem does not break easily from the spur, allow fruit to ripen for a few more days.

DISEASES AND PESTS

Scab and fireblight are the most destructive diseases of pears. Common pears are more susceptible to fireblight than Asian pears. Check for varietal resistance in the charts.

Insects attacking pears include codling moth, mites and pear slug. See pages 38 and 39.

ABOUT THE CHARTS

● The pear varieties most often recommended and with widest adaptation are 'Bartlett', 'Comice', 'Bosc' and 'Anjou'.

● Choose 'Bosc' or 'Winter Nellis' for baking, 'Bartlett' for canning and 'Seckel' for preserves.

● If you want a pear to espalier, any variety can be kept to 8 or 9 feet by pruning. There are no completely proven dwarfing rootstocks. See page 70.

● If you plant Asian pears, you may want to combine an early variety such as 'Yali' with a later one such as 'Shinseiki'.

● In a booklet on Asian pears, the University of California says demand for these crisp, juicy pears has increased in recent years. Increased commercial plantings should result in further gains in popularity.

PEARS
Average picking dates at Davis, California.

E = European, A = Asian, H = Hybrid

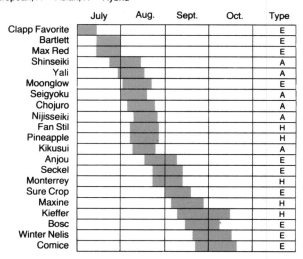

	July	Aug.	Sept.	Oct.	Type
Clapp Favorite					E
Bartlett					E
Max Red					E
Shinseiki					A
Yali					A
Moonglow					E
Seigyoku					A
Chojuro					A
Nijisseiki					A
Fan Stil					H
Pineapple					H
Kikusui					A
Anjou					E
Seckel					E
Monterrey					H
Sure Crop					E
Maxine					H
Kieffer					H
Bosc					E
Winter Nelis					E
Comice					E

'Comice'   'Starkrimson'   'Bosc'   'Rogue River'   'Anjou'

A selection of pear varieties shows the many differences available in size, shape and color.

EUROPEAN PEARS

VARIETY	ORIGIN	ZONE	HARVEST SEASON	FRUIT AND TREE	REMARKS
'ANJOU'	Belgium.	2, 4-8, 10, 11, 16, 19.	Midseason.	Fruit is large. Light green at harvest, cream to green after ripening. Flesh is fine textured, mild, juicy. Vigorous, upright tree is slow to begin bearing.	Use for eating fresh. Ripens after a month's storage under refrigeration. Slightly less prone to blight in Northwest. Susceptible to cork spot in hot summer areas. 'Red Anjou' is a red-skinned variation.
'BARTLETT'	England.	1-11, 16, 18, 19.	Early.	Medium-large fruit is green at picking, yellow when ripened to maturity. White flesh is sweet and tender. Vigorous tree.	Standard summer pear of supermarkets. Use for eating and canning. Tree is subject to fireblight. Thrives in summer heat if there is adequate winter cold. Quality is poor if summer is too cold. Ripens without cold storage. May need a pollinizer in Zones 3 and 6.
'BOSC'	Belgium.	2-8, 10, 11, 16.	Late.	Fruit is large, green to dark yellow with russeting. Narrow shape with a long neck distinguishes it from other pear varieties. White flesh is tender, juicy and sweet. Large, vigorous tree has upright growth habit.	Use for canning; excellent when eaten fresh. Ripens well at room temperature. Very susceptible to fireblight.
'CLAPP FAVORITE'	Mass.	1-8, 10, 11, 16.	Early.	Large, lemon-yellow fruit with red blush. Soft, sweet, breaks down at core if picked too late. Resembles 'Bartlett'. Attractive tree is hardy, very productive. Bears annually.	Softens very quickly after picking. Tree is very susceptible to fireblight.
'COMICE'	France.	2-8, 10-16, 19.	Late.	Fruit is large, greenish yellow when mature, yellow with russet dots when ripe. Flesh is buttery, sweet, tender, juicy and aromatic. Large, vigorous tree is extremely slow to bear fruit.	Considered the best winter pear. Moderately susceptible to fireblight. Unusually low chilling requirement. Requires cold storage to ripen.
'MAX RED BARTLETT'	Washington.	1-8, 10, 11, 16, 18, 19.	Early.	Fruit is medium, striped brownish red, changing to bright red when picked. A budsport of 'Bartlett'. Tree is similar to 'Bartlett'. Growth is weak. Limbs frequently revert to producing green fruit.	Tree is susceptible to fireblight. Red coloring on branches and leaves of tree. May need a pollinizer in Zones 3 and 6.
'MOONGLOW'	Maryland.	2, 4-8, 10, 11.	Midseason.	Large fruit is shaped similar to 'Bartlett'. Soft, juicy flesh is low-acid with little grit. Vigorous, upright tree bears when young. A heavy cropper.	Tasty eaten fresh or canned. Stores well. Tree resistant to fireblight.
'SECKEL'	New York.	2-11, 19.	Midseason.	Fruit is small, reddish brown over yellow-brown with russet. Flesh is creamy white and sweet—tops in flavor. Semidwarf tree is productive. Extensive thinning is required to achieve medium-size fruit.	Surpasses all other varieties in dessert qualities. Great for eating fresh or in preserves. Tree is somewhat fireblight resistant. Not compatible with 'Bartlett' for cross-pollination.
'SURE CROP'	Arkansas.	2-8, 10, 11, 16, 19.	Late.	Fruit is large, yellow, resembling 'Bartlett' in looks and flavor. Prolonged blooming period, good for areas with late frost. Bears annually. Tree is vigorous and upright.	More resistant to fireblight than any other variety.
'WINTER NELIS'	Belgium.	2, 4-11.	Late.	Medium fruit is yellow-green to green with russet. Flesh has fine texture but is gritty toward center. Moderately juicy. Vigorous and heavy-cropping tree.	Use for baking. Stores well. Susceptible to fireblight. Adapted to hot summer areas if provided with winter cold. Tends to alternate-bear. Requires another variety nearby for cross-pollination.

'Red Anjou'   'Bartlett'   'Seckel'   'Reimer Red'   'Chojuro'   'Shinseiki'

HYBRID PEARS

VARIETY	ORIGIN	ZONE	HARVEST SEASON	FRUIT AND TREE	REMARKS
'FAN STIL'	Texas.	2-16, 19.	Midseason.	Medium fruit, yellow, with a red blush. Flesh is white, crisp and juicy. Tree grows upright and vigorous.	Low chilling requirement. Resists fireblight and damage from extreme temperatures.
'KIEFFER'	Pennsylvania.	2-16, 19.	Late.	Medium to large fruit is yellow with a red blush. White, crisp, coarse flesh is juicy but gritty. Tree is vigorous, upright, good for mild winter areas.	Poor to fair flavor for eating or any fresh use. Use for cooking and canning. Stores well. Tree highly resistant to damage from extreme hot or cold temperatures. Low chilling requirement.
'MAXINE' ('STARKING DELICIOUS')	Ohio.	2-16, 19.	Late.	Large, yellow fruit. Flesh has average firmness and moderate grit, with sharp flavor and above-average quality for hybrid pears.	Suitable for eating fresh and rated high as a canned product. Appears to be more tolerant of fireblight than 'Kieffer'.
'MONTERREY'	Mexico.	2-16, 19.	Midseason.	Large, yellow fruit is shaped like an apple. Flesh is soft, smooth with very little grit. Vigorous tree, good for mild winter areas.	Good eaten fresh or canned. Stores well. Tree very resistant to fireblight.
'ORIENT'	Chico, California.	2-16, 19.	Late.	Large, yellow skin is russeted. Flesh is white, smooth and sweet. Tree is a heavy cropper, strong and very easy to train. Bears fruit in approximately 4 years.	Relatively low chilling requirement. This tree has the highest fireblight resistance of any hybrid pear. Tree produces regularly. Requires another variety for cross-pollination.
'PINEAPPLE'	Texas.	2-16, 19.	Midseason.	Large, heavily russeted fruit. Tree is vigorous and productive.	Flesh has the taste of pineapple.

'Bartlett' pear shown in three stages of ripeness: green at left, medium ripe at center and ready to eat at right.

'Chojuro' Asian pear

ASIAN PEARS

Asian pears are rapidly becoming popular. Also known as Oriental pear, Chinese pear, salad pear and apple pear, Asian pears are delicious and distinctively flavored. Trees are exceptionally ornamental with bright, white, spring flowers, leathery green leaves and beautiful fall color. They can easily be espaliered or trained to fence or hedgerow.

Asian pears basically comprise two species: *Pyrus ussuriensis* and *Pyrus pyrifolia*. They differ from *Pyrus communis*, the common pear, in that they remain firm and are especially crisp and juicy when ripe. This fact has probably led to the misleading name apple pear. Asian pears have a totally different texture and flavor than apples. The difference can be appreciated only when the fruit is tasted.

Asian pears should be allowed to ripen on the tree.

Other than these differences, Asian pears are almost identical to common pears in culture and climate adaptation. They need to be pruned a little more severely, but training and pruning methods generally follow the same guidelines.

Asian pears are self-fertile, but the close presence of another variety will greatly increase yield. Suitable pollinizers for each variety are included in the variety chart.

Ripe fruit can be stored for 10 to 14 days at room temperature and much longer under refrigeration.

ASIAN PEARS

VARIETY	ZONE	POLLINIZER	FRUIT AND TREE	REMARKS
'CHOJURO'	2-12, 16, 19.	'Kikusui' 'Shinseiki' 'Nijisseiki' 'Bartlett'	Fruit oblong and lopsided. Skin is greenish brown, russetted, thick, medium tough, smooth. Flesh is white, mildly sweet, somewhat bland. Core is sour, firm, somewhat coarse, pulpy and aromatic. Tree is medium size, vigorous, spreading, slightly drooping, dense.	Fruit quality is good to excellent. Midseason harvest time.
'KIKUSUI'	2-12, 16, 19.	'Chojuro' 'Seigyoku' 'Nijisseiki' 'Shinseiki' 'Bartlett'	Fruit medium to large, oblong and lopsided. Skin is yellowish green, slightly bitter, relatively tough, thick and smooth with conspicuous raised dots. Flesh is sweet, mild with a trace of tartness, firm, tender, juicy. Tree is of medium size and vigor, spreading, slightly drooping and dense.	Fruit quality is good to very good. Midseason.
'NIJISSEIKI' ('APPLE PEAR', '20th CENTURY')	2-12, 16, 19.	'Bartlett' 'Chojuro' 'Shinseiki'	Fruit round to oblong, often lopsided. Skin is greenish yellow mottled with green, thin, tender and smooth. Flesh is white, sweet to slightly tart, mild, firm, tender, juicy, somewhat coarse, pulpy and slightly aromatic. Tree is medium size, fairly vigorous, medium upright with spreading growth, dense.	Fruit quality is good to excellent. Midseason.
'SEIGYOKU'	2-12 16, 19.	'Chojuro' 'Kikusui' 'Nijisseiki' 'Bartlett'	Fruit large, round to oblong. Skin is light greenish yellow, tough and thick, smooth, free of russet, dots inconspicuous. Flesh is white, sweet, mild, slightly tart, firm, tender, juicy, somewhat coarse and pulpy. Tree is small to medium size. Medium vigor, open, spreading, somewhat drooping.	Fruit quality is good to very good. Midseason.
'SHINSEIKI'	2-12, 16, 19.	'Chojuro' 'Kikusui' 'Nijisseiki' 'Bartlett' 'Seigyoku'	Fruit round to oblong, uniform in shape. Skin is yellow, medium tough, thick and smooth, dots small, numerous, conspicuous. Flesh is white, sweet, mild, tender, crisp, juicy, faintly aromatic, pulpy and coarse. Tree is of medium size and vigor, spreading, medium dense.	Fruit quality is excellent. Early.
'YALI'	2-12, 16, 19.	'Nijisseiki' 'Chojuro' 'Shinseiki'	Fruit medium to large, pear shaped, light yellowish green and smooth. Flesh is white, mildly sweet, aromatic, crisp, juicy, coarse. Tree is large, upright, somewhat spreading, dense and productive.	Low chilling requirement. Fruit quality good to excellent. Midseason.

'Fuyu' persimmon

Persimmon

Two species of persimmon can be grown in the West. Oriental persimmon, *Diospyros kaki,* also called Japanese or kaki persimmon, is the most popular and widely grown. Trees bear heavy crops of delicious fruit. Oriental persimmon is extremely attractive in late fall when fruit hang on trees after leaves have fallen. Striking, dark green leaves turn stunning shades of yellow, orange or red in fall even in the mildest climates. Oriental persimmon is very attractive grown as shade trees, in containers or espaliered.

VITAL STATISTICS—PERSIMMON

	Standard	Dwarf
Height at maturity (feet)		
Unpruned	40	N/A
Pruned	10-30	
Spread at maturity with		
no competition (feet)	30	
Recommended planting		
distance (feet)	25	
Years to reach bearing age	5	
Life expectancy (years)	50-75	
Chilling requirement (hours)	100-400	
Pollinizer required	No	
Good for espalier	Yes	
Good for containers	Yes	

N/A = Not Available

Oriental persimmon is adapted to Zone 5, and Zones 7 to 14. It can also be grown in inland areas of Zone 6 and possibly warmer sites of Zones 3 and 4. Trees are hardy to 0° F (−18° C). It can be grown in desert climates but rarely fruits.

Native to parts of the eastern United States, American persimmon, *Diospyros virginiana,* is equally attractive and similar in appearance to Oriental persimmon. It does have two important differences. American persimmon is hardier and can be grown in Zones 2 to 14. It also bears much smaller fruit—from 1-1/2 to 2 inches in diameter. Fruit of Oriental persimmon are usually at least twice as large.

There are two types of persimmon fruit: *astringent* and *nonastringent.* Astringent fruit, which include all American persimmon, are acid tasting and make your mouth pucker unless fruit is soft-ripe. Many people make the mistake of picking and eating these fruit before they are fully ripe and are quite disappointed. However, if you wait until astringent fruit are ripe and very soft, you will be rewarded by a rich flavor.

Fruit of nonastringent varieties may be eaten when they are firm-ripe, much like apples.

Persimmon begin to ripen in late September and October. A frost will hasten the loss of acidity in astringent varieties.

VARIETIES

'**Hachiya**' is the most popular variety. It is the persimmon most commonly available in markets. Fruit are astringent until soft. Skin and flesh become yellow to orange when ripe. Fruit are large and oblong to cone shaped with a pointed tip. This is one of the largest-fruited persimmon grown. Fruit are 4 or more inches long and 2-1/2 to 3 inches across.

'**Fuyu**' is the most popular nonastringent variety. The reddish yellow flesh is sweet and mild. 'Fuyu' is not as large as 'Hachiya' and is about the size of a flattened tennis ball.

'**Chocolate**' grows into a large tree sometimes over 40 feet high. It produces dark-fleshed fruit that must be fully soft-ripe before eating.

'**Tamopan**' produces a large, turban-shaped fruit that can weigh up to a pound. It must be fully soft-ripe before eating. Because of thick skin, fruit of 'Tamopan' can be eaten with a spoon from its half shell. Flesh is light orange, very juicy but a little stringy. Flavor is excellent.

'**Tanenashi**' grows as a small, somewhat weeping tree with large, orange-red, tapered fruit. Flesh is astringent until soft and characteristically mealy or pasty when ripe. Fruit often develop an open core that collects dust, dirt and mold.

'Nishrazh' 'Tamopan' 'Tishihtzu'

'Fen Nio' 'Fugi' 'Hachiya' 'Hyakume'

'Tsuru' 'Jiru' 'Niv Nai' 'Chienting'

'Honanred' 'Yeddo' 'Moru' 'Fuyu'

Persimmon come in a myriad of shapes and sizes. Many of the varieties pictured above were obtained from the experimental station, University of California, Davis, and may be available to home gardeners at a future date.

SOIL, NUTRIENT AND WATER REQUIREMENTS

Persimmon succeed under widely varying soil conditions, but are not tolerant of poorly drained soils. Some persimmon have a rather long taproot, thus a deeper hole may be necessary for planting persimmon than for other deciduous trees.

Persimmon respond to an application of nitrogen if the soil is deficient. Best time to apply nitrogen is at dormant or nonfruiting times, such as late winter or early spring. However, excess nitrogen will cause young fruit to drop. Apparently persimmon do not respond to or need fertilizers other than those containing nitrogen. They are not troubled by excesses or deficiencies of other elements.

Persimmon are less susceptible to drought than other deciduous fruit trees. Vegetative growth and fruit production will be better with adequate and regular irrigation.

Persimmon are remarkably free from diseases and pests. They are among the best fruit for the gardener who has little time to spray.

Persimmon do not require a pollinizer to set fruit.

PRUNING

Persimmon need relatively little pruning except to keep them manageable and to remove dead wood. Fruit are borne on current season's growth and usually form on outer part of tree. Fruit thinning is not necessary. However, if crop is heavy it can break brittle branches. Prune young trees to create strong scaffold limbs and wide crotches. Supports for branches may be necessary in very heavy fruiting seasons. Persimmon can be pruned for container growing. They also make good espaliers.

HARVESTING AND STORAGE

Fruit stay attached strongly to tree. To harvest, cut fruit stem with shears. The tough, green *calyx*, the collar or crown, adheres to the fruit. Don't try to remove fruit without taking the calyx and short fruit stem with it.

Soft, astringent varieties are picked when firm-ripe. They may be left to become soft-ripe on the tree—if birds don't bother them. Firm, nonastringent varieties are picked when they turn characteristic golden yellow.

'Hachiya' fruit may be kept a month or more in the refrigerator. 'Fuyu' fruit may be kept for several months. At lower temperatures, the flesh will become pasty and tasteless. Fruit can also be dried.

The attractive winter color of 'Hachiya' persimmon.

Fruit of 'Hachiya' persimmon.

Persimmon **125**

'Satsuma' Japanese plum

Plum and Prune

Plums are a diverse group, available in a range of colors, sizes, tastes and forms. Many varieties are pleasant to eat fresh and have just enough tartness to make splendid jelly. Trees are well suited to gardens because they are comparatively small and bear consistent, quality crops.

European plums are blue or common plums. They usually mature during late summer or fall. Japanese or Oriental plums are the red, early-blooming types and include many popular commercial varieties. Native American plums, which are found along the Pacific Coast and in the eastern United States, are generally small and tart. Damson plums are small, usually blue and are most often used to make jellies and jams.

Prunes are a type of European plum with an extra-high sugar content. This permits them to be dried in the sun without fermenting at the pit. Varieties that are commonly dried are 'French Prune', 'Sugar',

'Brooks' and 'Italian'. 'Brooks' and 'Italian' are favored varieties for the Northwest. They can also be eaten fresh if you like very sweet fruit.

The wide choice of plum types makes it possible to grow some variety in almost every location in the West. However, each type does have limitations.

European plums and prunes are late blooming, enabling them to escape spring frosts. Most varieties have a moderately high chilling requirement and are quite hardy.

Damson plums are similar to European plums in climate requirements.

Climate requirements of Japanese plums are similar to those of apricots, except best quality is obtained in areas that have hot summer days. Like apricots, they bloom early so are particularly subject to spring frost damage. Also, they often fail to set satisfactorily in cold, damp, spring weather. Fruit are not the best quality under these conditions. They are as winter hardy as apricots or peaches. Their winter chilling requirement is similar to peaches. Some varieties such as 'Methley' and 'Mariposa' are known to do well in mild-winter climates.

There are many native American species of plum. Some are native to the Southwest, some to the Pacific Coast mountains and others to areas in central Canada. Varieties have been selected and propagated from wild forms of many of these species. They are available in areas where native forms are known to be adapted. Local nurserymen are often familiar with such plums.

The term *cherry plum* is often used to describe small native or wild plums. It also refers to a group of recently developed *interspecific hybrids*. These are hybrids developed between two different species of fruiting

VITAL STATISTICS—EUROPEAN PLUM		
	Standard	Dwarf
Height at maturity (feet)		
Unpruned	30	N/A
Pruned	15	
Spread at maturity with		
no competition (feet)	25	
Recommended planting		
distance (feet)	20-22	
Years to reach bearing age	4-5	
Life expectancy (years)	40	
Chilling requirement (hours)	700-1,000	
Pollinizer required	See chart, page 133	
Good for espalier	Yes	
Good for containers	Yes	

Comments: Some low-chill varieties are available.

N/A = Not Available

This prune orchard in spring is pleasant to the eye and nose.

'Sprite' cherry plum   'Burbank' Japanese plum   'Queen Ann' Japanese plum

plants. Cherry-plum hybrids are actually more widely adapted than either cherries or plums. Varieties include 'Sprite' and 'Delight'. Both are low chilling and bloom later than Japanese plums. They are described in the variety charts.

Plumcots, interspecific hybrids between plums and apricots, resemble apricots in fruit form. 'Plum Parfait' is a hybrid of Japanese plum and apricot. Fruit is similar to an apricot with red-blushed skin over dark yellow. Flesh is dark yellow marbled with red near the pit. Tree resembles a plum tree in form and is very ornamental.

POLLINATION

Many plums need cross-pollination from specific varieties to set adequate crops. Such requirements are included in the variety charts. Suitable pollinizers for Japanese and hybrid plums can be found in the pollination chart on page 129.

VITAL STATISTICS—JAPANESE PLUM

	Standard	Dwarf
Height at maturity (feet)		
Unpruned	30	N/A
Pruned	15	
Spread at maturity with no competition (feet)	25	
Recommended planting distance (feet)	18-22	
Years to reach bearing age	3	
Life expectancy (years)	40	
Chilling requirement (hours)	500-900	
Pollinizer required	See chart, page 132	
Good for espalier	Yes	
Good for containers	Yes	

Comments: Weeping types and low-chill varieties are available.

N/A = Not Available

PRUNING

When cared for properly, Japanese plums achieve tremendous shoot growth. For this reason they are pruned rather severely at all ages. Trees should be trained in a vase shape. This is readily accomplished because of the vigorous growth and free-branching habit of most varieties. Some tend to branch upright and should be cut to outside branches. Others tend to spread and should be cut to inside branches. After the initial training period of two to three years it is not necessary to cut back branches.

Japanese plums bear on long-lived spurs that are formed abundantly on all branches. They also bear a sizeable portion of their crop laterally on one-year-old shoots. This production can be sacrificed in the interest of shaping the young tree and regulating growth of the old tree. Shoots and water sprouts of vigorous trees require a great deal of thinning. This is the main pruning method on older trees. Large volume of growth makes it easy to replenish fruiting wood and develop new fruiting wood any place on the tree.

European plums branch less freely than Japanese varieties. There is often little choice for developing the framework of the tree. Some varieties branch freely only after one season's growth. Shoots do not branch during the season they are produced. But enough side buds develop the second year to ensure good growth.

Older European plums need little pruning because most fruit is borne on long-lived spurs. In the early life of the tree, spurs are quite long. They appear as short shoots approximately 4 to 6 inches long, covering the branches. Such growth should not be thinned out. To prune, just cut back annual shoot growth.

Damson plums should be pruned in the same way as European plums.

Native plum trees vary in size from small trees or shrubs to large forms. In general, their training and development are the same as for Japanese plums.

'Nubiana'

'Wickson'

'Kelsey'

'Late Santa Rosa'

'Elephant Heart'

A rainbow of colors in 5 plum varieties.

FRUIT THINNING

Many plums, especially Japanese varieties, tend to overbear. Pruning can seldom regulate a crop so that no thinning is needed.

Hand thinning of Japanese plums is done as soon as fruit is large enough to be seen and picked easily. The fruit should be spaced 4 to 6 inches apart and clusters should be broken up.

European plums are often not thinned unless fruit set is heavy. Damson plums are not thinned. Native plums are thinned only if the crop is very heavy.

HARVESTING AND STORAGE

For best quality, plums should remain on the tree until firm-ripe. Except for a few, early-maturing Japanese varieties, this stage is often very difficult to determine.

POLLINIZERS FOR JAPANESE AND HYBRID PLUMS

Variety to be Pollinated	'BEAUTY'	'BURBANK'	'BURGUNDY'	'CASSELMAN'	'DELIGHT'	'DUARTE'	'ELDORADO'	'ELEPHANT HEART'	'FRIAR'	'HOWARD MIRACLE'	'KELSEY'	'LARODA'	'LATE SANTA ROSA'	'MARIPOSA'	'METHLEY'	'NUBIANA'	'OZARK PREMIER'	'PIPESTONE'	'PLUM PARFAIT'	'QUEEN ANN'	'REDHEART'	'REDROY'	'SANTA ROSA'	'SIMKA'	'SATSUMA'	'SHIRO'	'SPRITE'	'STARK GIANT PLUM CHERRY'	'STARKING DELICIOUS'	'SUPERIOR'	'WEEPING SANTA ROSA'	'WICKSON'
'BEAUTY'	P						X				X											X	P									X
'BURBANK'	X	O																					X									
'BURGUNDY'			X																													
'CASSELMAN'				P																												
'DELIGHT'	X				O		X					X										X										X
'DUARTE'						O																						X				
'ELDORADO'	X						O				X	P	P						P	P												X
'ELEPHANT HEART'	P							O			X	P									X		X									X
'FRIAR'			X						O		X									X	X	X	X									
'HOWARD MIRACLE'										X																						
'KELSEY'	P						P				O																					X
'LARODA'	X								X			O				X				X			X									P
'LATE SANTA ROSA'	X							X					P	P									P									X
'MARIPOSA'	P											P	X	O		P			P	P												X
'METHLEY'		X													X											X						
'NUBIANA'	P						X	P			X	P				O						X	P									P
'OZARK PREMIER'												X	X				O							X								
'PIPESTONE'																		O												X		
'PLUM PARFAIT'																			X													
'QUEEN ANN'							X				X	X								O		X	X									P
'REDHEART'							X					X									O		X									
'REDROY'	X						X			P	X	P		X						X		P	P									P
'SANTA ROSA'															X							X	P									
'SIMKA'																								X								
'SATSUMA'	X																						X		O							
'SHIRO'	X			X								X										X	X			O						X
'SPRITE'						X																					O					
'STARK GIANT CHERRY PLUM'																						X						O	X			
'STARKING DELICIOUS'													X									X							O			
'SUPERIOR'																	X													O		
'WEEPING SANTA ROSA'																															O	X
'WICKSON'	P																						X									P

LEGEND:
X = Good fruit set most years—can be used to pollinate variety.
P = Fair fruit set most years—partially self-fruitful, but not recommended for solid planting.
O = Variety is self-fruitful—should not be used to pollinate variety.

Possibly the best guide to ripening is to watch for softening fruit. As soon as they appear, most fruit on the tree will be ready to harvest. Early-maturing varieties should be picked two or three times per season, taking the ripest at each harvest. Late-maturing varieties can be picked all at one time, or at two pickings spaced about a week or ten days apart.

Late-maturing varieties that hang well on the tree can be picked over a long period. Pick them for table use whenever the flavor is acceptable. Continue picking until harvesting is necessary to avoid losing fruit on the ground.

European plums are best picked just as they start to soften. Allow them to ripen at a moderate temperature in the house.

Prunes either fall naturally from the tree or are knocked off when they reach the proper stage for drying. If you knock them off, wait until a few fall naturally, then clear off all fruit at one time. Fruit that are to be eaten fresh should be harvested by hand.

Early-maturing varieties of all plums can be stored for up to a few weeks without noticeable deterioration of quality. They should be harvested a little less ripe than those that are to be used immediately. Late-maturing varieties can be stored for one to three months, depending on variety. Some European varieties will remain edible for several months if stored in a cool, dry place.

Damson plums are used mainly for jellies. For this purpose, they can be picked after developing full color.

DISEASES AND PESTS

Plums are subject to a variety of diseases and pests. Few are troublesome except in cool, humid regions. Among the most serious are leaf spot and brown rot of blossoms and foliage.

European plums—including prunes—are quite prone to mite attacks, especially if the trees are not well cared for.

ABOUT THE CHARTS

● Commonly recommended plum varieties for western gardens include: 'Santa Rosa', 'President', 'Satsuma', 'Italian' and 'Green Gage'. All are widely adapted to this climate. Check zone recommendations in the charts.

● Plum varieties are numerous, and have been introduced for different qualities. Some are important because of their time of ripening. Others are good shippers. Some are useful for making jams and jellies.

● In the Northwest, if you are looking for four hardy European plums to plant in one hole for an extended harvest season or because of limited space, try 'Italian', 'Brooks', 'Stanley' and 'French'. If you are in California, substitute 'Sugar' for 'Brooks'. If you are looking for four Japanese plums for the same purpose, try 'Santa Rosa', 'Elephant Heart', 'Casselman' and 'Red Heart'.

● If you live in California and want three varieties that will pollinize each other, try 'Queen Ann', 'Laroda' and 'Santa Rosa'.

● 'Satsuma' plum and 'Italian' prune are recommended for jams and jellies.

● Good varieties for canning are 'Italian', 'Brooks' and 'Stanley'.

● The chilling requirement for Japanese plums is 500 to 900 hours. European plums require 700 to 1,000 hours. Variations of these chilling requirements are noted in the charts. If you live in a mild climate, look for low-chilling varieties.

PLUMS

Approximate dates of maturity at Davis, California

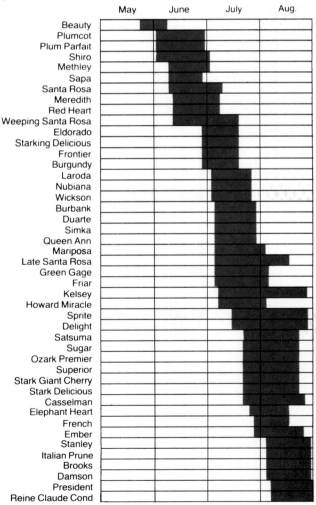

JAPANESE AND HYBRID PLUMS

VARIETY	ORIGIN	ZONE	POLLINIZER	HARVEST SEASON	FRUIT AND TREE	REMARKS
'BEAUTY'	California.	5, 7-18.	Yes.	Early.	Medium to large, heart-shaped fruit. Greenish yellow to bright red skin.	Good flavor fresh or cooked. Adapted variety for Arizona. Partially self-fruitful.
'BURBANK'	California.	2-5, 7-16.	Yes.	Midseason.	Large, bright red fruit is mottled yellow. Deep yellow flesh. Tree is low growing, flat topped, drooping. Tends to bear biennially, often overbears.	Fine flavor. Use for canning and fresh. Does well in cold-winter areas.
'BURGUNDY'	California.	5-14.	None needed.	Early to midseason.	Small, cherry-red fruit. Flesh is deep red. Tree is upright, heavy producer, requires thinning.	Use fresh and canned. Keeps well on tree. Good for mild-winter areas.
'CASSELMAN'	Exeter, California, 1959.	2, 5, 7-14.	Yes.	Late.	Large, cone-shaped fruit. Light, red-blushed skin with yellow specks. Yellow flesh. Upright tree.	A sport of 'Late Santa Rosa'. Ripens very slowly. Partially self-fruitful.
'DELIGHT'	Modesto, California, F. Zaiger.	2, 5-15.	Yes.	Midseason.	Small, round fruit. Almost black skin with thick, blue-gray bloom. Amber, clingstone flesh. Flavor is between plum and cherry—mild, tangy, tart at skin.	Cherry plum. Low chilling requirement. Fruit holds well on tree without loss of quality. Hybrid of Japanese plum and 'Mahaleb' cherry.
'DUARTE'	Japan.	2-5, 7-12, 16, 18, 19.	Yes.	Midseason.	Medium-large, dull red fruit with silver markings. Flesh is deep red.	Good flavor, tart when cooked. Keeps well. High chilling requirement. Cold hardy.
'ELDORADO'	California.	5-14, 16.	Yes.	Early.	Large, oblong, dark red fruit with amber, clingstone flesh. Tree is very upright.	Fruit is somewhat dry, good for canning. Slow ripening. Stores well.
'ELEPHANT HEART'	Santa Rosa, California, L. Burbank.	2, 5-14, 16.	Yes.	Late.	Large, heart-shaped fruit. Dark reddish purple skin. Purple-red, free-stone flesh is sweet and juicy.	Very good fresh, frozen or canned.
'EMBER'	Minnesota.	1, 2, 16, 19.	Yes.	Late.	Medium to large fruit is bright red. Yellow flesh is juicy and sweet. Tree is low, spreading, hardy but only moderately productive.	Sand cherry hybrid. Use for eating and cooking. Adapted to cold climates.
'FRIAR'	Fresno, California, 1968.	5-14.	Yes.	Midseason.	Large, oblong, black fruit with free-stone, amber flesh. Tree is vigorous, upright, productive.	Fruit is high quality, resists cracking. Softens slowly after harvest.
'HOWARD MIRACLE'	Montebello, California, 1947.	5-14, 16, 18, 19.	Yes.	Midseason to late.	Medium-large fruit. Skin is yellow with red blush at maturity. Flesh is yellow, firm and juicy. Rather tart pineapple flavor. Tree is very vigorous.	Low chilling requirement.
'KELSEY'	Japan.	5-11, 13, 14, 16.	None needed.	Midseason to late.	Large, heart-shaped fruit. Skin greenish yellow with red blush. Flesh is yellow, firm, juicy, good quality. Small pit. Medium-size, upright tree is willowy with narrow leaves and gray branches. Moderately vigorous.	Fruit ripens slowly, becoming very sweet when left on tree.
'LARODA'	Winters, California, C. Hesse, 1954.	5-11, 13, 14, 16.	Yes.	Midseason.	Large, cone-shaped fruit with deep reddish purple skin. Amber flesh is light red near skin. Flesh is firm, sweet, aromatic. Tree is vigorous and upright with many spurs.	Fruit is best when used fresh.
'LATE SANTA ROSA'	California.	5-14.	Yes.	Late.	Large, cone-shaped fruit. Deep purple skin. Flesh is yellow, red near skin. Upright tree.	Bud mutation of 'Santa Rosa'. Fruit may split badly, otherwise, resembles parent. Flesh never completely softens. Partially self-fruitful.
'MARIPOSA'	Pasadena, California, J. Thompson, 1935.	5-14, 16.	Yes.	Midseason.	Large, heart-shaped fruit. Skin is mottled greenish yellow to red. Flesh is blood-red, tender, juicy, sweet, slightly acid. Freestone. Tree is medium-large, vigorous and upright.	Low chilling requirement. Fruit holds on tree two to three weeks after ripening.
'MEREDITH'	Texas.	6-14.	None needed.	Early.	Medium-size fruit. Skin is green with a red cheek. Yellow, crisp, juicy flesh is very sweet. Medium-size, broad, hardy tree is vigorous and productive.	Low chilling requirement. Fruit holds well on tree two to three weeks after ripening.
'METHLEY'	South Africa.	2, 4-14, 16.	None needed.	Early.	Small to medium, round, reddish purple fruit. Flesh is red, soft, juicy and delicious. Tree is vigorous, upright, productive.	Low chilling requirement. Good pollinizer.

JAPANESE AND HYBRID PLUMS

VARIETY	ORIGIN	ZONE	POLLINIZER	HARVEST SEASON	FRUIT AND TREE	REMARKS
'NUBIANA'	Winters, California, C. Hesse, 1954.	2-14, 16, 18, 19.	None needed.	Midseason.	Large fruit, very oblong or flattened. Skin is deep reddish blue. Amber flesh is moderately sweet. Medium upright tree is vigorous and very productive.	Fruit turns red when cooked. Fine flavor when eaten fresh. Fruit ripens very slowly.
'OZARK PREMIER'	Mt. Grove, Missouri, P. Shepard, 1946.	1, 4-14, 16, 18, 19.	Yes.	Midseason to late.	Very large fruit, round to slightly heart shaped. Bright red skin. Yellow, clingstone flesh is firm, fine grained, juicy and tart. Hardy, vigorous, productive tree.	Good fresh, canned or use in jellies and sauces.
'PIPESTONE'	Minnesota.	1, 13, 14.	Yes.	Early.	Large, deep red fruit with yellow flesh. Tree is hardy and vigorous.	Flesh is high quality though somewhat stringy. Use for eating fresh and for cooking. Adapted to cold-winter areas.
'QUEEN ANN'	Winters, California, C. Hesse, 1954.	2, 4-11, 13, 14, 16.	Yes.	Midseason.	Large, heart-shaped fruit. Dark purple skin. Flesh is light amber, sweet, firm and juicy. Tree is medium size, upright, weak.	Very high-quality fruit. Stores well. Tip of pit often breaks off. Fruit ripens slowly.
'REDHEART'	California.	2, 4-14, 16.	Yes.	Early.	Medium-large fruit is slightly oval to heart shaped. Skin is dull green covered by medium dark red with heavy, gray bloom. Bright red flesh is sweet, firm, melting, fine grained and aromatic. Upright tree is spreading, vigorous and productive.	Excellent when eaten fresh, canned or used in preserves. Fruit keeps well. Moderate chilling requirement. Partially self-fruitful.
'SANTA ROSA'	Santa Rosa, California, L. Burbank.	2-19.	Yes.	Early.	Large, cone-shaped fruit has deep purple skin. Flesh is yellow with pink coloring. Firm, juicy, slightly tart. Tree is large, vigorous, hardy, upright and productive.	One of the best Japanese plums. Widely adapted. Slow ripening. Eat fresh, can or use for desserts.
'SATSUMA'	Santa Rosa, California, L. Burbank.	2, 3, 5-13, 16, 18, 19.	Yes.	Midseason.	Small to medium, round fruit. Skin is solid dark red. Red flesh is juicy, sweet, firm. Has very good flavor. Semifreestone, small pit. Upright tree.	Use for desserts or preserves.
'SHIRO'	California.	2-13, 16.	Yes.	Early.	Medium, round, beautiful yellow fruit. Flesh is yellow. Tree is low growing, very hardy and prolific.	Considered one of the best yellow plums. Use for cooking, canning and desserts. Productive in western Oregon and western Washington.
'SIMKA'	Fowler, California.	12, 13.	None needed.	Midseason.	Large, oblong to cone-shaped fruit. Skin is ebony. Flesh is yellowish white and sweet. Freestone at maturity. Vigorous, medium-size tree. Moderately productive and regular.	Fruit is slow ripening, keeps well on tree. Stores well.
'SPRITE'	Modesto, California, F. Zaiger.	5-15.	Yes.	Midseason.	Small, round fruit with almost black skin has thick, blue-gray bloom. Flesh is yellow, sweet, juicy. Has abundant flavor. Semidwarf tree is vigorous, upright.	Cherry plum. Low chilling requirement. Fruit holds on tree long without losing quality. Hybrid of 'Mahaleb' cherry and Japanese plum.
'STARK GIANT CHERRY PLUM'	Missouri.	2, 4-13, 16, 18, 19.	Yes.	Late midseason.	Large, bright red fruit. Flesh has sweet, spicy flavor. Tree is a heavy cropper.	Use for eating fresh or in jams and jellies.
'STARKLING DELICIOUS'	Oklahoma.	12, 13.	Yes.	Midseason to late.	Large, dark red fruit. Deep red clingstone flesh is tough and tart. Tree is very hardy, productive and disease resistant.	Eat fresh or use in desserts and jellies. Good for canning.
'SUPERIOR'	Minnesota.	12, 13.	Yes.	Late.	Large, dark red fruit with russet dots. Yellow, clingstone flesh has sprightly flavor, slightly acid near skin. Tree is a vigorous, early cropper. Tends to overbear and needs thinning.	Good dessert quality. Sand cherry hybrid. Fine tree for cold regions.
'WEEPING SANTA ROSA'	Sutter County, California, G. McFeely, 1969.	2-19.	None needed.	Midseason.	Large, cone-shaped, dark purple fruit has gray bloom. Fruit resembles 'Santa Rosa'. Flesh is amber. Tree has a weeping growth habit and is very productive and vigorous. Stake when young.	A sport of 'Santa Rosa'. Blooms approximately one week after 'Santa Rosa'. Self-fruitful in California's central valleys.
'WICKSON'	California.	2, 3, 5-13, 16.	Yes.	Midseason.	Large, heart-shaped fruit. Skin is greenish yellow with red blush, white bloom. Yellow flesh has fine flavor. Medium, upright, vigorous tree.	Eat fresh or use in sauces. Keeps well.

'Brooks' European plum   'President' European plum   'Stanley' European plum

EUROPEAN PLUMS AND PRUNES

VARIETY	ORIGIN	ZONE	POLLINIZER	HARVEST SEASON	FRUIT AND TREE	REMARKS
'BROOKS'	Oregon.	2, 4, 5, 7.	None needed.	Late.	Large fruit. Flesh is yellow and sweet with some acid. Tree overbears, breaks easily.	Oregon prune suitable for canning or drying.
'DAMSON'	England.	2-17.	None needed.	Late.	Small, blue to purple fruit. Flesh is golden yellow, melting, juicy, slightly acid. Small tree.	Use for preserves and canning.
'EARLY ITALIAN'	Washington.	2-4, 16.	None needed.	Early.	Fruit resembles 'Italian Prune' but matures earlier. Tree is less vigorous and weaker than 'Italian Prune'.	Also known as 'Milton' and 'Richards'. Subject to internal browning.
'FRENCH PRUNE'	France.	2, 4-7, 9-12, 16.	None needed.	Late.	Medium, long, oval fruit is red to dark purple. Sweet, mild-flavored flesh. Tree is large and long-lived.	Use for drying. Too sweet for canning.
'GREEN GAGE'	Europe.	2-13, 16.	None needed.	Midseason.	Medium, round to oval fruit. Skin is greenish yellow with brown spots. Flesh is greenish yellow, aromatic, sweet and mild. Very good juicy flavor. Medium-size tree.	Use for canning, preserves and eating fresh. 'Jefferson' is a selected strain of 'Green Gage'.
'ITALIAN PRUNE'	Germany.	2-7, 9-12, 16.	None needed.	Late.	Large, long, oval fruit. Skin is purple to dark blue with greenish yellow flesh. Hardy tree often overbears. Heavy summer fruit drop. Moderate growth habit. Irregular producer in cool spring weather.	Also known as 'Fellenburg'. Sweet fruit is good for eating fresh, canning or drying.
'PRESIDENT'	England.	2, 4-12, 16.	'Stanley'	Late.	Large, blue fruit with fine-textured, yellow flesh. Tree has moderate growth habit.	Use for cooking. Slow ripening.
'REINE CLAUDE CONDUCTA'	Hungary.	2-13.	None needed.	Late.	Fruit has purplish red skin. Greenish yellow clingstone flesh is juicy and delicious. Tree is very productive.	Also known as 'R. C. D'Althan'.
'STANLEY'	Geneva, New York, 1926.	2-12, 16, 18, 19.	None needed.	Late.	Large, bluish purple fruit. Greenish yellow flesh is juicy and sweet but flavor is inferior to 'Italian Prune'. Tree is large, spreading and productive. Bears young.	Highly susceptible to brown rot. Fruit doubles in hot climates.
'SUGAR'	California.	2-12.	None needed.	Midseason.	Large, dark purple fruit. Purple flesh is sweet, highly flavored. Tree is a heavy cropper. Bears alternately.	Use for eating, canning and drying.

'Wonderful' pomegranate

Pomegranate

This shiny-leafed tree is normally planted as an ornamental. Its red, carnation-like flowers bloom for several weeks. Large, round fruit may be 3 to 5 inches in diameter. They are quite showy, especially in autumn, when they turn bright red.

Pomegranates withstand temperatures from 10° to 15° F (−12° to −10° C) but are subject to damage from late spring frosts. They thrive in hot valleys of California and in desert regions. The accumulation of heat makes the fruit sweeter than those grown in mild climates. Chilling requirement is very slight. In warm, southern climates growth is resumed shortly after leaves fall. Trees grow well in cool climates, but the fruit is less sweet.

Pomegranates are very easy to grow and are subject to very few pests or diseases. They do well in a wide range of soils, including those that are somewhat saline. They do not need much water or fertilizer. Pomegranates can be trained as a tree by selecting one or more strong shoots or they can be grown as a shrub or espalier.

VARIETIES

Although there are many varieties of ornamental pomegranates, 'Wonderful' is the best-known fruiting variety. It has attractive, yellowish red foliage in the fall, with large fruit and flowers. When grown near the coast, it is an inconsistent bearer. Fruit will crack if soil is allowed to become alternately wet and dry.

'Fleishman's' is a newer, very sweet, large-fruited variety selected by Paul Thomson of the California Rare Fruit Growers. See page 189 for their address.

HARVESTING AND STORAGE

Pomegranates are harvested when they have attained full color. Fruit split open if left on the tree. They may be stored in a cool, dry place for two to three months. Cut fruit from tree and store only those showing no cuts or splits. Split fruit deteriorate quickly.

VITAL STATISTICS—POMEGRANATE

	Standard	Dwarf
Height at maturity (feet)		
Unpruned	12-15	N/A
Pruned	6-15	
Spread at maturity with		
no competition (feet)	12-15	
Recommended planting		
distance (feet)	10	
Years to reach bearing age	4	
Life expectancy (years)	75-100	
Chilling requirement (hours)	100-200	
Pollinizer required	No	
Good for espalier	Yes	
Good for containers	Yes	

Comments: Not available as true dwarf but size can be controlled by pruning.

N/A = Not Available

Here's an easy way to enjoy pomegranates: Roll fruit between your hand and a hard surface to rupture juice sacs. Enjoy the sweet juice through a straw.

'Pineapple' quince

Quince

Quince is an unappreciated fruit tree that deserves to be planted more often. It is an attractive ornamental with a profusion of large, white to pinkish spring flowers. It features bold, dark green leaves with whitish undersides and a gnarled branching pattern. Round or pear-shaped fruit may reach up to 5 inches in diameter and weigh up to a pound. They are sweetly fragrant, covered with downy hairs.

Quince is adaptable to more regions than perhaps any other fruit tree, but does least well in low deserts. Flowers appear late and are seldom subject to frost damage. It is subject to very few pests or diseases.

VARIETIES

'**Champion**'—Greenish yellow, tender flesh with a delicate flavor. Imparts an exquisite quince taste and odor to anything with which it is cooked. Produces an abundance of pear-shaped fruit even at a young age.

'**Cooke's Jumbo**'—Large, yellowish green fruit with white flesh. Fruit reaches 6 to 8 inches in diameter.

'**Orange**', '**Apple**'—Names applied to a group of very similar quinces. Flesh is orange-yellow and fine grained with a smooth, golden skin. Flavor is rich and aromatic. Matures very early—usually in late August. Some people prefer it to 'Smyrna'.

'**Pineapple**'—Originated and distributed by Luthur Burbank in 1899, this variety is the result of a long effort to find a quince that would cook tender like an apple. White flesh has a slight, pineapple flavor. Skin is smooth and golden yellow.

'**Smyrna**'—Extremely large and handsome fruit. Flesh is light yellow and tender with lemon-yellow skin. Fruit can be stored in the refrigerator longer than other varieties. If you plant a single variety, this is probably the best one.

SOIL, NUTRIENT AND WATER REQUIREMENTS

Quince does well in a wide range of soils and is better adapted to heavy or wet soils than many fruit trees. Trees seem to thrive on neglect but will do much better with regular care. They seldom need fertilizing. Do not promote extra-vigorous growth. This increases the likelihood of fireblight, to which quince are very susceptible. Water regularly, although trees are somewhat drought resistant.

PRUNING

Trees should be trained to a vase shape. Because branches tend to droop and become leggy, they should be headed to keep foliage full and productive. Quince can also be trained as shrubs.

Mature trees are seldom pruned other than to remove suckers. Black knots that commonly develop on trunk and branches are natural and should not be removed. Quince fruit are not thinned unless there is an extra-heavy crop that would cause limbs to break.

HARVESTING AND STORAGE

Quince are ready for harvest during fall months after the skin loses its greenish color and assumes the characteristic, golden yellow of most varieties. Fragrance becomes more pronounced as maturity is reached. Although quince fruit is hard, it bruises easily and should be handled carefully. Fruit will keep for only a few weeks when stored in a refrigerator.

The "wool" on the skin rubs off easily with your fingers. If you are not going to prepare fruit immediately, it is best left on. Fruit are inedible unless cooked. Quince are most often used to make jams and jellies.

VITAL STATISTICS—QUINCE		
	Standard	Dwarf
Height at maturity (feet)		
Unpruned	12-15	N/A
Pruned	8-10	
Spread at maturity with		
no competition (feet)	12-15	
Recommended planting		
distance (feet)	10-15	
Years to reach bearing age	3-5	
Life expectancy (years)	40	
Chilling requirement (hours)	100-450	
Pollinizer required	No	
Good for espalier	Informal only	
Good for containers	Yes	

N/A = Not Available

Berries

Berries offer the western gardener tremendous opportunity. The West has the greatest variety of berries maturing over the longest season. Fruit grown here is of the highest quality.

Commercial growers have taken advantage of this quality for some time. Premium wine grapes are grown in northern California's Napa and Sonoma valleys. The finest strawberries are harvested by the ton along the coast of southern California. Superb raspberries flourish in Oregon's Willamette Valley and Washington's Puget Sound.

Berries are small only in terms of individual fruit. Yields are large because most berries are borne in clusters and bunches. Surprisingly few plants can produce a bountiful harvest. Under ideal conditions, 25 strawberry plants yield up to 30 quarts of fruit. Just 6 blueberry plants produce up to 15 quarts. And two currant shrubs yield up to 12 quarts.

Berries offer versatility in the garden. A few strawberry plants can be tucked in almost anywhere. Massed

Berries: Where they will grow

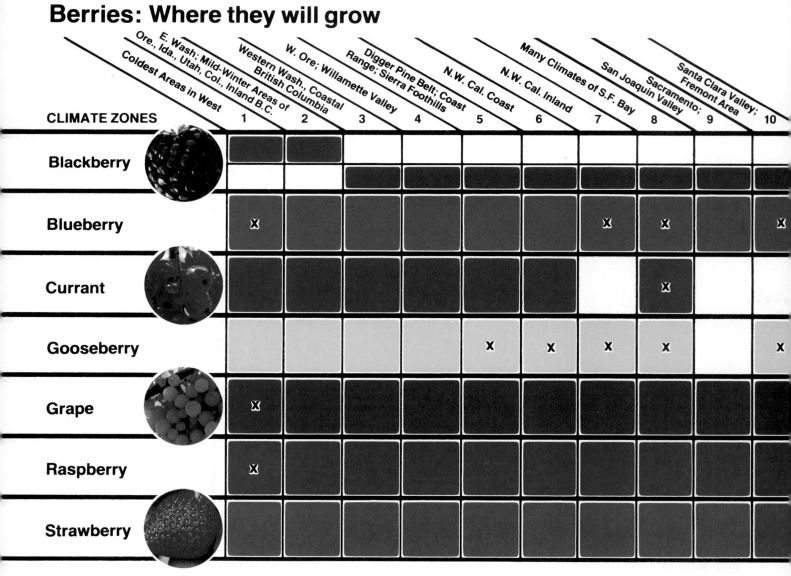

CLIMATE ZONES	1 — E. Wash; Mild-Winter Areas of Ore., Ida., Utah, Col., Inland B.C.; Coldest Areas in West	2 — Western Wash., Coastal British Columbia	3 — W. Ore; Willamette Valley	4 — Digger Pine Belt; Coast Range; Sierra Foothills	5 — N.W. Cal. Coast	6 — N.W. Cal. Inland	7 — Many Climates of S.F. Bay	8 — San Joaquin Valley	9 — Sacramento; Santa Clara Valley; Fremont Area	10
Blackberry	●	●	●	●	●	●	●	●	●	●
Blueberry	X	●	●	●	●	●	X	X	●	X
Currant	●	●	●	●	●	●		X		
Gooseberry	○	○	○	○	X	X	X	X		X
Grape	X	●	●	●	●	●	●	●	●	●
Raspberry	X	●	●	●	●	●	●	●	●	●
Strawberry	●	●	●	●	●	●	●	●	●	●

X — See fruit description for special cultural requirements, planting site selection or variety adaptation needed to be successful in this zone.

together, strawberries can be used as a small-scale ground cover. They can also be grown in containers ranging from vertical planters to half-barrels.

Currants, gooseberries and blueberries are attractive ornamental shrubs with beautiful spring blooms, colorful berries and bright fall color.

Blackberries and raspberries are usually grown on a trellis but flourish just as well on a fence. Grape vines can be trained on arbors, fences, trellises and walls.

Most berries need a supporting structure. There are many attractive ways to build a trellis or arbor. If you want permanence, design the structure to complement your landscape. Build it strong to last.

Reaping the bountiful harvest of 'Sequoia' strawberries.

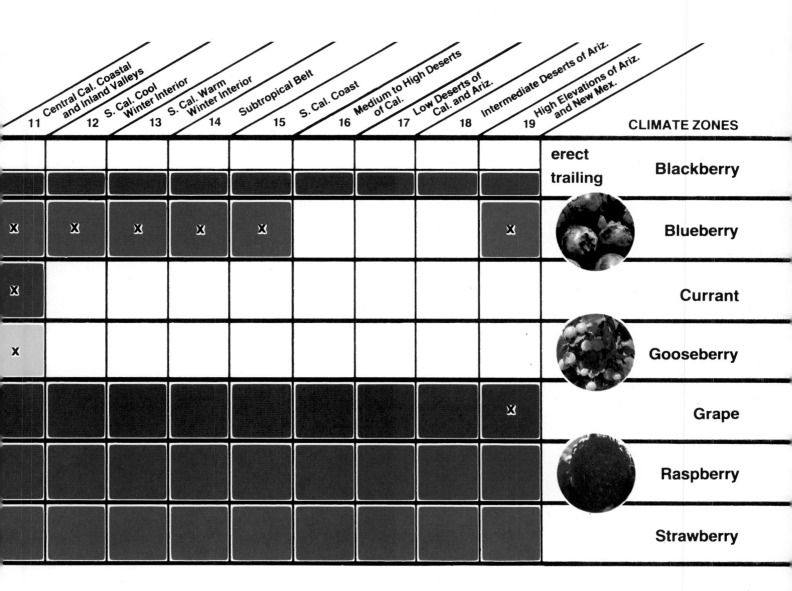

	11 Central Cal. Coastal and Inland Valleys	12 S. Cal. Cool Winter Interior	13 S. Cal. Warm Winter Interior	14 Subtropical Belt	15 S. Cal. Coast	16 Medium to High Deserts of Cal.	17 Low Deserts of Cal. and Ariz.	18 Intermediate Deserts of Ariz.	19 High Elevations of Ariz. and New Mex.	CLIMATE ZONES
Blackberry — erect										
Blackberry — trailing	■	■	■	■	■	■	■	■	■	
Blueberry	X	X	X	X	X				X	
Currant	X									
Gooseberry	x									
Grape	■	■	■	■	■	■	■	■ X	■	
Raspberry	■	■	■	■	■	■	■	■	■	
Strawberry	■	■	■	■	■	■	■	■	■	

Blackberries ready for harvest.

Blackberry

Blackberry varieties are derived from native species of *Rubus*, originating in many parts of the United States. Some are hybrids between species. Plants vary among varieties from trailing to erect or bushy. Some varieties come in thornless forms. Fruit color at maturity varies from black to reddish purple. Blackberries are often referred to as *dewberries* in some areas. *Loganberries* and *boysenberries* are common names for blackberry varieties 'Logan' and 'Boysen'.

VITAL STATISTICS—BLACKBERRY

	Standard	Dwarf
Height at maturity (feet)		
Unpruned	Cane trails	N/A
Pruned	5-6	
Spread at maturity with no competition (feet)	20-40	
Recommended planting distance (feet)		
Between plants	4-8	
Between rows	6-9	
Years to reach bearing age	2	
Life expectancy (years)	6-25	
Pollinizer required	No	
Good for espalier	No	
Good for containers	Yes	

N/A = Not Available

Blackberries grow best in regions that have cool, fairly humid summers such as western Washington, western Oregon and northwestern California. However, there are varieties adapted to almost every climate in the West. 'Olallie' blackberry, although originating in Corvallis, Oregon, is widely adapted to California. See variety chart on page 140. 'Boysen', introduced to the public by Walter Knott of Buena Vista, California, is widely grown throughout the Pacific Northwest. Other widely adapted varieties include 'Logan', 'Young' and 'Marion'.

Climate limitations of blackberries are related to winter cold and high summer heat. Most varieties are definitely susceptible to winter injury in coldest parts of the West. These include the high elevations of eastern Washington and Oregon and high desert regions of the Southwest. Canes can be protected to a certain degree with a heavy winter mulch. In areas where daytime temperatures are high in summer, vines are short-lived and yield small amounts of low-quality fruit.

PRUNING

Blackberries bear fruit on canes that grew the previous season. When 2-year-old canes are fruiting, new shoots are sprouting from the base. They bear the following year. Canes fruit only once. The object of pruning is to remove fruited canes and select strong canes for fruiting the following year. 'Thornfree' branches very little and usually does not need pruning.

The easiest way to grow blackberries is on a trellis. Build a two-wire trellis about 5 feet high with 18 inches between wires. An existing fence will serve the same purpose. The idea is to raise canes that will produce fruit above new canes, placing them within easy reach for harvesting. Illustrations on the opposite page outline the training steps.

SOIL, NUTRIENT AND WATER REQUIREMENTS

Like other berries, blackberries prefer deep soil and constant moisture. They also demand excellent drainage. Blackberries respond well to nitrogen applied in winter at a rate of 1/4 pound actual nitrogen per year per plant.

HARVESTING AND STORAGE

Blackberries develop maximum flavor and sweetness when they begin to turn their characteristic color. Usually they change from bright red to blackish red. Ripening usually extends for at least a two-week period. This begins as early as mid-May for early varieties and extends into fall for late-ripening varieties.

Varieties grown in warm climates will ripen before the same varieties grown in cooler areas. Berries are tender and must be handled with care.

Blackberry pruning

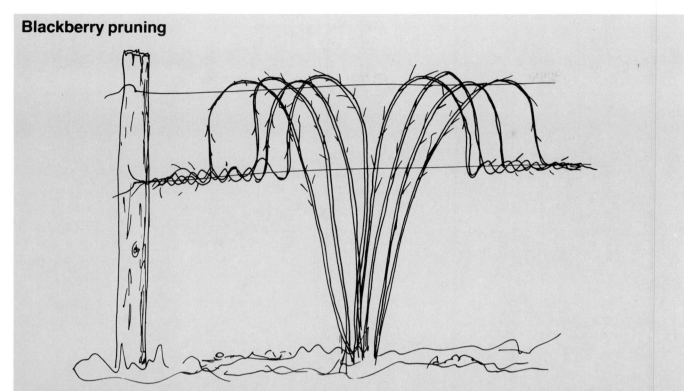

1. Immediately after harvest remove fruited canes and train new ones on trellis. In hot climates new canes will sunburn if left on ground. Trellis only strong, new canes and remove weaker ones. About 8 to 10 canes are sufficient for established plants. A fan-like arrangement of canes is best because it allows for good fruit and leaf development. Several canes can be bundled together for ease of handling. Erect blackberries send up root suckers in addition to new canes that rise from the crown. Pull root suckers out.

   Head canes at about 6 to 8 feet in hot climates, 8 to 10 feet in cool climates. The farther berries are borne from the base of the plant, the smaller they will be at maturity.

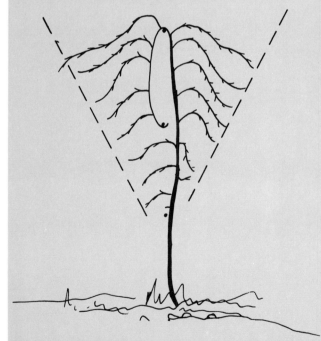

2. In winter after leaf fall, remove all laterals within 2 feet of the ground. Head any long laterals to 12 to 15 inches. Head shorter laterals less to increase fruit size. The result should look similar to above.

3. Where space is limited, blackberries can also be tied to a post with a crossbar.

BLACKBERRIES

VARIETY	ZONE	HARVEST SEASON	FRUIT AND PLANT	REMARKS
'BOYSEN'	All zones.	Midseason.	Black, very large fruit, 1-1/4 inches long, 1 inch thick. Covered with a dusty bloom. Reddish black at maturity. Trailing, vigorous, on productive plant. Fruit is borne on canes of previous season only. Small thorns. Thornless strain has small fruit, is less productive.	Very fine flavor but not as sweet as 'Young'. Soft, distinct aroma. Flavor suggestive of raspberries.
'CHEHALEM'	3, 4.	Late.	Glossy black, medium fruit. Thorny and trailing plant.	Excellent for pies and preserves. Mainly grown in home gardens.
'DARROW'	1, 2.	Ripens over prolonged period.	Black, glossy fruit, 1 inch long, 3/4 inch wide. Firm, mildly acid flesh. Good quality. Vigorous plant is reliably heavy producer. Relatively cold hardy. Erect habit, no trellis necessary.	Very hardy. Originated in New York.
'LOGAN' ('THORNLESS LOGAN')	All zones.	Late.	Dusty maroon to reddish fruit, 1-1/4 inches long, 3/4 inch thick. Covered with fine hairs that dull its color. Plant is productive and trailing. Best with some trellis support. Thornless.	Flavor is tastier, more acid than 'Boysen'. Excellent for canning and pies. Used for wine production in the Northwest. A cross between red raspberry and California wild blackberry. Can be grown in eastern Washington with winter protection.
'MARION'	All zones.	Late.	Black, medium to large fruit, longer than wide. Flesh is medium-firm. Trailing and vigorous plant with only a few long canes. Spines are large and numerous. Higher yields for a longer period than 'Boysen'.	Excellent flavor, great for canning, freezing, pies and jam. Needs winter protection in eastern Washington.
'OLALLIE'	5-15.	Midseason.	Black, large fruit, slightly longer and more slender than 'Boysen'. Glossy, black, firm flesh. Plant is productive, vigorous, thorny and trailing. Lower chilling requirement than 'Boysen'.	Better adapted to California than the Pacific Northwest. Not cold hardy.
'THORNFREE'	3-11.	Late.	Glossy black, medium-large fruit, blunt in shape. Only fair quality. Unlike most thornless types, all canes of 'Thornfree' are thornless. Bush canes are semiupright, 7 to 8 feet long. Best with some trellis support.	Tart flavor. Fruiting laterals bear 20 to 30 berries. Productive, moderately winter hardy.
'THORNLESS EVERGREEN'	3, 4, 6, 8, 10, 11.	Late.	Black fruit, 1-1/2 inches long, 3/4 inch thick. Very firm and sweet. Seeds are large. Fair quality. Very vigorous and productive plant. Disease resistant.	Commercial blackberry of Oregon. Must be propagated from tip layering to preserve thornless trait. Similar to 'Thornless Logan'.
'YOUNG'	All zones.	Midseason.	Wine-colored fruit, similar to 'Boysen', but shiny and somewhat sweeter. Plant is similar to 'Boysen'.	Does not produce as well as 'Boysen'.

Properly trained blackberries are easy to harvest.

Blueberries fresh from the bush.

Blueberry

Blueberry culture is limited by two factors: soil and climate. Plants must have acid soil. Optimum fruit quality occurs in areas having cool summers. Blueberries are best adapted to cool, coastal areas of northern California, Oregon, Washington and British Columbia. But they are worth trying in other areas. Blueberries can be grown in containers. Use an acid soil mix with at least 50 percent peat moss or other acidifying soil amendment. In hot summer areas grow them in partial shade.

Blueberries are long-lived shrubs. They present no special cultural problems other than soil requirement. Plants are quite ornamental with a neat, compact, growth habit. Glossy foliage changes to bright orange, red and yellow in the fall.

VITAL STATISTICS—BLUEBERRY

	Standard	Dwarf
Height at maturity (feet)		
Unpruned	7-8	N/A
Pruned	6-8	
Spread at maturity with		
no competition (feet)	8	
Recommended planting		
distance (feet)	3-4	
Years to reach bearing age	3-4	
Life expectancy (years)	Indefinite	
Pollinizer required	Yes*	
Good for espalier	Yes	
Good for containers	Yes	

*Best production with cross-pollination.

N/A = Not Available

Rabbit-eye blueberries are widely grown in the southeastern United States where they are known for their great heat and drought tolerance. Fruit are small and black with a somewhat gritty flesh. Their cultural and pollination requirements are the same as regular blueberries, but acid soil is not absolutely necessary. Varieties that are occasionally available in western nurseries include 'Woodward', 'Garden Blue', 'Tifblue', 'Menditoo' and 'Homebell'.

SOIL, NUTRIENT AND WATER REQUIREMENTS

Blueberries require 1/4 pound of actual nitrogen per year per plant. Acidifying forms of nitrogen such as ammonium sulfate are best.

Blueberries demand constant moisture and excellent drainage. Roots are shallow and should not be disturbed. Apply a thick mulch at the base of plants. This will eliminate weeding, retain moisture and cool the soil.

PRUNING

Plants should be allowed to develop fully the first two years, so little pruning is needed. The University of California recommends that blossoms be stripped the first two years to prevent fruiting and favor plant growth. See illustration on page 142.

POLLINATION

Blueberries require cross-pollination with another variety for best fruit production. Always plant more than one variety.

HARVESTING AND STORAGE

Plant will reach full production in 6 to 10 years. Berries ripen over a period of 6 or 7 weeks. Not all berries within one cluster ripen at the same time. Select ripe ones and leave others for later picking. Ripe berries hold on the bush for about a week without deteriorating or dropping.

Berries are very tender so handle them carefully. You will probably want to use them fresh after picking but they can also be frozen or made into jams or jellies.

Blueberry bird protection.   Harvesting blueberries.

Blueberry pruning

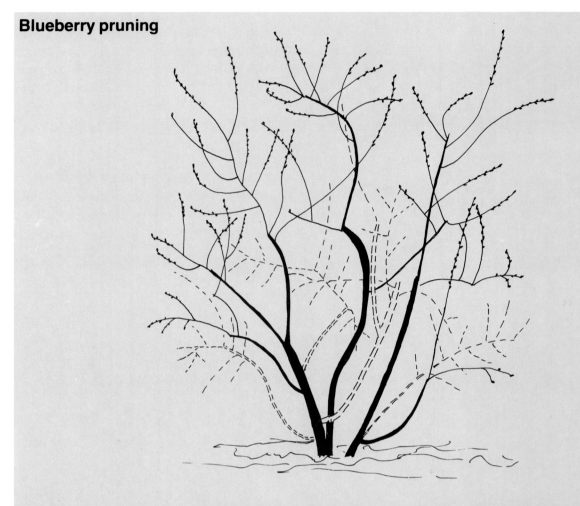

Prune in winter or early spring. Remove weak side shoots in top of plant. If shoots appear too crowded, remove some older shoots entirely. To increase fruit size, head back shoots that have an abundance of flower buds.

BLUEBERRIES

VARIETY	ZONE	SEASON	FRUIT AND PLANT	REMARKS
'BERKELEY'	2-11.	Late midseason.	Fruit very large, light blue skin, firm flesh, mild flavor. Plant vigorous, open, spreading and productive.	Fruit stores well, does not drop from plant. Excellent for pies or eating fresh.
'BLUECROP'	1-11.	Midseason.	Fruit medium-large, light blue skin, flesh very firm. Good flavor. Plant vigorous, erect and tall. Drought tolerant.	Unusually productive, tends to over-produce unless properly pruned.
'BLUERAY'	2-11.	Midseason.	Fruit large, medium light blue, crisp, aromatic. Fine flavor. Plant hardy, very productive, upright and tall growing.	Heavy yields, not quite as flavorful as 'Berkeley'.
'DIXI'	2-11.	Late.	Fruit large, medium blue, tender and luscious. Plant tall, open.	Fruit not good for shipping—too tender.
'EARLIBLUE'	2-11.	Very early.	Fruit large, light blue, very firm flesh, mild, slightly acid, very good flavor. Plant upright, hardy, well shaped, moderately vigorous.	Fruit does not drop. Plant not very productive. Good dessert quality.
'HERBERT'	2-11.	Late midseason.	Fruit large, medium dark blue, tender flesh. Plant vigorous, open, spreading, consistently productive.	Special mountain-huckleberry flavor. Fruit does not drop from bush.
'PATRIOT'	2-11.	Early to midseason.	Fruit medium, excellent color and flavor. Plant has medium vigor, is open and productive.	Disease resistant and winter hardy.
'SPARTAN'	2-11.	Early.	Fruit large, light blue, firm, good flavor. Plant erect, open, productive.	Adapted to machine harvest.
'STANLEY'	2-11.	Early.	Fruit firm, aromatic with spicy flavor. Plant erect, medium-tall, attractive foliage.	One of the tastiest.

Red currants ready for harvest.

Currant and Gooseberry

Currants and gooseberries belong to *Ribes* species. They are attractive plants with bright spring flowers, colorful berries and attractive, lobed foliage. Their small, tart berries are used to make pies, jams, jellies and preserves. Cultural requirements are identical.

Both plants are best adapted to the cool, moist, coastal areas found in Zones 2, 4, 6, 8 and 11. This includes western Oregon and western Washington and the north and central coast of California. In many areas of California it may be illegal to grow currants and gooseberries. These plants can serve as an alternate host to white pine blister rust. Check with your local extension service before planting currants or gooseberries in California.

VITAL STATISTICS—CURRANT & GOOSEBERRY

	Currant	Gooseberry
Height at maturity (feet)		
Unpruned	4-6	6-8
Pruned	3-4	5-7
Spread at maturity with no competition (feet)	2-4	2-4
Recommended planting distance (feet)	3-4	2½-5
Years to reach bearing age	3	3
Life expectancy (years)	15-30	15-30
Pollinizer required	No	No
Good for espalier	Yes	Yes
Good for containers	Yes	Yes

Comments: Dwarf currants or gooseberries are not available.

Currants and gooseberries are hardy and can be grown in protected locations of eastern Washington. They are also grown in many areas of Zone 1. They may do well in the interior valleys and other warmer areas of California if planted in a shady location such as the north side of a wall or fence.

VARIETIES

'Red Lake' and **'Perfection'** are the two most productive currants. Both have medium-size, red fruit borne in loose clusters. Both are good quality but 'Red Lake' is preferred in California. Plants are upright with dense foliage.

'Wilder', a productive variety with similar characteristics to 'Red Lake', is grown widely in the valleys of eastern Washington.

'Cherry' and **'Fay's Prolific'** are often grown in western Oregon.

'White Grace' and **'White Imperial'** are white-fruited varieties of currant.

'Oregon Champion' is the most common gooseberry in western gardens. Berries are medium to large in size and light green to yellow in color. Bushes are thornless and fairly vigorous.

'Pixwell' and **'Poorman'** are red-fruited gooseberries.

SOIL, NUTRIENT AND WATER REQUIREMENTS

Currants and gooseberries are easy to grow and do well in a wide range of soils. Soil must be well drained and relatively free of salts. Keep soil constantly moist but do not allow it to become too soggy. Cultivation around plants should be kept near the surface so that the plant's shallow roots are not disturbed. Plants respond to regular applications of nitrogen.

PRUNING

After first season's growth, prune all but 6 to 8 of the strongest shoots to the ground or to plant crown. At end of the next season keep 3 or 4 of the best 1-year-old shoots, along with 4 or 5 of the best 2-year-old shoots. Remove all other growth.

After the third year, retain 3 or 4 shoots of each growth period—1, 2 and 3 years. Select the strongest canes each year and try to space canes evenly.

Do not save canes 4 or more years old. They are less fruitful than younger canes.

HARVESTING AND STORAGE

Currants and gooseberries are ripe when all berries in a cluster reach full color. They ripen slowly and will remain on the bush for long periods in cool climates.

If fruit are to be used for jelly, pick when slightly underripe. They contain more pectin at that stage.

'Perlette' grape

Grape

Two major types of grapes, *American* and *European,* are available to fruit growers. A third and increasingly important group is *hybrids,* crosses of popular grape varieties.

American grapes, *Vitus lambrusca,* are *slip-skin* grapes, meaning the pulp slides easily out of the skin. They have soft flesh and a distinctive, musty flavor and aroma. Varieties were developed primarily in the eastern United States and are moderately vigorous. American grapes are hardy to 0° F (−18° C) and resistant to many insects and diseases. They also mature early in the season. 'Concord' is the most famous American grape variety.

American grapes are most commonly grown in eastern Washington, other parts of Zone 2 and milder areas of Zone 1. They are often used for grape juice, although many people like them fresh.

European grapes, *Vitis vinifera,* differ from American grapes in fruit, vine and climate adaptation. Fruit are firm with nonslip skin and relatively mild flavor. Compared to American grapes, which prefer a more humid, cooler climate, European grapes have a defined heat requirement and usually prefer a long, warm growing season. In areas with fewer than 170 frost-free days, only American or hybrid grapes are assured success. Early-maturing European types require at least 170 to 180 days. In areas of more than 180 frost-free days, a wider range of European grapes can be grown as well as many American grapes and hybrids.

European grapes are less hardy than American grapes. They survive without damage to 10° F (−12° C). They produce vigorous, upright growth that normally requires trellising. Susceptibility to many insects and diseases often limits their adaptation.

American and French hybrids are intermediate between American and European grapes. Plants are more vigorous than American varieties. Most require a warmer and longer growing season to mature the crop and develop resistance to fall and winter cold. Their growth, foliage and fruit are more characteristic of European varieties. Although they retain some of the strong flavor and aroma of American grapes, they usually have firmer flesh and do not have the characteristic slip skin of American varieties. To the home

VITAL STATISTICS—GRAPE

	Standard	Dwarf
Height at maturity (feet)		
Unpruned	Canes trail	N/A
Pruned	4-5	
Spread at maturity with		
no competition (feet)	100	
Recommended planting		
distance (feet)	6-12	
Years to reach bearing age	3	
Life expectancy (years)	40-60	
Pollinizer required	No	
Good for espalier	Yes	
Good for containers	Yes	

N/A = Not Available

gardener, their most important traits are resistance to cold and a wide range of adaptation.

WINE GRAPES

Most premium wines are made from European grapes. In the eastern United States and colder areas of the West, American varieties are used to make wine.

Many areas of the West are experimenting with wine grape production. From Arizona to Washington, wine makers are having success with varieties previously thought reserved for famous wine-growing regions of northern California.

Variety adaptation is critical to quality grapes and the resulting wine. Some varieties, such as many white wine grapes, prefer cool weather. Many standard red varieties prefer hotter climates.

The University of California has divided California into five *viticultural* or wine-grape growing regions based on available heat. Extension offices of other western states will have similar helpful information. Their addresses can be found on page 189.

Region I, the coolest zone, includes the towns of Guerneville, Napa and Saratoga. It is best for dry, white table wines.

Region II, which is moderately cool, includes the towns of St. Helena, Los Gatos and Hollister. Red and white table wines are superior here.

Region III includes the towns of Ukiah, Livermore and King City. Climate is moderately warm and produces good quality, standard red and white wines.

Region IV, a warm area represented by Davis, Modesto and Escondido, produces naturally sweet wines and standard table wines.

Region V includes the area from Sacramento north to Red Bluff, from Merced south to Bakersfield and the eastern slope of the Sierra Nevadas. It is a hot area and produces primarily sweet dessert wines.

WINE GRAPE VARIETIES

'Cabernet Sauvignon'—Red grape with excellent, peppery flavor. Best in cool climates.

'Chenin Blanc'—Produces white wines in cool to warm climates.

'French Colombard'—Very vigorous and productive. Good for white wines in warmer climates.

'Grenache'—Light red wine grape for warm climates.

'Pinot Chardonnay'—Excellent quality fruit for white wines in cool climates.

'Ruby Cabernet'—Very productive. Produces red wine in moderately cool to warm areas.

'White Riesling'—Good for white wines in cooler climates.

'Zinfandel'—A California exclusive. Excellent red wine grape for cool to warm climates.

PRUNING

Pruning and training grape vines have two objectives: first, to shape the vine to the gardener's needs; and second, to balance fruit production with vegetative growth.

There are two ways to prune mature vines. The method used depends on the variety. Some varieties, including many European and wine grapes, are *spur pruned.* Healthy canes are selected and cut back to two or three buds. These buds produce fruit the following season. Other varieties, including many American grapes such as 'Concord', do not produce fruit close to the main trunk. Here, 6 to 18 buds, depending on the vigor of the vine, are retained for fruiting. The selection is made so that canes with fruiting buds are stretched out on a trellis wire. This second type of pruning is called *cane pruning.* The variety charts indicate whether a vine should be spur pruned or cane pruned. Each type of pruning is illustrated on pages 146 and 147.

Spur-pruned grapes are usually trained to a head or cordon. Cane-pruned grapes are either trellised to one or two wires or pruned to a head. By increasing the height at which the vines branch, you can train either type of grape over a pergola or arbor.

SOIL, NUTRIENT AND WATER REQUIREMENTS

Grapes are adapted to a wide range of soil types, as long as soil is well drained. If vines are not growing vigorously or show poor foliage color, they will respond to 1/4-pound of actual nitrogen per plant per year. Mature vines are deep rooted and require only occasional watering. However, they should not be allowed to dry out. Watering prior to harvest will increase fruit size.

In coldest parts of Zones 1 and 19 only the hardiest varieties should be grown. Use a mulch for added cold protection. American grapes may show signs of leaf burn due to alkaline soils in Zone 19.

FRUIT THINNING

Thinning is usually not practiced with American grapes. If you want picture-perfect clusters from European grapes, you can remove clusters of flowers or young fruit to divert energy into remaining clusters. Or, you can thin individual berries or parts of clusters to fill out the rest of the cluster.

HARVESTING AND STORAGE

As grapes mature, they become less acidic and noticeably sweeter, taking on their characteristic colors and

Training young grape vines

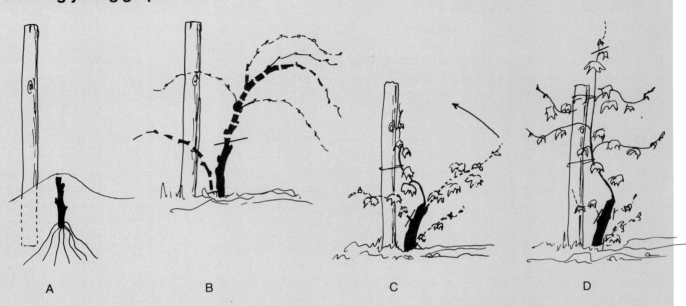

A   B   C   D

A. If a rooted, pruned cutting is planted, set it so the top bud is level with the ground. Mound a little soil over top of plant. Developing buds will push their way to the surface.

B. At the first dormant pruning, all but 1 strong cane is removed from the vine. This single cane is then cut back to 2 or 3 buds.

C. After a few inches of growth in the second summer, the best-placed and strongest shoot is saved and others are removed.

D. This shoot is trained along a stake, which should be placed at the time of planting. Tie shoot loosely to stake. Lateral shoots are allowed to develop but remove suckers from roots or crown.

Spur pruning of head-trained vines

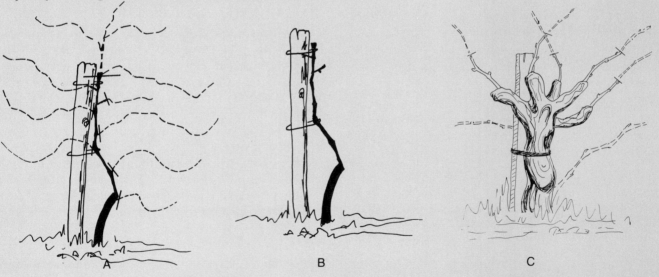

A   B   C

A. Canes of head-trained vines are cut off at the *node* (dormant bud) above where the head is to be formed. Cut through node so that bud is destroyed at that point. Tie cane tightly to top of supporting stake. Tie it again loosely about halfway to the ground.

B. All lateral canes below the middle of the trunk are removed entirely. Weak laterals in the upper half are also removed. Two to 4 laterals may be cut back to 2 to 3 buds each. The greater the vine vigor, the more spurs that are left. The greater the cane diameter, the more buds that can be left.

C. Mature, head-trained vines of European grapes are usually *spur pruned*. Because of limited space, pruning is very severe. Depending on vine vigor, remove all but 3 to 6 of the strong canes developing in the third summer. These are cut to 2, 3 or 4 buds, depending on vigor as indicated by diameter of the cane. These will be the fruiting spurs. More spurs are left each year as the vine ages, up to 10 to 20 per head.

Spur pruning of cordon-trained vines

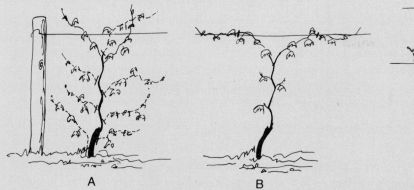
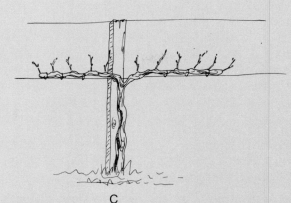

A. *Cordon* is a permanent, horizontal branch on a wall or trellis. In the second summer, cordon-trained vines are allowed to go unheaded. Two strong laterals—or the main shoot and a strong lateral—are chosen at a point 8 to 10 inches below the trellis wire. All other laterals as well as the main shoot are pinched back.

B. A bilateral cordon is the best method. Two canes are trained in opposite directions along the trellis. Keep ties at least a foot or more away from growing points.

C. During third dormant pruning of cordon-trained vines, fruiting spurs are retained along the cordon arm. They are spaced 8 to 12 inches apart from the arm bend to the tip. Spurs are cut to 2 to 3 buds, depending on the cane vigor. After cutting the spurs, retie and straighten the cordon arm. During the following summer, you may want to tie strong canes to an upper wire to avoid bending and twisting the cordon. Pinch back overly vigorous canes.

Cane-pruned vines

Vines to be *cane pruned* are cut in much the same fashion as head-trained vines, except canes with 6 to 18 buds are retained for fruiting. The number of buds depends upon vine and cane vigor. Select canes in a fan-shape rather than symmetrically around the trunk. In the third dormant season of the vine, 2 such canes are selected and tied to a trellis wire. All others are removed.

Kniffen-system training for cane-pruned vines

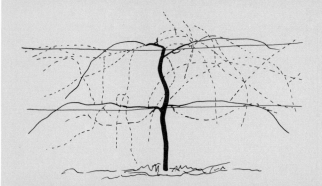
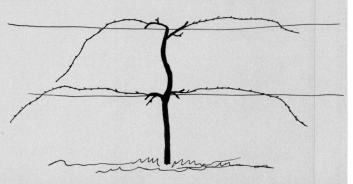

Train American grape vines by the *Kniffen system*. This is similar to cane pruning but with an additional upper wire. Tie the central cane to a stake to keep it straight. Head cane just above top wire. After the next season's growth, prune away all but 2 canes at each wire level. Cut them to 4 to 8 buds and tie them to the trellis wire.

In later years of Kniffen pruning, remove old fruiting canes and select vigorous canes for next year's fruiting. Tie them to the trellis and cut back to 6 to 10 buds, depending on their vigor. From the base of the old fruiting cane or the arms near the trunk, select 2 to 3 strong canes and cut these back to 2 to 3 buds each. Growth from these buds will supply next year's fruiting canes.

flavors. Red or black varieties rapidly change color. Green-berried varieties become yellowish or whitish. Maturity may be checked by tasting a few berries. To harvest, cut entire clusters from a vine rather than pulling them off.

Grapes that are to be dried into raisins should be allowed to stay on the vine longer to develop higher sugar content. However, be sure to pick early enough so grapes can dry before winter rains begin.

ABOUT THE CHARTS

• The grape is an easy-to-grow fruit that is widely adapted. But except in the commercial grape climates, varieties must be chosen with care.

• One way to avoid disappointment is to note the recommended zones for European and American grapes. Keep in mind that American grapes are hardy to −10°F (−24°C) and European grapes are hardy to 10°F (−12°C). In the cool areas of California, American grapes such as 'Senecca' and 'Diamond' may be more enjoyable than the European table grapes. European varieties generally need heat for sweetness. But some, such as 'Perlette' and 'Black Monukka', require less heat than the famous 'Thompson Seedless'.

• To maximize available heat, give vines a full quota of sunshine. Avoid shady planting sites.

For more on how to increase heat and resulting sweetness of grapes, see the information on microclimates, page 4.

EUROPEAN GRAPES

VARIETY	ZONE	SEASON	PRUNING	REMARKS
'BLACK MONUKKA'	2, 3, 5-13, 16-18.	Early midseason.	Cane or spur.	Medium, reddish purple, seedless berries. Fruits in large, loose clusters. One of the hardiest European grapes.
'BLACKROSE'	7-13, 16-18.	Early midseason.	Cane or spur.	Large, jet black clusters with a light gray bloom. Attractively formed and more flavorful than 'Ribier'. Vine vigorous and productive.
'CARDINAL'	7-13, 16-18.	Early.	Spur, short cane.	Large, dark red berries with firm texture. Slight muscat flavor. Vine very productive. Thin flower clusters to increase cluster size.
'CSABA' ('PEARL OF CSABA')	2, 4, 7.	Very early.	Spur.	Small to medium light gold berries with slight muscat flavor. Hardy vine often grown in central Washington.
'EMPEROR'	9, 12, 13.	Late.	Cane or spur.	Large, light red to reddish purple berries. Very firm and crisp. Thick skin. Very vigorous and productive vine. Ships and stores well. Leading California table grape.
'EXOTIC'	7-13, 17.	Early midseason.	Spur.	Large, round, black berries resemble 'Ribier'.
'FLAME SEEDLESS'	5, 7-13.	Early.	Cane or spur.	Medium, round, light pinkish red, seedless berry. Crisp, crunchy, sweet, very good flavor. Fruits in loose, medium-size, cone-shaped clusters. Can be left on vine for long period after ripening without loss of quality.
'ITALIA' ('ITALIAN MUSCAT')	7, 9, 11-13, 16-18.	Midseason.	Spur.	Large, golden berries with mild muscat flavor. Vine very productive and moderately vigorous.
'LADY FINGER'	7, 9, 11-13, 16-18.	Midseason.	Cane.	Large, very elongated berries, green to greenish white. Firm, tender, neutral flavor, low in acid, easily bruised. Two other grapes sold as 'Lady Finger': 'Olivette Blanche' and 'Rish Baba'.
'MALAGA, RED'	7, 9, 11-13, 16-18.	Early midseason.	Spur or cane.	Light reddish purple berries. Firm, with neutral flavor. Large, irregular clusters. Vine vigorous, good for an arbor.
'MALAGA, WHITE'	7, 9, 11-13, 16-18.	Midseason.	Spur or cane.	Large, greenish yellow berries with thick, tough skin. Flesh is sweet but less flavorful than 'Thompson Seedless'.
'MUSCAT' ('MUSCAT OF ALEXANDRIA')	7, 9, 11-13, 16-18.	Late midseason.	Spur or cane.	Large, round, dull green to yellowish berries. Famous for its strongly aromatic, musky character.
'OLIVETTE BLANCHE' ('LADY FINGER')	7, 9, 11-13, 16-18.	Late midseason.	Cane.	Long, slender berries are broader, darker green than those of 'Rish Baba'. Sometimes tinged pink. Grows in large, tight, cone-shaped clusters. More popular than 'Rish Baba'.
'PERLETTE'	2, 3, 4, 5, 7-13, 16-18.	Very early.	Spur or cane.	Medium berries in large, translucent yellow clusters. Distinctive flavor but less sweet than 'Thompson Seedless'. Requires less heat than most European grapes.
'RIBIER'	5, 7-13, 16-18.	Early midseason.	Spur.	Large, deep purplish black berries in loose clusters. Sweet and juicy but less flavorful than 'Blackrose'.
'RISH BABA' ('LADY FINGER')	7, 9, 11-13, 16-18.	Late midseason.	Cane.	Berries are long, slender, greenish white, sometimes slightly curved. Skin is tender and crisp. Slender and loose clusters.
'RUBY SEEDLESS' ('KING'S RUBY')	7-13, 17.	Late midseason.	Spur or cane.	Very large clusters of medium dark red, seedless berries. Sweet flavor, good for raisins. Vine very vigorous and productive.
'THOMPSON SEEDLESS'	7, 9, 11-13, 16-18.	Early to midseason.	Cane.	Small to medium, greenish white to golden yellow berries in large bunches. Sweet but mild flavor. Planted in many areas, but requires heat for best quality.
'TOKAY'	7-13.	Late midseason.	Spur or cane.	Large, oval, brilliant red to dark red berries. Crisp texture with distinctive, wine-like flavor. Reaches perfection in moderately warm areas such as Napa Valley, Hollister and Gilroy in California.

Fall brings vivid colors to grapevines in California's Napa Valley.

'Niabell' grape

AMERICAN AND AMERICAN-HYBRID GRAPES

VARIETY	ZONE	SEASON	PRUNING	REMARKS
'CACO'	1, 2, 5.	Midseason to late.	Cane.	Light red berries have thick skin. Aromatic, wine-like flavor.
'CAMPBELL EARLY' ('ISLAND BELLE')	1-6, 10, 11.	Early.	Cane.	Dark purple berries. Moderately vigorous vine. 'Concord' type, grows well where climate is too cool for 'Concord'.
'CATAWBA'	2, 7, 8, 10, 11.	Late.	Cane.	Large, round, deep coppery red berries with distinctive flavor. Aromatic, wine-like and slightly musty.
'CONCORD'	1, 2, 4, 5, 7, 8, 10-12.	Midseason to late in Northwest.	Cane.	Very large, oblong, blue-black, seeded grape. Sweet flavor. Grows well in inland, coastal climates such as Sonoma and Napa. Not adapted to Puget Sound or hot summer areas. Tolerates cold. Resists powdery mildew.
'DELAWARE'	2-5.	Early midseason.	Cane.	American hybrid. Small, round berries. Light red color with lilac bloom.
'FREDONIA'	1-6.	Early.	Cane.	Black berries larger than 'Concord'. Tough, thick skin. Vigorous vine is handsome in appearance.
'GOLDEN MUSCAT'	1, 2, 4--16.	Early midseason.	Cane.	American hybrid. Yellowish green berries have muscat flavor. Vigorous vine. Grows in coastal areas of California.
'HIMROD'	1-5.	Very early.	Cane.	American hybrid. Greenish white grape produces low yield and poor set. Often winter damaged. Loose bunch in Northwest.
'INTERLAKEN SEEDLESS'	1-5.	Very early.	Cane.	American hybrid. Greenish white berries are small, crisp and firm. Seedless, with excellent flavor. High vigor, low yield and loose bunch. Berry size varies in the Northwest. Recommended table grape for the Northwest.
'NIABELL'	5, 7-12.	Early.	Spur or cane.	Large, blue-black, seeded fruit, similar to 'Concord'. Vigorous and productive. Excellent arbor grape. Grows and fruits well even in shade. Tolerates cold, resistant to powdery mildew. Weak rooted.
'NIAGARA'	2, 4, 5, 10, 11.	Midseason.	Cane.	Large, light green to white berries have sweet, tangy flavor. Vigorous vine is excellent for arbors. Needs warmth to ripen. Resists powdery mildew.
'ROMULUS'	2, 4, 5.	Late midseason.	Cane.	American hybrid. Medium to large, seedless fruit is high quality. White to yellow skin. Vigorous grower with medium winter hardiness. Fruits in small clusters. Fruit similar to 'Interlaken'.
'SCHUYLER'	2-5.	Early.	Spur or cane.	American hybrid. Large clusters of blue, medium-size berries. Very juicy and sweet. Low yield. Maturity time varies in the Northwest.
'SENECA'	1-6.	Very early.	Cane.	Large uniform berry. White, aromatic and sweet with thin, tender skin. Sometimes produces loose bunches, especially in Northwest. Susceptible to powdery mildew. Medium-high vigor, good set.
'VAN BUREN'	1, 2, 4, 5.	Very early.	Cane.	'Concord' type. Uniformly bunched grapes. Good vigor, heavy yield, good set in the Northwest. Excellent table and juice grape.
'WORDEN'	1, 2, 4, 5.	Midseason.	Cane.	Large, round, purplish black berries. High, 'Concord' quality but ripens two weeks earlier.

Red raspberies ready for harvest.

Raspberry

Raspberries are ideally suited to Zones 2 to 4 in the Pacific Northwest. They also do well in portions of Zones 6 to 8 and 10 in California where coastal influence moderates summer temperatures. In spite of climatic limitations, raspberries often produce acceptable crops of quality fruit in many other regions.

Raspberries come in a wide range of colors: red, yellow, purple and black. They are the hardiest cane fruit but should be heavily mulched during winter in Zone 1. Raspberries differ from other *brambles*, species of *Rubus*, in that the fruit separates from the core when picked.

VITAL STATISTICS—RASPBERRY

	Red	Black
Height at maturity (feet)		
Unpruned	6-10	6-7
Pruned	6-10	4-5
Spread at maturity with	Indefinite	
no competition (feet)	suckers	6
Recommended planting		
distance (feet)		
Between plants	2-4	
Between rows	6-7	
Years to reach bearing age	2	2
Life expectancy (years)	6-30	6-30
Pollinizer required	No	No
Good for espalier	No	No
Good for containers	Yes	Yes

PRUNING

Raspberries can be divided into two types by bearing habit: *standard* and *everbearer*. Canes of both are *biennial*—living two years—but canes of standard raspberries don't fruit until the second year. Everbearers produce fruit on ends of heartiest canes late in the first season, and laterally on the same canes early in the second season. With both types, canes die after fruiting in the second season. New canes start as shoots from the base of an old cane or as suckers from root-like, underground stems.

By pruning out all canes of an everbearing raspberry after it has fruited the first year, you can limit the harvest to one, late-spring picking. This pruning also eliminates the need for staking or trellising, and has been very successful in warm climates. Otherwise, follow the same pruning procedures as for standard varieties. 'Heritage' and 'September' are recommended everbearing varieties.

Every bud on a raspberry cane can produce fruit. Because of this, there isn't much difference in production between canes 5 feet or more tall and canes headed at 4-1/2 feet or lower. Lower buds produce larger, later-maturing fruit than buds near end of cane. Heading forces lower buds to produce and can also eliminate the need for trellising. In cold areas, delay heading until spring. Absence of new growth will tell you canes have been damaged by cold and should be removed.

SOIL, NUTRIENT AND WATER REQUIREMENTS

Cultural requirements of raspberries are identical to blackberries. Refer to page 138.

HARVESTING AND STORAGE

Pick raspberries at the peak of ripeness, just as fruit develops full color and characteristic flavor and aroma. Raspberries deteriorate rapidly and can be held for only a few days in the refrigerator. Eat them fresh right after picking, freeze or make jams or preserves.

These red raspberries are supported by two parallel, horizontal wires. See illustration on page 151.

Raspberry pruning

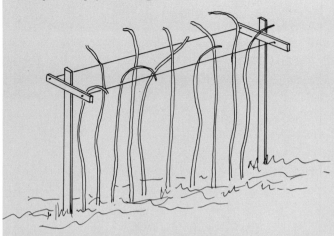

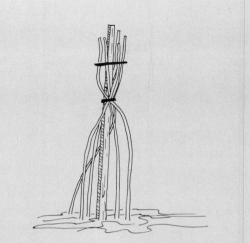

Red raspberries are frequently supported by two parallel, horizontal wires about 18 inches apart held by crossbars. Headed canes are pulled up between the wires. With a one-wire trellis no crossbar is used and canes must be tied to wire.

Single red raspberry plants can be trained to a single stake.

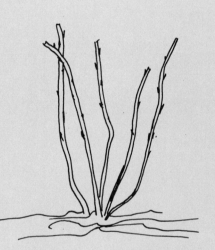

Black raspberries before and after pruning. Black and purple raspberries are not as vigorous as red raspberries and are usually pruned heavily and left freestanding.

Red raspberries can be left freestanding by heading back below 4-1/2 feet. Canes any higher may bend so fruit rubs against ground.

Permanent trellis for raspberries or any cane fruit should be strong and built to last. As shown above, a trellis can also be attractive.

RED RASPBERRIES

VARIETY	ZONE	HARVEST SEASON	FRUIT AND PLANT	REMARKS
'CANBY'	3, 4, 6-8, 10.	Early.	Large, bright red fruit has thick flesh, delicious flavor. Canes are completely free of thorns. Exceptionally vigorous plant.	One of the best red raspberries. Excellent dessert berry and superior shipper. Good soil drainage required.
'HERITAGE'	2-4, 6-8, 10.	Late.	Large, dark fruit. Mild flavor. Plant is sturdy with upright canes. Usually bears first season after planting.	Everbearing. Large crop in fall. Cold hardy in central and eastern Washington.
'MEEKER'	3, 4, 6-8, 10.	Midseason to late.	Large, bright red fruit is thimble shaped. Firm with superior flavor. Long-lived. Plant is vigorous, suckers well.	Good for freezing. Developed by Washington State University. Excellent home garden variety.
'NEWBURGH'	2-4, 6-8, 10.	Midseason.	Large, attractive, bright red fruit is shallow cupped, firm, with very good flavor. Not as good quality as 'Meeker' or 'Willamette'. Plant is highly resistant to freezing.	Good home and market berry. Ships and stores well. Quite hardy. One of the best in adverse climate conditions. Very easy to grow. Cold hardy in central and north Washington and eastern British Columbia.
'SEPTEMBER'	6-8, 10.	Late.	Medium to large, bright red fruit, good flavor. Plant has vigorous growth.	Hardy. One of the best fall-bearing varieties. Bears later than 'Heritage'. Matures too late in Oregon and Washington.
'SOUTHLAND'	6-8, 10-15.	Early.	Medium, light red fruit is firm and does not crumble. Slightly acid flavor. High quality. Plant has moderate vigor. Hardy and disease resistant.	Originated in North Carolina. Extends adaptability into warmer areas, where it produces a fall crop. Probably best in southern California but might do well in northern California.
'WILLAMETTE'	2-4, 6-8, 10.	Midseason.	Largest raspberry. Dark red, firm and rather long. Vigorous and productive plant. Canes are medium to large, tall, straight and spiny. Suckers freely.	Principal commercial variety. Use fresh in pies or jam. Best for freezing and canning. Ships well. Large crop in summer; new canes produce a second crop in fall. Recommended for western Washington, Yakima Valley and west to coast. Not recommended for hot, dry climates.

BLACK RASPBERRIES

VARIETY	ZONE	HARVEST SEASON	FRUIT AND PLANT	REMARKS
'CUMBERLAND'	2-8, 10.	Late.	Large, firm fruit. High quality. Vigorous plant.	More seeds than other varieties. Use fresh in jams and jellies. Adapted to cold regions.
'MUNGER'	2-8, 10.	Midseason.	Large fruit, plump and firm, with sweet, delicious flavor. Free from crumbling or seediness. Plant has stout canes. Very hardy and disease resistant.	Best blackcap-type raspberry. No other black has been grown as extensively or is as popular in all berry-producing areas. Excellent for preserving, satisfactory for freezing.

'Sequoia' strawberry

Strawberry

Strawberries can be grown in nearly every part of the West. There are two types of common strawberry—*spring-bearing* varieties and *everbearing* varieties. A third type of strawberry, *fraise de bois*, is usually sold as a novelty.

Spring-bearing strawberries depend on long winter nights to trigger flowering. They produce one heavy crop over a short season in spring. In California or the Southwest, this crop comes in April and May. In the Northwest and colder climates it appears later in spring and early summer. In some areas there may be a light, fall crop. This is especially likely in coastal areas of California.

Everbearing strawberries do not depend on long nights to initiate flowering and are often referred to as *day neutral.* They flower and fruit throughout the growing season but do not bear heavily at any one time. For this reason, many plants are needed to provide sufficient harvests. An advantage of everbearing strawberries is that even though the first flowers may be harmed by frost, more flowers and fruit will follow. This is especially helpful in regions with short growing seasons.

Fraise de bois, or European strawberries, are often available as seed from catalogs and nurseries. They bear very small but delicious fruit on plants that do not produce runners. They are ideal for growing in containers.

PLANTING

Strawberries are usually planted in fall or spring. Fall planting is preferred in California and the Southwest except in the coldest winter areas. Plants in cold regions are put in the ground in early spring as soon as soil can be worked. In the Northwest, strawberries can also be planted in fall if plants will be established before cold winter weather. Mulching in winter will prevent alternate freezing and thawing of soil and resulting cold damage to plants.

Strawberries are usually purchased bare root and require special care when planted. First, trim off any old leaves and cut roots to about 4 inches long. Do not let roots dry out.

Take care in setting plants in the soil. If strawberries are planted too high the roots will dry out. If planted too low, with soil over the crown, they are likely to rot.

Normally, strawberries are planted according to a plan. Because they multiply by runners, they can be

VITAL STATISTICS—STRAWBERRY		
	Standard	**Dwarf**
Height at maturity (feet)		
Unpruned	1/2-1	N/A
Pruned	1/2-1	
Spread at maturity with		
no competition (feet)	1/2-1	
Recommended planting		
distance (feet)		
Between plants	1	
Between rows	12-15	
Years to reach bearing age	1	
Life expectancy (years)	1-10*	
Pollinizer required	No	
Good for espalier	No	
Good for containers	Yes	

*Low yields, poor vigor and greater likelihood of pest and disease problems after 3 years.

N/A = Not Available

Plastic mulch keeps strawberries away from soil-borne insects and conserves soil moisture.

Planting bare-root strawberries

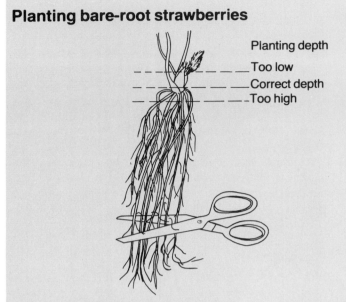

Planting depth
— Too low
— Correct depth
— Too high

It is important to plant strawberries at correct height—not too high or too low. Trim roots before planting to stimulate growth.

Strawberry spacing

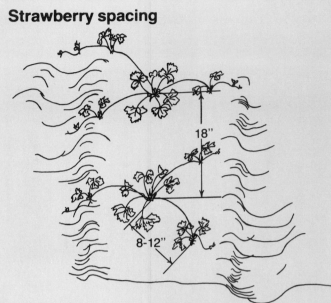

18"

8-12"

Strawberries are easy to water when planted on mounded beds. Properly spaced runners will soon fill out bed.

planted at wide intervals and runners will fill in the gaps. Usually only selected or properly positioned runners are allowed to root because overcrowding will reduce yield. Runners transplanted to new areas should come only from healthy beds. Viruses carried by infected mother plants are transmitted to its runners.

Fall-planted strawberries should not be allowed to flower or fruit until the following spring. Pick off any flowers that form. Spring-planted, everbearing strawberries should not be allowed to flower and fruit until midsummer. This gives the plant time to become established and results in a bigger fall crop.

The life of a strawberry plant varies somewhat with region and climate. In a coastal area, it seldom lasts more than three or four years. Inland, it may last considerably longer. Everbearing varieties do best if replanted every year or at least every other year. Older plants of either type are healthier and more productive if runners are cut off.

Strawberries are perfectly suited to containers. This is especially advantageous in desert regions where they can be difficult to grow because of salt content in soils and water. They can be grown in raised beds, hanging baskets, vertical planters, strawberry pots and strawberry barrels.

SOIL, NUTRIENT AND WATER REQUIREMENTS

Strawberries do well in a variety of soils, except in soils containing high concentrations of salts. Do not confuse stunting and leaf burn, symptoms of excessive salts, with nitrogen deficiency. See page 33.

Because they have shallow roots, strawberries must have a constant supply of moisture. Never allow plants to dry out. Mulches, especially plastic, are very helpful in conserving moisture. They also help to keep the berries clean and away from soil-borne insects.

Strawberries must have good soil drainage. Soggy soils promote root rots. Red stele is an especially troublesome root rot common to soggy soils and older plantings. Grow resistant varieties or plant in containers or raised beds.

Strawberries have deep green foliage when they are growing vigorously. They benefit from applications of nitrogen. Use about 1/4-pound of actual nitrogen per 100 square feet of bed. Divide this into two applications—one in spring and the second after the first crop.

'Olympus' strawberry

HARVESTING AND STORAGE

Strawberries must be picked as soon as they reach maturity. This is indicated by the typical red color of the fruit. If they are allowed to remain on the plant they will deteriorate. They also draw energy from the plant, which could be used to ripen more berries. Remove decayed fruit from plants at each picking.

Fruit ripen rapidly. You may need to harvest every other day in warm areas or at least weekly in cool locations.

Berries are usually picked with the *calyx,* the green, leafy shoulder, still attached to the fruit. If berries are to be used immediately, calyx can be pulled free, eliminating extra work later.

STRAWBERRIES

VARIETY	CLIMATE ADAPTABILITY	FRUIT AND PLANT	REMARKS
'BENTON'	Excellent performance in western Washington and Oregon's Willamette Valley.	Fruit large, soft, excellent fresh. Plant has erect habit. Very productive. Produces many runners.	New variety. Too tender for shipping, but makes good preserves. Fair sliced and frozen. Good vigor. Virus tolerant and resistant to mildew and root diseases. Used for local fresh market.
'FORT LARAMIE'	Cold hardy if well mulched. Excellent in mountain, coastal and other cool-winter areas.	Everbearing. fruit very firm and large. Good yield over long season. Excellent flavor. Better than 'Gem' or 'Ogallala'.	Fruit good for freezing. Very good dessert fruit. Produces more berries at one time than any other everbearer and is second to fruit in spring. Recovers quickly after blight or hailstorms. Foliage susceptible to mildew.
'FRESNO'	Tolerates some salinity. Suggested variety for San Joaquin Valley, southern California and California coastal valleys.	Fruit large, firm but not as firm as 'Tioga'. Very productive.	Low chilling requirement. Highly subject to verticillium wilt.
'GEM'	Extra hardy.	Everbearing. Fruit small, glossy red. Plant very hardy.	Tart flavor, good dessert quality. Resistant to wilt, yellows. Being replaced by everbearers 'Fort Laramie', 'Ozark Beauty' and 'Quinalt'.
'HOOD'	Similar to 'Northwest'.	Fruit large, medium firm. Excellent color and flavor. Plant has good vigor, erect habit.	Crop ripens over a short period. Makes excellent preserves. Fair when sliced and frozen. Resistant to red stele and mildew. Not virus tolerant. For many years was leading commercial cultivar in Oregon and is still a very popular home garden variety.
'NORTHWEST'	Formerly popular in Washington and Oregon. Lacks winter hardiness.	Fruit medium size, red flesh. Compact habit.	Good quality for eating fresh, freezing or preserving. Resistant to virus diseases. Not resistant to red stele. Susceptible to leaf spot and mildew. Needs good drainage.
'OGALLALA'	Very cold tolerant. Blossoms fairly frost resistant.	Everbearing. Fruit dark red, soft, medium size. Vigorous grower.	Pleasant flavor and good for freezing. Being replaced by everbearers 'Fort Laramie', 'Ozark Beauty' and 'Quinalt'.
'OLYMPUS'	Good in southwestern Washington and northwestern Oregon.	Fruit medium size, very productive. Tart, medium-firm, good red color. Plant has poor runner production. Fruit hidden by foliage.	Produces few runners so plants are well adapted to hill system. Needs constant moisture or fruit size and vigor are reduced. Good red stele resistance, but moderate virus resistance.
'OZARK BEAUTY'	Wide climate adaptability. Tolerates much cold. Does well in most cooler California climates, excellent in central part of state.	Everbearing. Fruit large, often elongated, with firm flesh and skin. Produces many runners. Vigorous and productive.	Very sweet, good for freezing. Very good dessert fruit. Resists leaf spot and scorch. Late harvest season for everbearer, but well worth the wait. Good for hanging baskets.
'QUINALT'	Does fine in inland valleys, with wide range of adaptability to most central California climates. Best flavor at 2,000-3,000 feet elevation.	Everbearing. Fruit very large, soft texture, tender skin. Vigorous, compact growth. Produces many runners.	Sweetest of the everbearers, excellent for freezing. Most disease-resistant everbearer. Main crop from crown, also produces some fruit on rooted runners.
'RAINIER'	Best in Northwest, west of Cascade Mountains.	Fruit very large, very firm, uniformly red, rich flavor. Produces many runners.	A standard of quality in frozen packs. Caps hard to remove. Some resistance to viruses, fair resistance to root rot, mildew.
'SEQUOIA'	Grows best in inland valleys, desert and warm-winter areas. Performs extremely well in southern California climates. Performs like an everbearer in mild climates.	Fruit very large, soft flesh, tender skin. Medium firmness. Plant bears for many months. Very productive.	Outstanding flavor. Good for freezing, excellent dessert quality. A fine choice for home gardens and U-pick farms where fruit can be harvested when mature and flavorful.
'SHUKSAN'	Very cold hardy. Tolerant of alkalinity. Especially suited to northwest Washington and British Columbia.	Fruit large, medium-firm, dark red, good flavor. Plant has good vigor, moderately productive. Low growing.	Excellent color and flavor for freezing. Makes very good preserves. Some resistance to diseases.
'TIOGA'	Excellent performer in warm-winter areas—desert and inland valleys.	Fruit large, sweet, very firm texture and skin. Plant very productive.	Important commercial variety because it ships well. Average resistance to strawberry diseases. Most prolific of spring-bearers. Highest yield second year or if planted the previous summer. A fine producer once established.

Nuts

Nut trees serve as dual-purpose plants. Most are large, beautiful shade trees and provide bountiful harvests. Unfortunately, many people forget about nuts and keep popular fruit such as apples, pears or strawberries in mind when they plant their fruit garden. Most nut trees are large and require a considerable amount of room to grow. But some such as almonds and pistachios are small and fit perfectly into nearly any garden scheme.

Consider larger nut trees as functional parts of your landscape, rather than merely something to be fitted into the fruit garden. For example, plant a pecan instead of a sycamore or ash. In addition to lush shade, you will enjoy a nutritious harvest that is long lasting and easy to store.

Recent breeding has developed many nut varieties with exceptional characteristics. Walnut breeding at the University of California is aimed at developing walnuts that produce heavy crops of thin-shelled, meaty nuts late in the season. Late-maturing nuts are able to escape many pests and diseases that plague early-ripening walnuts.

The USDA Pecan Field Station in Brownwood, Texas has introduced the Indian series of pecan varieties. Until recently, pecans were limited to the hottest desert areas of the Southwest. Varieties with Indian names such as 'Choctaw', 'Cherokee' and 'Mohawk' are now being grown successfully throughout the San Joaquin and Sacramento Valleys in California.

There is increased interest in many nuts that have been in cultivation for years. A large-fruited hybrid chestnut, 'Colossal', developed by Charles Parsons of

Nuts: Where they will grow

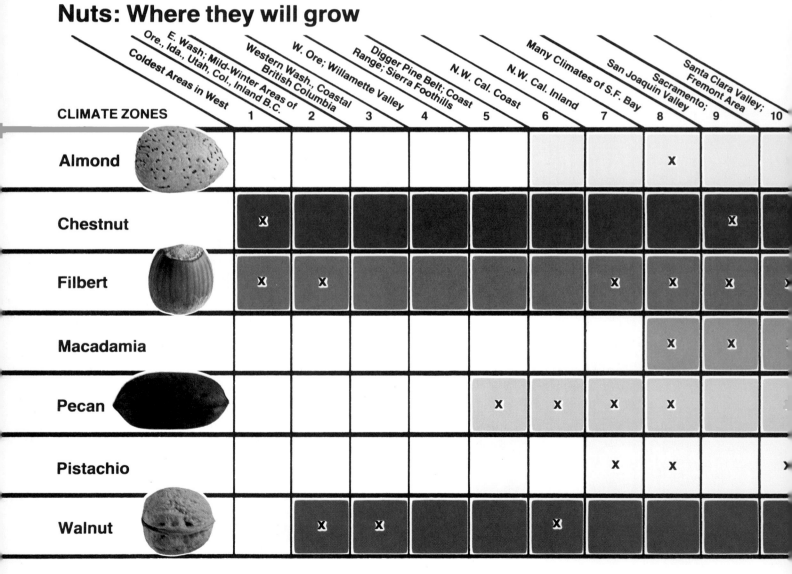

CLIMATE ZONES	Coldest Areas in West	1	2	3	4	5	6	7	8	9	10
Almond									X		
Chestnut		X								X	
Filbert		X	X					X	X	X	
Macadamia									X	X	
Pecan						X	X	X	X		
Pistachio								X	X		
Walnut			X	X			X				

X — See fruit description for special cultural requirements, planting site selection or variety adaptation needed to be successful in this zone.

Nevada City, California is becoming available to home gardeners. Filberts, *Corylus* species, are being planted with renewed interest in many parts of the California foothills.

As with all fruit, pay close attention to climate adaptation when selecting a nut tree. Many nuts can be grown as ornamentals out of their area of adaptation but may not produce crops. Some nuts such as almonds and pecans require long, hot summers to fill their shells. If you grow them in areas without ample heat, the shells will be empty or partially filled.

Many nuts have to be dried and/or hulled before they can be stored. The *hull* is the leathery covering over the shell that encloses the kernel or meat.

Before selecting and planting the tree, consider how the fruit will be harvested. Some nuts must be knocked or shaken from the tree; others fall naturally.

A sign of ripeness in macadamias is when the husk splits before nuts drop to ground.

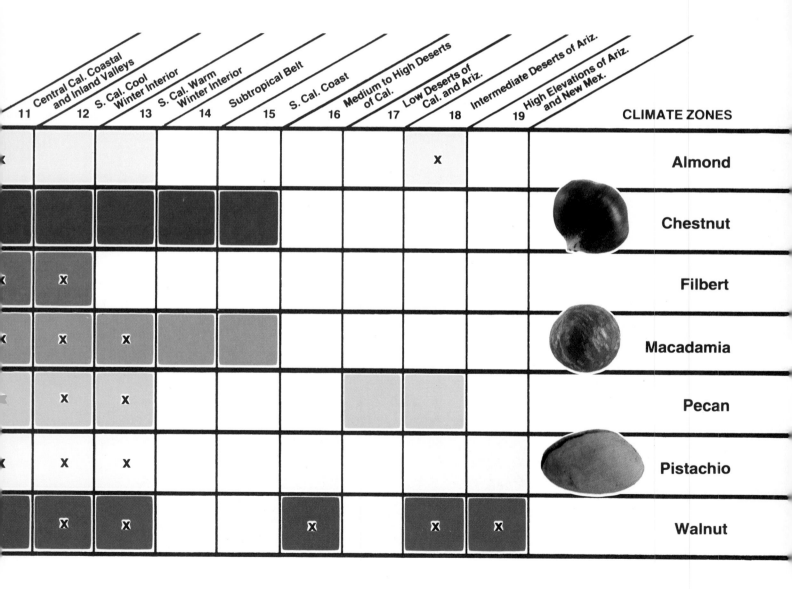

CLIMATE ZONES

11 Central Cal. Coastal and Inland Valleys	12 S. Cal. Cool Winter Interior	13 S. Cal. Warm Winter Interior	14 Subtropical Belt	15 S. Cal. Coast	16 Medium to High Deserts of Cal.	17 Low Deserts of Cal. and Ariz.	18 Intermediate Deserts of Ariz. and New Mex.	19 High Elevations of Ariz. and New Mex.	
X							X		**Almond**
◼	◼	◼	◼	◼					**Chestnut**
X	X								**Filbert**
X	X	X	◼	◼					**Macadamia**
X	X	X			◼	◼			**Pecan**
X	X	X							**Pistachio**
◼	X	X		X			X	X	**Walnut**

Walnuts

Chinese Chestnuts

Butternuts

Almonds

Pecans

Filberts

Macadamias

Pistachios

Almond blossoms

Almond

Prunus dulcis dulcis

Almonds are the earliest-blooming of all deciduous fruit or nut trees. They should be grown only in regions where there is relative freedom from frosts during blooming period and early spring when nuts begin to form. Small, immature nuts are even more frost sensitive than blossoms.

Almonds are best adapted to areas with warm, dry summers. These are needed for nuts to properly mature. Nuts will not reach maturity if summers are cool and humidity is high.

VITAL STATISTICS—ALMOND		
	Standard	**Dwarf**
Height at maturity (feet)		
Unpruned	40	8-10
Pruned	25	6-8
Spread at maturity with		
no competition (feet)	30-32	6-8
Recommended planting		
distance (feet)	24-30	10-12
Years to reach bearing age	3	3
Life expectancy (years)	50	50
Chilling requirement	Low to medium	
Pollinizer required	Yes	No
Good for espalier	No	No
Good for containers	No	Yes

POLLINATION

With a few exceptions such as 'All-in-One' and 'Garden Prince', almonds require cross-pollination with another variety to produce a crop. Suitable pollinizers for each variety are included in the variety chart.

SOIL, NUTRIENT AND WATER REQUIREMENTS

Almonds do well in most soils as long as soil is well drained. They do not tolerate salty soils. Trees are quite drought resistant once established but produce better with regular watering. If trees make 8 to 15 inches of new growth each year, they do not need to be fertilized. If they are slow to grow, trees will respond to nitrogen applied at a rate of 1-1/2 pounds actual nitrogen per tree per year.

PRUNING

Prune young almond trees to a vase shape. See the pruning section, page 49. Nuts are borne on spurs that remain fruitful for about 5 years. If an abundant almond crop is your goal, prune with thinning cuts to replace branches that have spurs past their prime. Extensive pruning is not usually required. A few large cuts will normally do the job.

HARVESTING AND STORAGE

Harvest almonds after hulls have cracked open and are partially dried. Nuts can be knocked or shaken from tree. Allowing them to fall naturally takes weeks and risks rain damage.

Remove hulls and place nuts in sun to dry for one to two days. When kernels rattle in their shells they are dried enough. A properly dried kernel will snap in two rather than bend.

Almonds in the shell will keep up to six months stored in a cool, dry, well-ventilated place.

Almond

ABOUT THE CHART

● Almond is a useful tree—primarily for its delicious nuts. Commercially it is grown from Redding, California, southward to the San Francisco Bay Area. It can be grown in home gardens over a much wider area. The varieties most recommended are 'Nonpareil', 'Ne Plus Ultra', 'Mission' ('Texas') and 'Thompson'.

● Through grafting, you can have a tree that will produce not only almonds but peaches and nectarines as well. Grafting 'Redhaven', 'Nectar', 'Springtime' and 'Fay Elberta' to an almond variety will give you fruit and nuts from early May to mid-September.

● Even almond shells are useful. In almond-growing areas like Butte County, California, they are crushed and used as an attractive, sand-colored mulch. Unlike walnut shells and leaves, almond shells are nontoxic.

ALMONDS
Average picking dates at Dave Wilson Nursery, Hughson, California, just south of Modesto.

	Aug.	Sept.	Oct.
Nonpareil			
Price			
Ne Plus Ultra			
Peerless			
Thompson			
Merced			
Garden Prince			
Texas (Mission)			
Carmel			
All-in-One			
Hall			

ALMONDS

VARIETY	ZONE	HARVEST SEASON	POLLINIZER	FRUIT AND TREE	REMARKS
'ALL-IN-ONE'	7-13, 18.	Late.	Self-fruitful.	'Nonpareil'-type nut. Very good to excellent quality, with soft shell and sweet flavor. Shell is well sealed. Tree is small, vigorous, medium upright. Bears heavily.	Valuable as an ornamental with showy, white blossoms that bloom late. Bloom overlaps 'Nonpareil' and 'Texas'.
'CARMEL'	7-13, 18.	Late.	'Nonpareil' 'Merced' 'Price'	Kernel is small, thick and long, with soft shell and good flavor. Small to medium tree produces early and heavily.	Regular producer of small nuts. Blooms midseason.
'GARDEN PRINCE'	7-13, 18.	Late.	Self-fruitful.	Medium kernel is sweet 'Nonpareil' type. Well sealed with soft shell. Tree is a genetic dwarf, approximately 8 to 10 feet tall at maturity.	Productive. Good for container planting. Blooms with 'Nonpareil'. This variety and 'All-in-One' are the only almonds that do not need pollinizers.
'HALL' ('HALL'S HARDY')	7-13, 18.	Late.	Partially self-fruitful or 'Texas'.	Good-size nut with a hard shell. Bitter flavor, which some find objectionable. Tree is hardy and bears heavily.	Blooms late. Good for late-frost regions. Partially self-fruitful.
'MERCED'	7-13, 18.	Midseason to late.	'Nonpareil' 'Carmel'	Shell is paper-thin, well sealed. Small, broad kernels. Tree is small to medium, vigorous and upright.	Blooms midseason. Produces heavily. Cross between 'Texas' and 'Nonpareil'.
'NE PLUS ULTRA'	7-13, 18.	Midseason.	'Peerless' 'Nonpareil' 'Price'	Nut is large, long and broad with soft shell. Kernel is average quality. Tree is small to medium and spreading.	Blooms early. Subject to frost damage. Relatively low chilling requirement.
'NONPAREIL'	7-13, 18.	Early.	'Ne Plus Ultra' 'Carmel' 'Price' 'All-in-One'	Large nut with soft, paper-thin shell. Flat, light-colored kernel with excellent, sweet flavor. Large tree.	Leading almond in California. Easily harvested and hulled. Blooms midseason but subject to bud failure in hot climates.
'PEERLESS'	8-13, 17, 18.	Early.	'Nonpareil' 'Ne Plus Ultra'	Very large nut with hard shell. Kernel is medium size, good quality. Tree is medium and spreading.	Early bloomer. Susceptible to late frost. Low chilling requirement.
'PRICE' ('PRICE CLUSTER')	7-13, 18.	Midseason.	'Nonpareil' 'All-in-One' 'Merced' 'Carmel'	Soft shell like 'Nonpareil' but plump and poorly sealed. Medium tree is a heavy bearer.	Nuts borne in clusters along branches. Blooms midseason.
'TEXAS' ('MISSION')	7-13, 18.	Late.	'Thompson' 'All-in-One'	Nut is small and round with a hard, well-sealed shell. Slightly bitter flavor. Tree is large, upright and vigorous.	Second most important almond in California. Late blooming, so it is safe for late-frost areas.
'THOMPSON'	7-13, 18.	Midseason.	'Texas' 'All-in-One'	Small nut with soft shell, well sealed and paper-thin. Good quality kernel is plump with a mild, bitter flavor. Tree is medium size.	Late blooming. Pollinizes best with 'Texas' in late-frost areas.

Burred hulls and toothed leaves of chestnut.

Chestnut
Castanea species

Chestnuts grow into spectacular, ornamental shade trees with a minimum of care. As long as they are given drainage and adequate attention when young, they are bothered by few pests or diseases and require little care. Chestnuts are widely adapted to Zones 2 to 15, but they can also be grown in Zone 1 to elevations of 3,500 to 4,500 feet.

Chestnuts grow from 40 to 100 feet high and spread 60 feet wide. Long, toothed, green leaves turn golden yellow in fall. Flowers grow in long, slender clusters. They completely cover the tree with a sweet-smelling, golden yellow crown in spring. Flowers are followed by spiny burrs, which contain one to three nuts.

VARIETIES

Four species of chestnut have been propagated and hybridized in the West.

Castanea sativa, European chestnut, is the best commercial and ornamental tree. It is more heat tolerant than other chestnuts and is the best for southern California. Large, sweet nuts are the ones most commonly seen in supermarkets. They dry easily and store well. Trees are resistant to oak root fungus, the only disease that threatens chestnuts.

C. mollisima, Chinese chestnut, usually produces large nuts at three years of age. Nuts do not store well. It is the smallest of the four chestnut trees, reaching about 40 feet high. Trees are susceptible to oak root fungus.

C. dentata, American chestnut, was virtually eliminated in its native eastern United States by chestnut blight. This disease does not occur west of the Rocky Mountains. American chestnut is the tallest-growing chestnut, reaching over 100 feet high. Nuts are small and sweet, taking about 100 to make a pound. Trees are resistant to oak root fungus.

C. crenata, Japanese chestnut, bears the largest nuts. However, they are inferior in quality. Trees are susceptible to oak root fungus.

These four species have been propagated and hybridized by many nurserymen in the past. Numerous named varieties have been sold. Felix Gillet of Nevada City, California, is recognized as the pioneer in chestnut hybridizing. With his successor, Charles Parsons, they introduced and propagated such varieties as 'Lyon', 'Combale', 'Castiva', 'Colossal' and 'Large American Sweet'. Unfortunately, due to lost records, only 'Colossal' has been located and positively identified.

All chestnut trees are normally propagated as seedlings, with two trees needed for cross-pollination. In recent years no named varieties have been propagated. It is doubtful any named hybrids other than 'Colossal' can be produced until identification of trees is made positive. Even the Chinese chestnut is available in nurseries only on rare occasions.

'Colossal' has just recently become available through seedling propagation by the Dave Wilson Nursery, Hughson, California. Their address can be found on page 189. Seed of 'Colossal' are provided to the nursery by Bob Bergantz, Placerville, California.

'Colossal' is a European hybrid with Chinese and Japanese traits. It is a superb commercial and ornamental tree with a fast growth rate. Nuts are large, about 12 to a pound. They peel easily and dry and store well.

HARVESTING AND STORAGE

Chestnuts drop to the ground in late summer or fall. They should be gathered every day. Nuts can be eaten fresh. To store for later use, remove nuts from burrs and dry in the sun. On hot days, dry nuts in shade rather than direct sunlight. Store nuts in a cool, dry place to prevent them from becoming rancid or moldy. Properly stored nuts will keep for several months.

VITAL STATISTICS—CHESTNUT

	Chinese	European
Height at maturity (feet)		
Unpruned	30-40	50
Pruned	20	25
Spread at maturity with		
no competition (feet)	30-50	40-50
Recommended planting		
distance (feet)	25-30	40
Years to reach bearing age	3-4	4
Life expectancy (years)	50	50
Chilling requirement	Low	Low
Pollinizer required	Yes	Yes
Good for espalier	No	No
Good for containers	No	No

Left: Filbert blossom cluster. Right: Nearly mature nut.

Filbert

Corylus avellana

Filbert varieties are derived from the wild hazelnut. They are attractive in form and foliage and small in size. Although they are best adapted to western Oregon and Washington, filberts are worthy garden plants in Zones 1-12, even though crops may be light and unpredictable.

In California, filberts bear best in the foothills of the Sierra Nevada between 1,500 and 3,000 feet. Some winterkill of branches may occur at higher elevations. Flowers are damaged at 15° F (−10° C). Because filberts blossom late winter to early spring, frost damage is a problem in colder areas.

VITAL STATISTICS—FILBERT		
	Standard	**Dwarf**
Height at maturity (feet)		
Unpruned	20	N/A
Pruned	15	
Spread at maturity with no competition (feet)	15-20	
Recommended planting distance (feet)	20	
Years to reach bearing age	4	
Life expectancy (years)	50	
Chilling requirement	Medium to high	
Pollinizer required	Yes	
Good for espalier	No	
Good for containers	No	

N/A = Not Available

Trees grow well in hot, dry valleys but often fail to set fruit. Because of a high chilling requirement, filberts are most successful in the coldest areas of the north and central coastal valleys. They are not recommended for southern California or desert areas.

POLLINATION

Filberts must be planted near another variety for cross-pollination. Pollinizing varieties must produce male flowers at the same time fruiting varieties produce female flowers. Proven pollinizers are listed in the following variety descriptions. Climate variations will influence your success with each variety.

VARIETIES

1. **'Barcelone'**—Perhaps the best variety. Excellent nuts. Slow-growing tree. Pollinized by 2, 3 or 4 (below).

2. **'Du Chilly'**—Large, long nuts of good quality. Slow to drop and difficult to husk. Pollinized by 4.

3. **'Royal'**—Large, early nuts. Pollinized by 4.

4. **'Daviana'**—Long nuts. Excellent pollinizer. Pollinized by 1 or 5.

5. **'Hall's Giant', 'Bolwyer'**—Large nuts. Pollinized by 1, 3 or 4.

PRUNING

Filberts are easiest to care for when allowed to grow naturally as a shrub. In this form they need very little pruning. If a tree is desired, remove suckers and unwanted branches. Train as a central leader. See page 50. In hot climates, cover trunks of young trees with white latex paint to protect against sunburn.

SOIL, NUTRIENT AND WATER REQUIREMENTS

Filberts produce best yields when planted in deep, well-drained soil. Adequate results can be achieved in shallow soil. As long as growth continues and leaves are dark green, there is no need to fertilize. If growth is poor and foliage color pales, give 1/2 to 1 pound of actual nitrogen per year per tree. Filberts in the Northwest seldom need irrigation. In California, follow regular watering practices and don't allow trees to dry out.

HARVESTING AND STORAGE

Nuts should be gathered from the ground as often as possible. 'Du Chilly' nuts may have to be knocked from the tree and husked. If it rains during harvest, wash nuts to remove dirt. Filberts can be sun dried in the same manner as almonds and walnuts. To test dryness, bite the kernel. If it snaps, it is dry enough.

Filberts in the shell may be stored for several months at cool basement temperatures. Shelled meats will keep for several weeks at room temperature.

Left: Macadamia blossom cluster and immature nuts. Right: Macadamia hulls split before nuts drop to the ground.

Macadamia

Macadamia species

Macadamias, slow-growing natives of Australia, are relatively new to the Pacific Coast. They are attractive, evergreen trees with glossy, dark green leaves. New growth is coppery red. White to pink flowers form in long clusters. Nuts mature about six to seven months after blossoms, which generally open in late winter to early spring. Nut kernels are high in oil content—up to 60 to 80 percent oil by weight—and have excellent flavor. They are enclosed by thick, hard, round shells that are very difficult to crack.

Two species of macadamia are commonly available. They are often confused with each other.

Macadamia integrifolia, Queensland nut or smooth-shelled macadamia, is the more common. It is widely grown in Hawaii as a commercial crop. *M. tetraphylla,* rough-skinned macadamia, has a pebbled shell, a more open tree habit and spiny, holly-like leaves.

High-quality varieties of each species, some with easier-to-crack shells, are available but difficult to find. Varieties of *M. tetraphylla* include 'Cata', 'Stephenson', 'Burdick' and 'Elimbah'. One variety of *M. integrifolia* is 'Beaumont', possibly a hybrid. Others are 'Keauhou', 'Ikaika' and 'Kakae'.

Macadamias are hardy to about 25° F (−4° C) and are best adapted to coastal regions of southern California. They can be grown in areas farther north with moderate winter temperatures and high humidity, such as around San Francisco Bay. Although fruiting is unpredictable, macadamias have survived and produced fruit in thermal belts above the San Joaquin Valley.

The two species and varieties within the species have slightly different climate adaptations. Smooth-shelled macadamia does best close to the coast. Rough-skinned macadamia grows better slightly inland. The best source of information on variety adaptation is the California Rare Fruit Growers. See page 189.

SOIL, NUTRIENT AND WATER REQUIREMENTS

Macadamias grow best in deep, fertile, well-drained soil. They are slighty drought resistant but produce better with regular watering. Trees respond to applications of nitrogen fertilizer. Light doses are recommended. Little is known about ideal amounts. Trees require little pruning other than to ensure strong crotch angles, to remove unwanted or dead branches and to shape trees.

HARVESTING AND STORAGE

Nuts drop naturally to the ground over a long period and should be gathered as often as possible. Do not pick or shake nuts from trees. Remove hulls and dry in the sun.

Macadamias are delicious without processing but taste even better after roasting and salting.

Macadamia shells are notoriously hard to crack. Everything from hammers to bricks has been tried, usually resulting in a smashed kernel. The most successful method of cracking a macadamia is to wrap a coat hanger wire as tightly as possible around the nut, place it on a hard surface and hit the wire encircling the nut with a hammer. The shell should crack cleanly without crushing the kernel. Kernels may be dried after cracking and stored for several months in a dry place.

Inventing easy-to-use devices to crack the hard shells is a pastime for members of the California Macadamia Society. Their nut crackers are described in their annual yearbook. The society's address is listed on page 189.

VITAL STATISTICS—MACADAMIA	Standard	Dwarf
Height at maturity (feet)		
Unpruned	30	N/A
Pruned	30	
Spread at maturity with		
no competition (feet)	30	
Recommended planting		
distance (feet)	30	
Years to reach bearing age	4-6	
Life expectancy (years)	Indefinite	
Chilling requirement	Low	
Pollinizer required	No	
Good for espalier	No	
Good for containers	No	

Pecan tree loaded with nuts.

Pecan

Carya illinoinensis

The graceful, billowing pecan is an asset to any garden big enough for a large tree. Trees do well in moderate summer climates, but the yield is dissappointing. Nuts require long, hot summers to fill the shells properly. Summers in California, except in the central valleys and desert regions, are not hot enough to mature pecans. Some varieties require less heat than others. But even those with the lowest heat requirement will not fill nuts well in coastal areas. In regions where available heat may be insufficient, early-leafing varieties will take advantage of the longest possible season.

Pecan trees are very resistant to high summer temperatures and can be grown in areas too hot for English walnuts. Pecans are ideally suited to the desert regions of the Southwest where most of the commercial crop is grown.

POLLINATION

Pecans will set light crops unless cross-pollinated with other varieties. If maximum yield is desired, plant more than one variety. Suitable pollinizers are included in the variety chart.

SOIL, NUTRIENT AND WATER REQUIREMENTS

Although pecans tolerate rather unfertile soils, best results are obtained in deep, fertile soils. A soil at least 6 to 8 feet deep is preferred.

For quality nuts, it is imperative that pecans grow vigorously at all times. Any deficiency in nutrients or water during the growing season will result in poorly filled nuts.

Pecans are not tolerant of even low amounts of salinity. Trees respond to nitrogen application with more vigorous growth but generally do well without the addition of nitrogen. Pecans trees tend to suffer from zinc deficiency. See pages 32 and 33.

PRUNING

Pecans should be pruned lightly and trained to a modified central leader. See page 50. Particular attention should be paid to selecting scaffold limbs with wide crotch angles because wood is brittle. Otherwise, pruning consists of shaping or removing crossing and wayward branches.

HARVESTING AND STORAGE

Pecans are generally harvested and stored like walnuts. See page 168. Nuts remain on trees and must be shaken down with poles. Allow nuts to stay on trees until they are well filled. Remove nut meats from hulls as soon as possible. Shelled meats can be kept frozen for over a year.

VITAL STATISTICS—PECAN		
	Standard	Dwarf
Height at maturity (feet)		
Unpruned	100	N/A
Pruned	60	
Spread at maturity with		
no competition (feet)	50	
Recommended planting		
distance (feet)	50-60	
Years to reach bearing age	5-6	
Life expectancy (years)	100	
Chilling requirement	Low to medium	
Pollinizer required	Yes	
Good for espalier	No	
Good for containers	No	

Comments: Some cultivars are reliably self-fruitful.

N/A = Not Available

Pecan

Consider available space when you plant pecan trees. They can grow large—up to 70 feet high or more with an equal spread.

Pecan shade trees are a common sight in many parts of the desert Southwest.

PECANS

VARIETY	ZONE	HARVEST SEASON	POLLINIZER	FRUIT AND TREE	REMARKS
'CHEROKEE'	5, 9, 17, 18.	Early.	'Choctaw' 'Mohawk' 'Wichita'	Medium-size nut has thin, soft shell. Kernel has excellent flavor. Tree very productive, vigorous, branches freely. Bears at a young age.	Well adapted to shelling by commercial machinery.
'CHEYENNE'	5, 9, 17, 18.	Midseason.	'Choctaw' 'Mohawk' 'Wichita'	Medium-size nut has blunt, rounded ends and a semisoft shell. Kernel is plump and high quality. Excellent flavor. Small tree is heavy bearer. Bears at a young age.	Suitable for high-density plantings. Lateral branching habit. Tree size can be reduced by pruning.
'CHOCTAW'	5, 9, 17, 18.	Midseason.	'Cheyenne'. 'Western Schley'	Large nut with thin shell. Kernel has excellent flavor. Tree is vigorous, branches freely, leafs out fairly late. Disease resistant. Very productive. Bears at a young age.	Leaves appear to be resistant to disease. Very good for home orchard.
'MOHAWK'	5, 9, 17, 18.	Midseason.	'Cheyenne' 'Western Schley'	Very large nut with a blocky shape. Thin shell and smooth kernel. Fair to good kernel quality. Tree is vigorous and semispreading. Makes an attractive shade tree, usually self-fruitful.	Somewhat resistant to disease.
'WESTERN SCHLEY'	5, 9, 17, 18.	Late.	'Mohawk' 'Wichita'	Long, tapered nut pointed at the ends. Medium size with thin shell. Kernel is high quality with a rich flavor. Tree is vigorous, hardy, tolerant of zinc deficiency. Easier to grow than many pecans. Produces heavily.	Planted over a wider area than any other pecan. One of the best for the Southwest. Recommended for single-tree plantings in home gardens according to University of Arizona Cooperative Extension.
'WICHITA'	5, 9, 17, 18.	Midseason.	'Cheyenne' 'Western Schley'	Medium-size, long, well-filled nut with large kernel. Shell has purplish black stripes and blotches. Very good quality kernel. Tree attractive, upright, fast growing. Sensitive to frost, subject to wind breakage. Weak crotches. Bears at a young age.	Tree bears heavily. Planted nationwide. Popular commercial variety in Arizona.

Pistachio blossoms

Pistachio
Pistacia vera

Pistachios require many years to become large trees. By pruning they can be kept small almost indefinitely. Their open habit and large, divided, grayish leaves provide considerable ornamental value.

Light-colored, pink-blushed nuts are borne in clusters. Although yield per tree is less than other nuts, quality and flavor are excellent.

Pistachios have about the same cold resistance as almonds but have a longer chilling requirement and are much less susceptible to late spring frosts. They are drought resistant and very tolerant of high summer temperatures. Pistachios are best adapted to the hot, interior valleys and desert regions of California and the Southwest—Zones 5, 9, 16, 18, 19. These areas have ample heat required to fill nuts and sufficient cold to break dormancy. They can also be grown in warm spots of Zones 7, 8, 10-13, where winter cold provides sufficient chilling. However, crops will be unpredictable.

POLLINATION

Pistachios are *dioecious*—meaning male and female flowers are on separate trees. Therefore, male and female trees must be present for fruit set or a branch from a male tree must be grafted to a female tree.

VARIETIES

Pistachios are somewhat difficult for the home gardener to find. The most common male pistachio is 'Peters'. It is a prolific source of pollen but a rather spindly, weak tree. The most common female pistachio is 'Kerman'. It is a commercial variety with good productivity and kernel quality. Tree is vigorous and spreading.

SOIL, NUTRIENT AND WATER REQUIREMENTS

Pistachio trees are able to withstand drought, poor soil and unfavorable climate conditions. If regular production of nuts is desired, it is best to supply regular water and nutrients as for any fruit tree.

Trees tend to be naturally low, spreading and round-headed. They are easily trained to a modified central leader with 4 or 5 main scaffold limbs branching about 4 feet above the ground. After initial training, little pruning is needed except to remove interfering branches. Heavy pruning reduces yield.

HARVESTING AND STORAGE

Nuts are harvested when the hull, the crisp covering around the shell, becomes fairly loose. Normally nuts can be shaken from the tree. Remove hulls soon after harvesting. Dip hulled nuts in water to moisten the shell and spread them in the sun to dry. Many of the shells will split. One method of processing is to boil the nuts in a salt solution for a few minutes, then redry and store. Stored in plastic bags, pistachios will last at least 4 to 6 weeks in the refrigerator. Frozen, they will last several months.

VITAL STATISTICS—PISTACHIO

	Standard	Dwarf
Height at maturity (feet)		
Unpruned	25-30	N/A
Pruned	20	
Spread at maturity with		
no competition (feet)	25	
Recommended planting		
distance (feet)	25	
Years to reach bearing age	7	
Life expectancy (years)	50	
Chilling requirement	Medium	
Pollinizer required	Yes	
Good for espalier	No	
Good for containers	No	

N/A = Not Available

Pistachio

English walnut tree serves as an integral part of the landscape.

Walnut

Juglans species

The walnut family includes species of large, ornamental, deciduous trees. Walnuts make dramatic shade trees where space allows.

The most commonly grown and familar walnut is English or Persian walnut, *Juglans regia,* which is described in the Vital Statistics on this page. With English walnuts, variety selection is critical in obtaining an edible harvest.

English walnut varieties are categorized according to when they leaf out in spring: *early, midseason* or *late.* Early varieties are very susceptible to spring frost damage, attack by codling moth and infection by *walnut blight,* a bacterial disease spread by spring rains. Early

varieties are therefore not recommended in cold or moist climates.

VARIETIES

The most widely grown English walnut variety is 'Payne', which is one of the earliest to leaf. It is rarely recommended for home planting. Late spring frost damage is likely, and extensive pest and disease controls are required to secure an edible harvest. It is grown commercially in California's central valleys because of its great productivity at a young age.

Active breeding at the University of California is resulting in many excellent, widely adapted, midseason-leafing and late-leafing varieties. They are fully described in the variety chart. Established midseason and late varieties such as 'Hartley' and 'Franquette' are also widely adapted and recommended in cool, moist climates.

Carpathian strains, originating from the Carpathian Mountains of eastern and central Europe, are the hardiest varieties of English walnut. They are often sold simply as Carpathian walnuts without specific varietal names.

English walnuts have a moderate chilling requirement of between 500 to 1,000 hours. When not properly chilled in winter, spring foliation is delayed and yields are poor. In mild-winter areas plant low-chill varieties such as 'Placentia'. English walnuts are not grown in desert areas because nuts are susceptible to sunburn.

BUTTERNUT AND OTHER SPECIES OF WALNUT

Butternut, *J. cinerea,* is similar in appearance to the English walnut except the tree grows slightly smaller.

Walnuts are one of the easiest nuts to crack. If you don't have a nutcracker, try a light tap with a hammer.

VITAL STATISTICS—WALNUT

	Black	English
Height at maturity (feet)		
Unpruned	70	60
Pruned	40	50
Spread at maturity with		
no competition (feet)	50-60	50-70
Recommended planting		
distance (feet)	50-60	60-70
Years to reach bearing age	5	5-8
Life expectancy (years)	100	100
Chilling requirement	Medium	Medium
Pollinizer required	Yes	No*
Good for espalier	No	No
Good for containers	No	No

*Better yields with a pollinizer.

Nuts are elongated rather than round. Butternut is adapted to Zones 1 to 11.

California black walnut, *J. hindsii*, is used primarily as a rootstock for English walnuts, although many admire its own stately character. It is rarely grown for nuts.

Eastern black walnut, *J. nigra*, is a hardy native of the eastern United States. It can reach up to 150 feet high. Trees are widely adapted to western climates, except for desert areas and coastal southern California. Nuts are hard to crack but delicious. 'Thomas' and 'Ohio' are recommended varieties although they are rarely seen in retail nurseries.

Southern California black walnut, *J. californica*, is rarely grown for its nuts, but is a useful landscape plant. It grows as a small, shrubby tree 15 to 30 feet high.

POLLINATION

English walnuts produce fertile male and female flowers on the same trees. But they sometimes open at different times, reducing effective pollination. This is related to variations in weather and is rarely a problem to the home fruit grower. There is usually sufficient overlap of bloom for adequate pollination and fruit set.

If walnut trees consistently produce light crops, graft a pollinizer limb to the tree or plant another variety nearby to provide pollination. Suitable pollinizers are listed in the variety chart.

SOIL, NUTRIENT AND WATER REQUIREMENTS

Once established, walnuts survive with very little attention. Best crops come from trees planted in a rich, deep soil with excellent drainage. Nuts will be plumper with regular watering, but avoid soggy soils. Young walnut trees are fertilized very lightly or not at all as long as leaf color is healthy and growth is vigorous. Mature trees benefit from nitrogen. Apply it at a rate of 3 pounds actual nitrogen per year per 1,000 square feet of surface area within the tree's drip line.

Walnuts are trained to a modified central leader system. See pruning, page 50. Mature trees require very little pruning.

Walnuts are so attractive that old orchard trees are often left in the landscape around new buildings or homes. Compacted soil from heavy equipment and grade changes can suffocate and kill walnut roots. Flowers, shrubs and lawns that are often planted under established walnuts usually require more water than the walnut can handle. This encourages root diseases. Consult your county extension agent before planting or building around mature walnut trees.

When planting young walnuts, consider eventual size of the tree, which can reach 60 to 100 feet high.

Fallen walnut leaves have a poisonous effect on some plants. They should not be added to compost piles or vegetable gardens.

HARVESTING AND STORAGE

Mature nuts fall naturally when the green hulls crack or split. Better quality is secured if nuts are knocked or shaken from tree while hulls are still intact. Gather nuts and remove hulls as soon as possible after they fall.

Hulled nuts should be rinsed with water to remove *tannin*, a chemical substance that may stain them. Spread the hulled nuts in the sun to complete drying of the meaty kernel inside. Do not allow them to get wet. If kernels break cleanly when bent, they have dried sufficiently for use or storage.

Nuts in the shell may be stored for many months if kept in a cool, dry place. Shelled nuts will also keep for several months if refrigerated.

English walnut

Butternut

QUID PUBLISHING Co., Inc.

BUSINESS PRINTING · BOOKS · MAGAZINES · BROCHURES · FULL COLOR PRINTING

230 WEST 1700 SOUTH · SALT LAKE CITY, UTAH

Tel. 487-5811

1) want to leave to Calif. by June 20th

2) by June 20th have 100 places of interest to apply to

— OSU } leads on
— State Dept. } Calif.
   may stay overnight

about Calif.

— Commerce   — company referrals
— Dept. of Ag   — mngmt company — mngr
— Universities, Extension service
— Corps
— Alumni "American Free Technologists"
— League A. Nursery Association

— Seek mngmt positions (Calif. newspaper , reg govmt may put ad in)   career advisors
— travel agency + study about Calif.   placement
— See Sutphil (Calif. Ag need map — carry in case   update resume and
   teaching)   job hunting
— plan mileage + other expenses. —   write to ? this now !!

Immature English walnut.

ENGLISH OR PERSIAN WALNUTS

VARIETY	ZONE	HARVEST SEASON	POLLINIZER	FRUIT AND TREE	REMARKS
'CHANDLER'	7-11.	Midseason.	'Hartley' 'Franquette'	Kernel quality excellent. Tree is medium to large with excellent production.	Midseason leafing—danger of spring frost damage slight. Most promising of University of California introductions.
'CHICO'	9-11.	Early to midseason.	'Serr'	Good kernel quality. Small to medium tree with good production.	Early leafing—moderate danger of spring frost damage.
'EUREKA'	9.	Late.	'Chico'	Kernel quality excellent. Large tree with good production.	Midseason leafing—moderate danger of spring frost damage. Slow to bear.
'FRANQUETTE'	3-5, 7, 8, 10, 11.	Late.	Partially self-fruitful.	Kernel quality good. Large tree with poor production.	Late leafing—no danger of spring frost damage.
'HARTLEY'	7-11.	Midseason.	Self-fruitful or 'Franquette'	Good kernel quality. Tree is medium to large with good production.	Midseason leafing—slight danger of spring frost damage. Only slightly susceptible to blight.
'HOWARD'	7-11.	Midseason.	'Hartley' 'Franquette'	Kernel quality good. Small tree has excellent production.	Midseason leafing—slight danger of spring frost damage.
'PAYNE'	9, 12.	Midseason.	'Chico'	Kernel quality excellent. Small to medium tree with excellent production.	Early leafing—great danger of spring frost damage. Very susceptible to blight.
'PLACENTIA'	12-14.	Midseason.	Partially self-fruitful.	Good quality nut. Large tree, excellent production. Early bearing.	Early leafing—great danger of spring frost damage.
'SERR'	9-11.	Midseason.	'Chico'	Kernel quality excellent. Medium to large tree has good production.	Early leafing—moderate danger of spring frost damage.
'SPURGEON'	2-4.	Late.	Partially self-fruitful.	Kernel quality excellent. Moderately productive tree.	Late leafing—no danger of spring frost damage.

Colorful subtropicals: sliced papaya, left, sliced kiwi, right.

Subtropicals

Perhaps the most appealing aspect of subtropical fruit is the image they create of exotic lands and different cultures. Unique fruit such as mango, papaya and guava are strange and unfamiliar to many palates. Yet these same fruit are mainstays in the diet of millions in tropical countries around the world.

Actually, the term *subtropical* is a misnomer as it applies to the plants in this chapter. Many are *tropical* in nature—native to areas where differences between day and night temperatures are minimal, humidity is high and rainfall is plentiful year-round.

The factor common to almost all of the plants in this section is that they are restricted to the mild, subtropical climate of California. This climate is characterized by low humidity, warm days and cool nights, and low amounts of rainfall with usually none in summer.

Many of the fruit described in this chapter require special care and close attention to planting site. An understanding of microclimates and frost protection as described on page 4 is essential. Exposure and wind protection can make the difference between success and failure. Taking advantage of microclimates also allows you to grow many subtropicals well out of their adapted temperature range.

Most subtropicals are perfectly suited to growing in containers. They can be used to make a spectacular display in the greenhouse or indoors.

Because many of these plants are new to the West, named varieties have not been selected. For some there may be varieties that originated in other parts of the world but do not perform well in the West. Still others may be available only from seed. Fruit quality of seedling-grown plants is not always predictable. Named varieties adapted to specific climates may also be difficult to find.

Due to their newness to western gardens, exact cultural requirements are not established on some subtropicals described in this section. Fertilizer requirements are often conspicuously missing. Application rates will have to be gauged by plant's response. See fertilizers, page 30. As more people grow subtropicals, the additional experience will help establish more exacting guidelines.

We have relied heavily on the California Rare Fruit Growers for much of the information in this chapter. Experience of its members has been invaluable in recommending varieties that are adapted to the West and where and how they can be grown. More information on a given plant may be obtained by writing the California Rare Fruit Growers. See address on page 189.

SUBTROPICALS

COMMON NAME BOTANICAL NAME	ORIGIN	ZONES	PLANT	FRUIT	ORNAMENTAL QUALITIES	COMMENTS
BANANA *Musa species*	Tropical Asia.	13-15.	Herbaceous and tree-like to 20 feet high.	Varies from green to yellow, and from 3 to 12 inches in length.	Large, yellow-orange flowers. Can be grown in tubs.	Frost sensitive. Plants should be protected from wind.
BARBADOS CHERRY *Malpighia glabra*	Tropical America.	13-15.	Semideciduous or evergreen shrub or small tree. Grows 10 to 15 feet high.	Cherry-like, 1/4 to 1 inch in diameter. Bright red, tinged yellow.	Small, white flowers in clusters similar to apple. Border or specimen plant. Clip to make a hedge.	Can be eaten fresh, or in jams, syrups, jellies. Highest vitamin C content of any fruit.
CAPULIN CHERRY *Prunus salicifolia*	High elevations of Central America.	12-15.	Fast growing, umbrella-like tree, reaching 15 to 30 feet high.	Resembles European cherry, 1/2 to 1 inch in diameter. Dark purple with green flesh.	Small, white flowers and glossy foliage.	A "true" cherry, but does not require chilling temperatures to bear fruit. Satisfactory along coast and 20 to 50 miles inland.
CHERIMOYA *Annona cherimola*	Northern Andes.	14, 15.	Evergreen or semi-deciduous tree, 20 feet high.	Green, strawberry-shaped fruit has the appearance of overlapping leaves. Fruit weigh up to 2 pounds.	Small, fragrant, yellow to yellowish green flowers bloom over a long period.	Delicious from tree. Will tolerate light frost. Protect from wind.
GUAVA, STRAWBERRY *Psidium littorale*	Brazil.	7-10, 12-15.	Evergreen shrub 6 to 10 feet high or multi-trunk tree 10 to 15 feet high.	*P. littorale littorale* fruit is yellow. *P. littorale longipes* is red. Both are 1-1/2 inches long.	Small, white, fragrant flowers. Excellent container plant.	Eat fresh or use in jellies and fruit salad.

SUBTROPICALS

COMMON NAME / BOTANICAL NAME	ORIGIN	ZONES	PLANT	FRUIT	ORNAMENTAL QUALITIES	COMMENTS
GUAVA, TROPICAL *Psidium guajava*	Lowland South America.	12-15.	Semideciduous tree 15 to 25 feet high.	2 to 4 inches. Yellow outside, flesh may be white, salmon or pink. Fruit of most varieties have a strong fragrance.	White flowers are 1 inch in diameter and slightly fragrant.	Eat fresh, also makes excellent jelly and guava cheese. Hardy to 26° F (−3° C). Grow 5 to 25 miles inland in warm spots.
JABOTICABA *Myrciaria cauliflora*	Southern Brazil.	14, 15.	Large, evergreen shrub or small tree, 15 to 25 feet high.	Grape-like fruit borne singly, doubly or in threes on trunk and larger branches. Skin is tough. Flesh is white, juicy and gelatin-like with a few small seeds.	Fruit preceded by small, white flowers. Can be pruned as a hedge.	Freezes well. Makes excellent jelly, juice and wine. Accepts temperatures down to 25° F (−4° C).
JUJUBE *Zizyphus jujube*	China.	5-19.	Small, deciduous tree. Occasionally reaches 25 feet high.	3/4 to 1-1/2 inches long, round or oblong. Green skin with brown-colored spots when ripe.	Small, insignificant, yellow flowers. Varieties 'Li' and 'Lang' are quite ornamental in form and foliage.	Use fresh, candied, dried or canned. Temperate zone plant, extremely hardy. Thrives in lawns. Excellent tree for low and intermediate deserts.
KIWIFRUIT *Actinidia chinensis*	East Asia.	3-15.	Vine form, reaching 30 to 60 feet long if allowed to grow.	Fruit is size and shape of an egg. Brown skin, green flesh.	Fragrant, white flowers. Can be grown in large containers or on a fence or trellis.	Eat fresh. Hardy to 10° F (−12° C). Not recommended for desert regions. Needs winter chilling.
LOQUAT *Eriobotrya japonica*	China.	5-15.	Evergreen tree 15 to 25 feet high.	Orange and yellow fruit is size and shape of small egg. Aromatic flavor is sweet and rich.	Attractive, fragrant, white flowers. Adapted to containers.	Use fresh, can or make jelly. Drought resistant.
LITCHI *Litchi chinensis*	Southern China.	14, 15.	Evergreen tree to 40 feet high.	Fruit 1 to 1-1/2 inches in diameter, borne in loose clusters of 3 to 20. Shell rough and brittle, flesh whitish with texture of firm gelatin.	Small, greenish flowers in large clusters. Dense, rounded tree canopy extends nearly to ground. Spectacular when fruit ripens and tree takes on reddish hue.	Can be frozen, dried or canned in syrup. Hardy to 25° F (−4° C).
MANGO *Mangifera indica*	India through Burma and Malaysia.	13-15.	Evergreen tree 15 to 25 feet high.	Green, yellow or red fruit is 6 inches long, oval.	Reddish yellow flowers in large clusters at the ends of branches. Dense foliage.	Use fresh or make jelly. Hardy to 30° F (−1° C).
NATAL PLUM *Carissa grandiflora*	South Africa.	12-15, 17.	Dense, evergreen shrub 8 to 10 feet high, sometimes to 20 feet.	Red, plum-shaped fruit, 1 to 2 inches in diameter.	1 to 2-inch, white, fragrant, star-shaped flowers and fruit appear at the same time. Attractive in containers or as hedge.	Resembles cranberries in flavor. Eat fresh, stew in a sauce, make into jellies, syrups and pies. 'Fancy' is recommended for fruit—it is self-fertile.
PAPAYA *Carica papaya*	Tropical America.	13-15.	Tree-like herb, 5 to 25 feet high.	Melon-like appearance. Weighs 2 to 10 pounds.	Insignificant, pale yellow or cream flowers. Plant in groups of three to five to ensure pollination.	Fresh fruit aids in digestion—contains tenderizing proteins and enzymes. Bears fruit when young.
PAPAYA, MOUNTAIN *Carica pubescens*	Mountains of Colombia and Ecuador.	13-15.	Shrub or multiple-trunk, upright tree to 12 feet high.	Smaller than regular papaya, 3 to 4 inches.	Insignificant, cream-colored flowers. Tropical foliage.	Tree hardier than *Carica papaya*. Fruit is barely edible. Hardy to 28° F (−2° C).
PASSION FRUIT *Passiflora edulis*	South America.	13-15.	Strong-growing vine to 30 feet long.	Purple, egg-shaped fruit is up to 2 inches long, depending on variety.	Fragrant flowers in various colors grow to 4 inches in diameter. Intricate foliage. Highly ornamental.	Use fresh or make jelly or juice. Grow in large tubs. Hardy to 29° F (−2°C).
PINEAPPLE GUAVA *Feijoa sellowiana*	Brazil.	5-18.	Tall, evergreen shrub or small tree 10 to 15 feet high.	Round or egg-shaped fruit is 3/4 to 3-1/2 inches long. Shiny to grayish green. Fragrant.	Small distinctive flowers have four, white, fleshy petals tinged purplish on the inside. Bright red stamens.	Eat fresh. Fleshy petals are edible, often used in salads and desserts. Unusually hardy—to 15° F (−9° C). 'Trask' produces the largest fruit.
SURINAM CHERRY *Eugenia uniflora*	Brazil.	12-15.	Small, slow-growing tree or evergreen shrub, usually 6 to 8 feet high.	3/4 to 1-1/4-inch fruit change from yellow to red to deep purple, at which time they are edible.	Small, white, fragrant flowers. Leaves change from greenish to coppery red in cold weather.	Use in jams and jellies, syrup, compote, wine and sherbets. Hardy to 28° F (−2° C).
SAPOTE, WHITE *Casimiroa edulis*	Highlands of Mexico and Central America.	10, 11, 13-15, 17.	Evergreen tree grows 25 to 30 feet high, width is slightly wider.	Fruit is 2 to 4 inches, very thin skinned and tender.	Flowers insignificant but fragrant. Rather large, 5-fingered leaves make this a delightful ornamental.	Eat fresh or frozen. Give plenty of space. Drops fruit which cover the ground, attracting squirrels, birds and fruit flies. Do not plant in lawn.

'Apple' banana

Banana

Musa species

Bananas are fast-growing, herbaceous perennials that spread by underground stems called *rhizomes* or *suckers*. Plants can reach up to 20 feet in height although many remain much smaller. They are attractive plants with a definite tropical appearance. Leaves are long and broad—up to 5 feet long and 2 feet wide—borne on thick, water-filled stalks.

The yellow-orange flowers, produced on drooping stalks, are large and showy. Fruit is usually ripe 13 to 15 months after planting and grows 3 to 12 inches long, depending on variety. Some bananas are eaten fresh; others must be cooked.

Grow bananas in moist soil that contains lots of humus. Because plants produce shallow roots, they do not need deep soil and are perfectly suited to containers. They are considered heavy feeders and benefit greatly from light, frequent applications of nitrogen.

Bananas are very sensitive to frost. Their large leaves are easily torn by wind. Plant them in protected sites.

Bananas are self-fruitful. Propagate bananas by dividing underground roots or suckers. In a few years one plant will usually produce at least three more suckers.

Field tests of banana varieties have been carried out in the Hollywood Hills of southern California. Results show success with 'Orinoco' and three-sided 'Lady Finger' banana. Another successful test variety was 'Apple'. When ripe, this short, plump banana is thin skinned, crunchy, creamy and absolutely delicious. It is also hardier than 'Orinoco'.

Other recommended varieties include 'Better Select', 'Chinese Dwarf', 'Dwarf Puerto Rican', 'Dwarf Brazilian Apple', 'Ice Cream', 'Lacatan', 'Manzano', 'Red Leaf' and 'Brazilian'.

'Better Select' banana

Bananas are usually harvested 12 to 15 months after planting.

'Chinese Dwarf' banana

Barbados Cherry, Acerola Cherry
Malpighia glabra

Acerola cherry is an evergreen shrub or small tree that grows slowly to 10 to 15 feet high. Not related to true cherries, it is native to the West Indies, where the fruit is prized for its nutritional value as well as its delicious flavor. Vitamin C content of the fruit is exceptionally high, more than 40 times that of an orange.

Although it can be trained as a small tree, acerola cherry is best grown as a shrub. A vigorous grower, it develops a number of strong, woody trunks as a framework for lateral fruiting branches. In warmer climates it is evergreen. In colder regions some leaves drop in the winter months.

Flowers are borne in clusters similar to apple blossoms. They reach up to 1/2 inch in diameter, range from white to pinkish and are self-fruitful.

The three-lobed fruit is cherry-like in shape and 1/4 to 1 inch in diameter. When ripe it is bright red tinged with yellow. It can be eaten fresh from the tree or used in jams, jellies or syrups.

Acerola cherry tolerates light frosts and is hardy to at least 30° F (−1° C). Young plants are especially sensitive to cold and should be protected. It does not have a chilling requirement. Acerola cherry can be grown indoors but is more commonly used outdoors as a border or specimen.

Acerola cherry must have excellent drainage to grow well and does best in a sunny location. Plant responds well to nitrogen fertilizers as long as they do not contain sulfur. It is semidormant from late November to early March and should not be fertilized during this period.

Do not prune plant during its first season of growth. Once established, prune in late summer or early fall to allow new growth to harden before onset of cold weather. Cut back inner, upright branches to promote new growth. This growth should bear fruit the following season.

Few fruit match the tropical appeal of bananas.

Fruit and foliage of Barbados cherry.

Capulin cherries

skin is thin and tender. Flesh is pale green, meaty, sweet and juicy. The flavor has been compared to that of wild cherries. Capulin cherries are delicious fresh or can be made into jams and preserves.

Paul Thomson of the California Rare Fruit Growers writes of his experience with capulin cherries in Vista, California: "After the fruit was picked the first part of August, the tree was not watered during the hot weeks that followed. By the end of September, cooler weather was at hand and the tree was given a good, deep watering. Within a week, a tremendous flush of growth appeared, with about half the number of flower clusters that normally form in spring. These set the usual light crop and matured slowly. This occurred during the exceptionally mild winter of 1972-1973. At the end of February, fruit were almost full size and were ripe by the end of March. The tree bore a crop of fruit among the flower *racemes*, which were about ready to open for spring bloom and would produce fruit at the end of summer. I conclude that it is possible to get two crops a year in some mild areas."

Capulin cherry is easily propagated by seed but fruit quality of seedling trees is quite variable. For reasons unknown, trees with gray bark seem to produce larger fruit than those with darker bark.

Stake young trees carefully and protect from strong winds. Plants can be grown as a fruiting hedge.

Capulin cherries respond well to light applications of nitrogen fertilizer when blossoms first appear in spring.

Capulin Cherry, Tropic Cherry
Prunus salicifolia

Capulin cherry does not require a period of chilling to bear fruit as do most other true cherries. Because of this, it extends the cherry-growing range into southern California.

Native to the highlands of Central America and northern South America, capulin cherry is an erect, semideciduous tree shaped like an umbrella. It is very fast growing and reaches a height of 10 feet in 12 to 18 months, eventually attaining a height of 30 feet.

Flowers are white, 3/4 inch in length and appear early in spring on slender stems 2 to 4 inches long. Leaves are about 4-1/2 inches long, slender, with serrated edges. They are deep green above and grayish green beneath. Where adapted, tree does not shed leaves in winter. It is frost tolerant and can withstand 19° F (−7° C) with some damage to the slender limbs.

Capulin cherry produces fruit two to three years after planting. Cross-pollination is not required. The fruit, which appear in heavy clusters in summer, resemble northern cherries. Deep, glossy dark purple

Cherimoyas

Cherimoya, Custard Apple

Annona cherimola

Cherimoya is an evergreen or semideciduous tree native to the cool, dry slopes of the Andes mountains in Ecuador and Peru. It reaches a height of about 20 feet with an equal spread. It produces unusual-looking, delicious fruit with a custard-like texture. In the western United States it develops best flavor inland, from Santa Barbara south to San Diego. Tree is less resistant to cold than 'Eureka' lemon. Young, tender growth may be killed by high summer temperatures.

Oval, 4 to 10-inch long leaves are light, dull green with fuzzy undersides. They emit an orange-like scent when touched. Leaves drop in late spring when flower buds begin to swell.

Flowers are single, about 1 inch in diameter, green, with a pleasant fragrance. They bloom over a period of three to four months.

Fruit is usually shaped like a large strawberry, weighing 1/2 to 2 pounds. Green skin is thick and leathery. Some varieties are smooth skinned; others are bumpy and look like a green pine cone. Fruit matures in 5 to 8 months. The inner flesh is creamy white and contains 30 to 40 black seeds the size of large beans. It has a custard-like texture and a sweet, spicy flavor akin to pineapple, spicy banana or papaya.

Harvest cherimoya when the fruit skin begins to turn yellow-green. Allow to soften at room temperature. Fruit can be stored up to a week when refrigerated.

Protect trees from wind and never allow to dry out. Young trees are usually not pruned but allowed to develop naturally. Prune mature trees annually to renew bearing wood.

POLLINATION

Cherimoya is characterized by light, irregular bearing. In its native South America, it is normally pollinated by insects. In California or other parts of the West it can be hand pollinated to improve the crop.

Dr. Arthur Schroeder, Professor of Botany at University of California at Los Angeles (UCLA), has studied cherimoya fruiting habits. He recommends this pollination procedure: "A watercolor paintbrush and a plastic 35mm film canister are all the materials needed. Hold the film canister under a fully open flower. Carefully brush the cream-colored pollen from the *anthers*. Anthers are the male part of a blossom which look like little pieces of straw at the base of the flower. One flower usually provides enough pollen for three to five flowers. When a flower is partially open the *pistils*, the female part of a blossom, are ready to be pollinated. Spread the petals with your fingers, dip the brush into the canister of fresh pollen and apply it to the cone-like pistil with an even, swirling motion. After a few flowers are pollinated, dip the brush in water to keep it moist and supple."

Pollination can be repeated at least weekly as long as new flowers continue to open. Choose flowers on the lower portions of limbs or near the main trunk where the fruit can easily be reached.

VARIETIES

'Bonita'—Introduced by Jonathan Brown, Carpinteria, California. Productive. Excellent quality fruit.

'Booth'—Originated in Hollywood, California. More tolerant of temperature extremes than others. Good quality. Handles well. Ripens late.

'Pierce'—Large, fast-growing tree. Prolific producer of large, excellent fruit. Sets a good crop without hand pollination. Starts ripening in November.

'White'—Originated on White Ranch in Lemon Grove, California. Large fruit with a semismooth skin.

Other excellent-flavored varieties include 'Chaffey', 'Bays', 'Deliciosa', 'Loma', 'Ott', 'Mariella' and 'Spain'.

Guava

Psidium species

There are two main guava species. One, *Psidium littorale (P. cattleianum)* is commonly represented by its two varieties, *P. littorale littorale*, the red-fruited strawberry guava, and *P. littorale longipes*, the yellow-fruited lemon guava. The second species, *Psidium guajava*, tropical guava, is seen less often in the western United States.

Guavas are used mainly to make a well-known, pleasantly flavored jelly. They can also be used to make

'Beaumont' guava

preserves. Fruit are high in vitamin C. Larger, improved varieties have thick flesh and are delicious eaten out-of-hand or as dessert or salad fruit.

P. littorale is a large, evergreen shrub or small tree growing 8 to 10 feet high, with a somewhat open habit. It grows slower than the tropical guava and makes a wonderful hedge. It is an attractive plant with glossy, dark green leaves that may have a bronze tinge when young. Greenish to golden brown bark is quite beautiful and decorative.

Flowers are white and small, about 3/4 of an inch; they appear in spring. Bright red or yellow, 1 to 2-inch fruit ripen in early fall. The inside is soft, aromatic and sweet tasting, with numerous hard seeds. Fruit is tangy and refreshing—tasting something like a tart cherry.

P. littorale is hardy to about 20° F (−7° C). Light pruning is desirable to encourage new fruiting wood. Pruning is usually done in spring. Heavy pruning is unnecessary.

P. guajava, tropical guava, is a semideciduous tree 15 to 25 feet high. It has large, deeply veined, 6-inch leaves that may drop in spring. Bark on the trunk and main branches is scaled and rough.

Flowers of the tropical guava are white, 1 to 1-1/2 inches and lightly fragrant. The yellow-skinned fruit is 2 to 4 inches long. Flesh, which may be white, salmon or pink, has a fragrance that can permeate a room.

Fruit ripens in fall. It tastes somewhat musky but is good eaten fresh. Also makes excellent jelly, juice and guava cheese.

Tropical guava is more sensitive to cold than strawberry and lemon guavas and is usually damaged at 26° F (−3° C). It is not as tolerant of cool summers as strawberry and lemon guavas and generally needs warmer temperatures for proper growth. Neither guava species can stand the high heat of desert areas or the warmest parts of central valleys in California.

Both guavas can be grown in containers and are especially attractive companions to citrus. They can also be grown indoors.

VARIETIES

A number of other types of guavas are commercially available as seed.

'Beaumont'—Commercial variety of the Hawaiian juice industry. Large, tropical-type fruit. Very productive and grows relatively true from seed.

'Mexican Cream'—A tropical guava with creamy consistency and chocolate flavor. Produces somewhat variable results when grown from seed.

'Pear Guava'—Tropical guava-type fruit with pear flavor. Relatively true from seed.

Fruit and foliage of jaboticaba.

Jaboticaba

Myrciaria cauliflora (syn. *Eugenia cauliflora*)

Jaboticaba is a large, evergreen shrub or small tree native to southern Brazil. It has an attractive shape and foliage. It forms a hedge when pruned or clipped. Unpruned, it can branch upward to 25 feet with a compact head.

Jaboticaba is best known for its spectacular fruiting habit. Grape-like fruit are borne singly or in clusters of two and three directly on the trunk and larger branches. This creates an unusual sight when plant is in full fruit.

Bark of jaboticaba is characteristically light brown and smooth and flakes off in patches. Dark green leaves are long and thin and give the tree a very fine texture.

Flowers are white with prominent yellow stamens. They appear on the trunk and larger branches during warm weather.

The 3/4 to 1-1/2-inch berries are purple and globular. Skin is thin but tough. Flesh is gelatin-like, juicy and translucent pink. When ripe, some have a sprightly, grape-like flavor; others taste more like cherries.

Fruit can be eaten fresh from the plant or used to make jelly, juice or wine. It can also be frozen.

Grow jaboticaba in partial shade or full sun. Keep soil constantly moist. Mulching is advisable. Plant will not tolerate moist, salty air and does not do well close to the coast. Jaboticaba is hardy to 25° F (−4° C).

Members of California Rare Fruit Growers report growing jaboticaba in the southern California cities of Encinitas, San Diego and Los Angeles. Farther north they report success with plants in Santa Maria, San Anselmo, El Cebrante and Santa Clara. One grower in southern California has had up to five harvests a year.

Jujube blossoms

Jujube, Chinese Date
Zizyphus jujuba

Jujube is a deciduous tree native to China. It is often called Chinese date because the shape and coloring of its fruit are similar to the common date. Shiny, reddish brown skin is much like parchment and covers mild, rather sweet, pithy flesh. When eaten fresh, fruit has a crisp texture. In China it is used principally as a candied or glazed fruit or dried and canned.

Tree is very ornamental with an upright habit, growing 20 to 25 feet tall. Leaves are 1 to 3 inches long, bright green and glossy. Leaves turn yellow in fall. Branches are spiny, slender, gnarled and zigzagged. They tend to droop due to the burden of fruit. These drooping branches add greatly to the tree's character.

Small, yellowish green to white flowers appear in clusters in late spring. This late-flowering time allows jujube to avoid injury from all but the latest frosts.

Two popular varieties come from China. 'Lang' is pear shaped, reddish brown and about 1-1/2 inches long and half as wide. 'Li' is round and larger, about 2 inches long, with mahogany-brown skin.

Trees of both varieties bear profusely at an early age. They may produce fruit the first year after planting and usually come into full bearing in three to four years. Fruit ripens during September and October and is harvested when it turns reddish brown.

Jujube is a hardy tree that accepts both heat and drought. It has a very low chilling requirement and does not ripen fruit or grow well in areas where summers are cool or short. An excellent choice for desert regions, it accepts alkaline and saline soils as long as they are deep and well drained. It grows poorly in wet or clay soils.

In southern Europe, jujube is used as a table dessert or is dried and used as a table sweet. Fruit for drying should be left on tree until skin darkens and wrinkles. It keeps very well after a short period of sun drying. Jujube, in the form of pastes, tablets and syrups, is also used as a remedy for throat ailments.

Paul Thomson of the California Rare Fruit Growers writes of growing the jujube in southern California: "Jujube has been carefully selected and cultivated for so long by the Chinese that a better fruit than 'Li' and 'Lang' varieties is hard to find. But it has been done. From several thousand seedlings planted at the USDA Plant Introduction Station at Chico, California, one has proven to be outstanding. I received wood of this selection in 1961 and it first fruited in 1967. Fruit are large, many 1-1/4 to 1-1/2 inch in diameter, and resemble a crabapple in general appearance. Most smaller fruit are seedless. The texture of the flesh is crisp with a more acid flavor than many varieties, giving it a character all its own. I have propagated it for several years and it has been distributed under the name 'Chico'. It is not suited to situations exposed to cool, ocean winds, and will not bear in such locations. It produces moderately heavy crops in protected spots and further inland. 'Chico' is also more thorny than other varieties.

Jujube tree

Kiwifruit

Kiwifruit, Chinese Gooseberry

Actinidia chinensis

Kiwifruit have attracted considerable attention in the western United States in the last few years. Native to parts of eastern Asia, they were first introduced to New Zealand in 1906 but weren't planted as a commercial fruit there until the late 1950s. They were introduced to California through the USDA Plant Introduction Station in Chico in 1935. But they weren't seriously planted as a commerical crop until the mid-1970s. Today, kiwifruit are gaining rapidly in popularity as a supermarket and back yard fruit.

Because kiwifruit were so recently introduced, some of the guidelines for their culture are still in the developmental stage. Although many growing practices are known, your experience and that of other kiwifruit growers in your climate may be your best teacher.

Fuzzy brown fruit are about the size and shape of a large egg. They are borne on vigorous, deciduous vines. The roundish leaves are 5 to 8 inches long, deep green above, fuzzy soft white beneath. New growth is usually covered with velvety red hairs. Vines can spread up to 30 feet and cannot support their own weight. Kiwifruit are usually grown on a trellis but are beautifully suited to an arbor or pergola or trained as an espalier against a wall.

Cream-colored flowers, 1 to 1-1/2 inches in diameter, appear in May. Fruit are covered with a fuzzy, leathery, brown exterior, which is peeled before eating. Concealed inside is striking, emerald-green flesh with small, black edible seeds. Uniquely flavored, the taste is described as minty, melon-like, strawberry-like or banana-like. Most people add the word "delicious." Kiwifruit are colorful additions to fruit salads and can be used in ice cream, jams, jellies, pies and many other desserts.

CLIMATE ADAPTATION

Kiwifruit grow to perfection in areas with mild spring and fall weather and high summer temperatures, such as California's central valleys. They also grow well in cool areas, such as the Puget Sound.

Female vines are hardy to 10° F (−12° C); males to 15° F (−10° C). Early fall frosts and late spring frosts are particularly hazardous. Kiwifruit grow best in planting sites protected from strong winds.

'Hayward', the most widely available kiwifruit, has a chilling requirement estimated at 600 to 800 hours below 45° F (7° C). 'Monty', 'Vincent' and 'Abbott' have lower chilling requirements. Inadequate chilling may result in low yield, dormancy problems and excessive sap flow after pruning.

POLLINATION

Kiwifruit produce male and female flowers on separate plants. For cross-pollination you must plant at least one male and one female plant. One male can pollinate up to eight surrounding females. Vines are usually spaced 15 feet apart.

PRUNING

Vines must be supported on some type of structure. A 6-foot-high T-bar trellis with 3 to 5 horizontal wires is the most common support. Pergolas, arbors and other types of trellises can also be used.

All fruit are produced on new growth that emerges from 1-year-old wood. Large, bulbous fruit buds are easy to distinguish from flat buds for foliage. The purpose of pruning is to maximize new fruiting wood and to balance vegetative growth with fruit production. Prune only when the vines are fully dormant. Pruning after buds have begun to swell causes excessive sap flow, which weakens the vine.

Fruiting lateral method of pruning is easiest for kiwifruit. This is done by training the *cordons*, permanent branches, to the middle wire of the trellis. After planting, allow the vine to grow straight up to the middle wire before it is allowed to branch. When vine is several inches above the wire, pinch it back to 2 to 3 inches below the wire. From the buds that grow select two canes to be the permanent cordons. Cut canes back to 24 to 36 inches the first dormant season.

If the vine does not reach the wire the first year, cut it back to 4 to 8 buds above ground and retrain a single, strong vine the next year.

The second season, select fruiting laterals spaced 24 to 36 inches apart along the main cordons. Allow cordons to continue to increase in length but cut fruiting laterals just beyond the outside wire. Laterals will fruit for two to three years, depending on their vigor.

In the second summer of fruit lateral growth, canes emerging from the lateral will produce fruit at their bases. During the growing season, usually May or June, cut these canes back to 6 to 10 buds beyond the last blossom. This will help avoid excess twining and channel energy to the fruit.

Remove most new laterals arising from the cordon, especially those with strong, upright growth. Leave enough laterals to replace old, fruiting canes that will need to be removed as their production declines.

During the second winter of a lateral's growth, cut it back, leaving only two or three canes that fruited the previous season. These will grow new fruiting wood the next season. As they fruit the following summer, cut them back to 6 to 10 buds past the last blossom. In its third dormant season, remove the fruiting lateral. Thus, pruning mature vines consists of renewing one-third of the fruiting wood each year. Also remove twining and crisscrossing canes during dormant-season pruning.

The *spur method* of pruning kiwifruit takes a good deal more work than the fruiting lateral method. It is often recommended to espalier less-vigorous varieties such as 'Bruno' or 'Monty'. To espalier, choose shorter, fruiting canes spaced at 12 to 15 inches apart. The first season cut them back to two or three buds. These spurs should grow slowly so do not pinch them the second or third fruiting seasons. After fruiting twice, remove them and replace with selected new spurs.

Methods of training over arbors or pergolas are similar to training on trellises. Vines are headed the

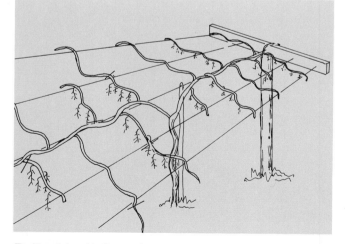

Fruiting lateral is the easiest method of pruning kiwifruit. Laterals produce fruit for 3 years then are removed.

first or second season, depending on the height of the supports. You will also want to develop secondary cordons off the primary ones.

SOIL, NUTRIENT AND WATER REQUIREMENTS

Kiwifruit can be grown in a wide range of soils as long as soil is well drained. Excess salts in soil or water will cause leaf burn. Iron deficiency may develop in alkaline soils.

Kiwifruit are usually sold as plants in containers or as bare-root plants. Planting site should be protected from strong winds. Long canes can break easily.

Because of the vigor and size of leaves, kiwifruit need a good deal of water for healthy growth. Do not let the vines dry out. Water frequently and deeply in very hot weather.

Kiwifruit also require nitrogen for vigorous growth. Mature kiwifruit vines should receive a total of 1 to 1-1/2 pounds of actual nitrogen per vine per year. Vines less than 5 years old should receive 1/4 to 1/2 the recommended rate. Divide fertilizer amounts into two or three applications—one in January and the remainder after fruit set. Avoid fertilizing and taper off watering in late summer or fall to avoid encouraging frost-tender new growth.

HARVESTING AND STORAGE

Kiwifruit are harvested like avocados. Pick fruit when hard and allow to soften at room temperature. If left on the vine, fruit will shrivel and will probably be damaged by birds.

Kiwifruit are usually picked in late fall but exact time is difficult to determine. Signs of ripeness are when a few fruit turn soft or when skin color goes from greenish to full brown. Experience will be your best guide. Some people believe a light freeze improves flavor. Fruit can be left on the vine after leaves have fallen.

If kiwifruit are picked too early, they will be tart. Picked too late, they won't store well or may be damaged by severe frost.

Kiwifruit can be stored in the refrigerator for up to four months. After refrigeration they must be ripened at room temperature. Not refrigerated, kiwifruit will keep about two weeks at room temperature.

VARIETIES

'Hayward' and 'Chico' are the most common female vines. They are very difficult to tell apart. They are vigorous and produce large, oval fruit. 'Vincent' is a seedling of 'Hayward'. It is very similar to its parent but has a lower chilling requirement. 'Monty', 'Bruno' and 'Abbott' produce heavy crops of smaller, oblong fruit. Male kiwis are usually sold simply as male kiwis.

Litchi

Litchi, Lychee

Litchi chinensis

Litchi is a delicious, aromatic and unusual fruit, native to China. Its cultivation can be traced back over 2,000 years. The common name of this fruit is spelled many different ways—litchi, lichee, lychee, lichi, leechee, laichi and others.

Litchi grows as a handsome, evergreen tree that can become 40 feet high. A dense, rounded canopy extends nearly to the ground. Trunk is smooth. Leaves are divided into three or more leaflets up to 6 inches long. They emerge a coppery color then turn glossy dark green.

Flowers, which appear in February and March, are small and greenish. They are borne in long clusters at branch tips and are self-fruitful.

Fruit are 1 to 1-1/2 inches in diameter, borne in clusters of 3 to 20 at the tips of branches. When ripe, they look like clusters of strawberries, enclosed in a rough, brittle shell. Flesh is whitish and has the texture of firm gelatin. One shiny, dark brown seed is enclosed in each fruit.

Litchi should be protected from strong winds and grown in full sun. It is hardy to 25° F (−4° C). It is considered a heavy feeder and benefits from regular applications of nitrogen. Exact amounts of nitrogen to apply have not been determined. In tropical countries mature trees receive liberal amounts of composted manure every three months. Mulching is also beneficial to protect the litchi's shallow root septum. Members of California Rare Fruit Growers report growing litchi in the southern California cities of Whittier, Los Angeles, San Diego, Encinitas and Vista. They also report success in El Cerrito and Santa Clara in the San Francisco Bay Area.

Litchi fruit is delightfully flavorful and can be eaten right from the tree. Whole branches can be used as dessert centerpiece, enabling guests to pick their own right at the table. Fruit can be kept in plastic bags under refrigeration for several weeks. They can also be dried, appearing somewhat like a raisin. When frozen or canned in syrup, the whitish flesh color is retained.

Abundant crop of litchi fruit ready for harvest.

Mature loquats

Loquat, Japanese Medlar

Eriobotrya japonica

Native to China, this evergreen tree or large shrub produces in early spring when other fruit are scarce. It reaches 15 to 25 feet tall and as broad when grown in full sun. Growth is somewhat more slender in shade. It has a well-rounded, handsome appearance, particularly when young.

The appearance of loquat changes as the plant matures. Young growth of leaves and stems is quite fuzzy and delicate bronze, later turning silver. Leaves harden with age. By the second year branches turn shiny brown. Third-year growth has a grayish cast.

Sharply toothed leaves are 6 to 10 inches long and 2 to 4 inches wide. Flowers, borne in clusters, usually set 3 to 10 fruit per cluster. They are small, fragrant and white. They appear in fall and bloom November to February, depending on climate. Loquats do not require cross-pollination from another variety.

Orange-yellow, somewhat fuzzy fruit are about the size and shape of a small hen's egg. Fruit have a sweet, rich, aromatic flavor and can be eaten fresh, canned or used for jelly.

Hardier than most subtropicals, loquat thrive almost anywhere in California except mountain and desert regions. They do best near the coast where higher humidity and cooler weather prevail. During hot summers or in inland areas, exposed fruit will sunburn

badly. Loquat will stand temperatures of 20° F (−7° C). If the temperature reaches 28° F (−2° C) during bloom, flowers will not set fruit and will drop shortly thereafter. To fruit in such a cold area, tree must be planted in a warm location or protected during very cold nights.

Fruit normally turn a characteristic golden yellow and are soft to the touch when ready to eat. Flesh will be smooth and mellow with a fine flavor. Each fruit has several seeds. After fruit have been picked, they may be kept for a few days under refrigeration. They bruise easily, resulting in browning and discoloration of the skin and flesh.

Although loquat is very drought resistant, it has a tendency to overbear. Branches break because of the weight of the fruit. Prevent this by thinning blossoms. Branches of young trees should be thinned to avoid crowding. Little pruning is needed unless more light is required for plants underneath mature tree.

VARIETIES

There are two types of loquat—white-fleshed and orange-fleshed varieties. One produces generally longer fruit with thin skin that is more easily peeled. Whitish to cream flesh is soft, sweet and juicy. The other is almost round or oblong and has a thick skin that is hard to peel unless fully ripened. Flesh is orange, firm and acid until well ripened. There are also differences in climate adaption. White-fleshed varieties do much better along the coast in a cooler climate. Orange-fleshed varieties need slightly more heat to obtain high quality and sweetness.

'Benlehr'—White flesh, finest for eating fresh.

'Champagne'—White flesh, very good quality.

'Day'—Bright orange flesh, very sweet.

'Gold Nugget'—Deep orange flesh, slightly acid to sweet.

'Miller'—Dull orange flesh, very good quality.

'Big Jim'—Both orange and white flesh.

Loquat tree

Mature mangoes ready to harvest.

Mango
Mangifera indica

Many consider mango to be one of the world's most delicious fruit. In tropical regions of the world this southeast Asian native is as popular as the apple in the United States. It is a large, evergreen, densely compact tree that reaches 25 feet in height, with a wide spread.

Leaves are long, narrow and leathery. When young, they range from shiny dark green to deep burgundy. Mature leaves are dull dark green. Leaves drop from tree all year.

Flowers are small and numerous, ranging from yellow to red, borne in long sprays. Although there may be hundreds of blooms to a cluster, only a few will set fruit. They do not require cross-pollination from another variety.

Fruit clusters usually ripen fall to winter. They produce a dramatic display as they hang outside the canopy of foliage. Each fruit is up to 6 inches long, shaped somewhat like a kidney bean. Color of the skin varies by variety from greenish yellow to orange and red. Yellowish orange flesh is aromatic and has an exotic, peach-like flavor. One large seed is found in the center of each fruit.

Mango is delicious fresh from the tree. Peel by making two longitudinal cuts 90 degrees apart around the entire fruit. Sections of skin can then be peeled off in quarters. Mango can also be sliced with the skin on.

Diced mango makes a unique ambrosia. Fruit can also be used to make breads.

Mango is tempermental as to climate. Warm days and nights are essential. Temperatures below 25° F (−4° C) can kill the entire tree. It is restricted primarily to frost-free areas of southern California.

VARIETIES

Many varieties are adapted to Florida, Hawaii and other tropical areas, but few perform well in California.

Paul Thomson of the California Rare Fruit Growers has had years of experience growing mangoes in southern California. He recommends the following:

'Villaseñor'—Coast to 10 miles inland. Rose-blushed fruit weighs 12 to 16 ounces. Small seed and no fiber. Flavor is good. Originated in Oceánside, California.

'Aloha'—Coast to 5 miles inland. Fruit weighs 8 to 10 ounces. Flavor is very good with little fiber. Originated in San Diego, California.

'Edgehill'— 10 to 15 miles inland. Fruit is green with a red blush and weighs 8 to 12 ounces. Excellent flavor and no fiber with a medium seed. Originated in Vista, California.

'Thomson Large Seedling'— 10 to 15 miles inland. Yellow fruit weighs 6 to 8 ounces. Flavor is excellent, with no fiber and small seed. Best mango for California. Originated in Vista, California.

'Cooper'— 15 to 25 miles inland. Green fruit is 14 to 16 ounces. Flavor is very good with little fiber. Medium seed. A very late February-to-April mango that keeps and ripens well. Originated in Hollywood, California.

Mangoes have an exotic, peach-like flavor.

Blossoms, fruit and foliage of natal plum.

Natal Plum
Carissa grandiflora

Natal plum is available in many sizes from low, ground-hugging types to larger, hedge-high forms. It is widely used as an ornamental because of its attractive foliage and the colorful flowers and fruit that often appear at the same time.

Natal plum is fast growing with an open habit. Leaves are oval, 3 inches long and shiny green. Branches are armed with sharp spines, calling for special thought as to plant placement. Taller types make formidable barriers. All parts of the plant contain a milky juice.

White, star-shaped flowers are up to 2 inches in diameter. They emit a wonderful, orange-like fragrance.

The 1 to 2-inch fruit are glossy red to deep maroon and plum shaped. Main crop is from June to October with some fruit borne all year. Planting more than one variety for cross-pollination may increase yields. When fully ripe, fruit taste somewhat like cranberries. Eat fresh, stew in a sauce or use for jellies and pies.

Natal plum is an easy-to-grow, drought-tolerant plant that can survive indoors or very near the coast. It is usually damaged at 26° F (−3° C).

VARIETIES

'Fancy' is best for edible fruit. It grows upright to 6 feet, and has showy flowers followed by large fruit. Of the many varieties available, the best include:

'Boxwood Beauty'—Thornless and very compact to 2 feet high and 2 feet wide. Leaves are deep green and look similar to those of a large-leaf boxwood. Excellent for shaping into hedges.

'Green Carpet'—Low growing to 1-1/2 feet high with a spread of 4-1/2 feet. Small leaves. Good ground cover.

'Horizontalis'—Low and spreading to 2 feet high. Dense foliage.

'Ruby Point'—Upright to 6 feet high. Reddish foliage.

'Tomlinson'—2-1/2 feet high, 3 feet wide. Shiny leaves have a deep red tint. Large flowers and wine-red fruit. Thornless and slow growing.

Papaya
Carica species

Native to tropical America, papayas are giant, herbaceous, evergreen plants that grow to 25 feet high. They are classed as herb plants because they have no woody tissues in their trunks. Trunks are straight and hollow and rarely branch. They are topped with broad, deeply lobed, fan-like leaves up to 15 inches wide and 24 inches long.

Papayas begin to produce inconspicuous, creamy yellow flowers about 5 months after seed are planted. Each plant can have one of three types of flowers: male, female or bisexual (hermaphrodite), which has both male and female parts. Only papayas with female or bisexual flowers can bear fruit. Female flowers must have a male or bisexual plant nearby to provide pollen.

To determine the sex of a plant you must examine the flowers. Female flowers are rather squat and round. Bisexual flowers are narrow and tubular. Male flowers are long, tubular and star shaped at the end.

Papaya seed may be obtained from fruit purchased at local markets. It is best to grow at least two plants near each other to help ensure male and female flowers are present for pollination.

Papayas bear fruit at a young age. Fruit require about 8 months to ripen after pollination. Flowers and fruit are borne in the *axil*, the upper angle between leaf and stem. As the plant grows taller, fruit is produced higher on the plant. Also, fruit and leaves tend to become smaller as tree grows older. For these reasons it is best to cut down tree after three or four years and start a new one. You may also want to grow trees at various stages of maturity.

Sliced 'Solo' papaya

SOIL, NUTRIENT AND WATER REQUIREMENTS

Warm soil in winter is the key to successful papaya culture. Cold, wet or soggy soils cause root rot. Good drainage is essential. Mulch should be kept out of contact with the base of the trunk to avoid crown rot.

Papayas are best adapted to warm, relatively frost-free areas along the coast of Southern California. Because plants fruit within a year after planting, it may be worthwhile to try papaya where frosts occur only every few years. They also do very well in a greenhouse. If they become too tall, cut them back or plant a new one. Papayas are considered heavy feeders but ideal amounts of nitrogen to be applied have not been determined.

VARIETIES

Papayas are divided into groups according to origin. Botanical nomenclature is a bit confused. According to *Hortus Third*, the standard reference for botanical nomenclature, Hawaiian and Mexican papayas are varieties of *Carica papaya*. The mountain papayas, from the highlands of Ecuador and Colombia, are varieties of *Carica pubescens*, formally *C. candamarcensis*.

Hawaiian papayas are the small fruit seen in supermarkets. There are two popular varieties. 'Solo', also known as 'Solo Waimanalo', is grown widely in Hawaii. It bears many hermaphrodites, some females and some males. Fruit have excellent flavor. Low, 6-foot height of plant makes harvesting easy. 'Solo' is ideal for a greenhouse. 'Strawberry', also known as 'Sunrise', produces smooth, pear-shaped fruit, much firmer than 'Solo'. Flesh is deep red with a delightful, strawberry-like flavor.

Mexican papayas bear large fruit up to 10 pounds. Trees are slightly hardier than Hawaiian papayas but fruit are not as sweet. Mexican papayas have a musky flavor and are available in red or orange-fleshed varieties.

Mountain papayas are the hardiest of the papayas. Small, rather bland fruit are usually eaten with sweetener or made into preserves. There are two varieties. 'Chamburro', the more prolific, bears small, football-shaped fruit that are bright yellow and emit a strong fragrance.

HARVESTING AND STORAGE

Papayas resemble melons in appearance and taste. They are actually large berries, often reaching 5 to 10 pounds under ideal conditions. Greenish yellow to orange skin has a smooth texture. Succulent flesh is orange-yellow, ranging from 1 to 2 inches thick. The center cavity of the fruit is filled with numerous, small, black seeds, which form on the inner walls of the flesh. Allow fruit to ripen as long as possible on the plant before picking. Fruit turn from green to yellow when mature. Do not store fruit at temperatures lower than 50° F (10° C) or the flesh may be damaged.

Papayas are usually eaten fresh with a squeeze of lemon or lime. They can also be used to make jams and jellies. Papayas are considered a digestive aid. The immature fruit contain tenderizing proteins and enzymes.

The milky sap from the plant or immature fruit will irritate your skin and should be washed off immediately.

Passion Fruit
Passiflora edulis

There are several kinds of edible passion fruit. The most familiar is the purple type, sometimes called purple granadilla.

This New World native grows as a woody, evergreen, perennial vine. Deeply toothed, three-lobed leaves are light yellowish green. The vine climbs by tendrils up to 30 feet high. Plant grows so rapidly that it has been known to cover the side of a fairly large house in two years. However, it can be controlled by pruning.

Unique, striking, intricate blossoms emerge during spring and early summer. Flowers are fragrant and vary in color. They reach up to 4 inches in diameter.

Vines bear fruit very early in life. Purple-skinned fruit are about 2 inches long, somewhat oval or shaped like a hen's egg. Numerous, small seed inside the parchment-like rind are surrounded by an aromatic, juicy pulp. This pulp has an unusual, pleasing, somewhat acid flavor. You may eat the pulp fresh, or use it to make jelly and juices, which often need sugar to improve flavor.

Allow fruit to become fully mature before harvesting. Characteristic flavor is the best indicator of ripeness. Because the leathery rind protects the soft interior, there are no special precautions to follow in harvesting. Use a pair of clippers or knife to cut fruit from

Fruit and foliage of passion fruit.

Yellow variety of passion fruit.

'Nazemetz' pineapple guava

vine. Even though the rind may shrivel after harvesting, the fruit interior will stay juicy for many days, even weeks.

Passion fruit is a tender subtropical. It requires attention to climate and planting location. Vine safely withstands only very light frosts. Do not grow where frost is frequent. If cold weather is not too severe, roots may put forth a new vine even though the top has been killed. Plant does very well in subtropical regions where winter temperatures do not fall below 29° F (1° C) and summer temperatures are relatively warm.

Passion fruit vine is exceedingly susceptible to crown rot caused by heavy, wet soils. Because it grows so rapidly and produces so many fruit, it responds well to applications of nitrogen. Vine withstands considerable drought, but growth is retarded and crops reduced without adequate moisture.

Rapidly growing vine is usually trained over an arbor or trellis or along a fence where sturdy support can be provided. Top of vine tends to become dense and must be pruned out. Best time to prune is when the plant is just beginning vigorous growth rather than when it is dormant.

'Golden Hawaiian' passion fruit

Pineapple Guava
Feijoa sellowiana

Native to southern Brazil and northern Argentina, pineapple guava is a tall, evergreen shrub or small tree of considerable ornamental interest. It is not a true guava, which belongs to *Psidium* species. Fruit are very tasty, with a slightly tart flavor. Taste is best described as somewhat like pineapple with overtones of spearmint. Plant can be easily pruned into any shape and is particularly handsome, especially when in bloom. Unpruned, it may reach 20 feet tall with several main trunks branching at or near the ground.

Oval, 2 to 3-inch leaves are attractive, bluish green above and soft, silvery white beneath. Wood is very dense, hard and brittle.

Striking 1-inch flowers have long, bright red stamens topped with large grains of yellow pollen. Flowers appear late, from May through June, thus escaping late frosts. The 4 to 6 fleshy flower petals are white, tinged with purple on the inside. They are mildly sweet and edible and can be used in salads or as ice cream topping.

Fruit ripen 4 to 7 months after flowering, usually between September and January, depending on the climate. They range from 3/4 to 3-1/2 inches long and may be round or egg shaped. Fruit blend in with foliage and don't add much to the plant's ornamental quality. Skin is shiny green to grayish green, but some varieties turn purplish on the side exposed to sun. Skin texture varies from smooth to rough and pebbly and is 3/16 to 5/8 inch thick. Pulp or flesh is amber to pale greenish white and very fragrant and juicy. Taste is slightly tart but some varieties are quite sweet. The flesh contains numerous, edible, black seeds, which have a distinctive flavor of their own.

Fruit can be tree ripened or picked early and allowed to ripen at room temperature. Flavor is excellent either way. Fruit drop to the ground when mature. Gather frequently to avoid decay.

Although pineapple guava grows well in warm climates, it produces the best quality fruit in cooler areas, especially around San Francisco Bay. It is extremely hardy—hardiest of the subtropicals—withstanding a range of temperatures from 15° to 115° F (−9° to 45° C).

VARIETIES

It is best to plant more than one variety of pineapple guava to ensure heavy crops. However, some are self-fruitful.

'Coolidge'—Self-fruitful and productive without cross-pollination. Small fruit with mild flavor.

'Nazemetz'—Large fruit of excellent quality. Self-fruitful. Good pollinizer for 'Trask'.

'Pineapple Gem'—Self-fruitful.

'Superba'—Self-sterile with round fruit. Plant with 'Coolidge' to ensure heavy crops.

'Trask'—Originated as a bud sport of 'Coolidge'. Large fruit with rough, dark green skin. Skin is thicker and grittier than parent but pulp quality is very good. Very productive and ripens early. Self-sterile.

'Trask' pineapple guava

Surinam cherry

Surinam Cherry, Pitanga
Eugenia uniflora

In its native Brazil, Surinam cherry, also known as pitanga, is greatly enjoyed as a fresh fruit. In western North America, it is used primarily as an ornamental landscape plant, valued for its attractive foliage, fragrant flowers and colorful fruit. These qualities have also been appreciated for decades in Brazil. In 1912 a Brazilian priest, Father Taveres, observed: "Surely Brazil does not need to envy Europe her cherry trees, bending in May under the weight of her ruby fruit. Our pitangas surpass them both in beauty and taste."

Surinam cherry can reach 20 to 25 feet high as an evergreen shrub or small tree but is usually kept smaller. Oval, 2-inch leaves are attractive green tinged with coppery red. When crushed, they give off a pleasant scent. In Brazil, the odor is thought to repel flies, so leaves are often scattered on floors.

Flowers of Surinam cherry are about 1/2 inch in diameter, white and intensely fragrant. Fruit are round, usually 1 inch diameter, with 8 prominent ribs. As they ripen they change from green to yellow to orange and finally to scarlet. They should be eaten only at this fully ripe stage when the delicious flavor is most distinctive and aromatic. Fruit can be eaten fresh or preserved in jams or jellies. They are also used to make sherbet and fresh juice.

Grow Surinam cherry in full sun or partial shade. It accepts pruning well and is often trained as a hedge. As a container plant, it displays fruit, flowers and foliage dramatically and is an attractive addition to a patio. Hardy to 28° F (−2° C).

White Sapote

Casimiroa edulis

White sapote is an amazing tree that produces thousands of fruit when mature. It is an exceedingly fast growing, evergreen tree that reaches 25 feet high with a spread of 30 to 40 feet. Native to the highlands of Central America, this tree has naturalized in southern California.

Branches of sapote are strong and capable of supporting large crops with little or no breakage, even in strong winds. Bark on new growth is bright green. In a short time it becomes marked with tiny gray lines. As growth matures, bark turns ash gray and retains that color throughout the tree's life. Trunk of a large tree is broadly fluted.

Roots of sapote are far reaching. Those of a large tree may extend 75 to 80 feet from the trunk. These roots contribute to drought tolerance. They can also be quite invasive, buckling sidewalks and entering flower beds. Care should be taken when choosing a planting site.

Foliage of sapote is nicely ornamental. Leaves are glossy green and divided into 3 to 7 finger-like leaflets.

Fruit is sweet, thin skinned and bruises easily. It is from 2 to 4 inches long, about the shape of an apple and weighs 3 ounces to a pound. It ripens from late summer through fall and sometimes into winter, depending on climate. White sapote is self-fruitful.

Sapote is generally eaten as a fresh fruit. When picked at the mature but still-firm stage, it ripens at room temperature in three to five days. It is ready to eat when soft to the touch. Jelly is often made from fruit, which is so sweet that considerable lemon juice must be added to give it character. Consequently, it often tastes more like lemon jelly.

Best way to store fruit is to freeze it, whole or just the pulp. It will keep indefinitely and retain its original flavor when thawed. Skin can be easily removed from frozen fruit by holding fruit under a stream of cold water. The remaining pulp can then be thawed and eaten. Pulp, minus seeds, can be added to milk and blended for a delicious sapote milk shake.

Fine specimens of sapote can be found from the Mexican border north to San Francisco Bay. Trees are generally confined to areas within 25 miles of the coast. Most trees will withstand temperatures of 25° F (−4° C), but not for prolonged periods.

Sapote is not a desirable lawn tree. It has invasive roots and produces many fruit that fall to the ground, making a mess and attracting squirrels, rats, birds, flies and other insects.

White sapote

VARIETIES

Identifying sapote varieties can be difficult. The two different types of sapote trees are hard to tell apart. One produces very large fruit, 3-1/2 to 5 inches long. Fruit has a prominent, rounded point and may weigh a pound or more. White flesh and skin remain green even when fully ripe. Flesh often has a bitter taste that is very objectionable to most palates.

A second type of sapote has fruit that are nearly round or flattened like a tomato and generally 3 to 5 inches in diameter. There is no distinct point on the end. Skin is dull, grayish green with immature. When ripe, skin attains a golden color and flesh is very sweet and juicy.

The following varieties reliably produce well-flavored fruit:

'May'—Medium fruit of very good quality. Only drawback is that it does not turn color when ripe, making it hard to know when to pick.

'Suebelle'—Medium fruit of good quality. Nearly everbearing within a mile of the coast.

'Vinmar'—Small fruit, 2 to 2-1/2 inches in diameter. Very sweet with a tough skin. Can be allowed to drop from the tree when ripe without damage.

Other Fruit

In this book we have described and illustrated the familiar fruit of the West. We have included many new and exciting fruit varieties. But a book of this size cannot include detailed information on all plants that bear edible fruit.

The aim of this section is to whet the appetite of the fruit grower who is looking for the unusual or appreciates some of the finer, native fruit. Some of these plants are known primarily as ornamentals and many will be difficult to find. All are worth the search.

Amelanchier **species**—This is a varied species with such common names as shadbush, shadblow, serviceberry and saskatoon. These plants are native to many parts of the United States including the Pacific Northwest. *Amelanchier* species are attractive, ornamental shrubs or small trees. They have white spring flowers and stunning fall color. Fruit are small and berry-like with the flavor of blueberries. They can be cooked in pies or canned and serve as a good source of vitamin C.

Prunus **species**—Many types of plums and cherries are native to the western states. Fruit quality usually varies from plant to plant but many are edible as well as ornamental. Some may even be locally available in improved forms. The Northwest produces one particularly good native plum, Klamath plum or *Prunus subcordata*. It bears small, tart yellow fruit. Native plums and cherries can be used to make delicious jams and jellies. Local nurserymen or native plant societies can lead you to other native plums and cherries.

Elderberries, *Sambucus* **species**—Elderberry shrubs or small trees are familiar in many parts of the West. The dark berries are key ingredients in many traditional jams, jellies and pies, as well as elderberry wine.

Cranberries, *Vaccinium macrocarpon*—Cranberries are adapted to many western climates. They require the same general care and acid soil as blueberries. Plants are attractive and spreading and are useful as ground covers. Small, red fruit are delicious in sauces and preserves. Many other closely related, western natives of *Vaccinium* species bear edible fruit. They include evergreen huckleberry, *V. ovatum,* and red huckleberry, *V. parvifolium.*

Cornelian cherry, *Cornus mas*—This fruit tree has many of the beautiful characteristics of its close relative, flowering dogwood, *Cornus florida.* In addition, it bears a useful crop of edible fruit. Bright yellow flowers appear on bare branches in late winter. Scarlet fruit follow in fall just as the foliage turns bright fall colors. Fruit is acidic but can be used to make jams and jellies.

Medlar, *Mespilus germanica*—Botanically, medlar is classed between a pear and a hawthorn. It is an odd-shaped fruit that is picked when hard and softened at room temperature until mushy. Medlar is popular in Europe where it is used in many desserts, including various types of mousse. It blends well with dessert wines and can be made into preserves. The shrub or small tree makes a fine ornamental. Its beautiful green foliage turns red in fall. Delicate, white spring flowers appear in spring.

Amelanchier alnifolia is native to portions of the Pacific Northwest. It is valuable as a small, ornamental tree, left, and for its fruit, above.

Fruit Growers

If you wish to expand your knowledge of fruit growing, here are addresses of catalogs and organizations we have found helpful.

CATALOG SOURCES

Apple Country Nursery, Inc.
Box 398
Brewster, WA 98812
Specialists in fruit trees. Brochure and price list available.

Armstrong Nurseries
Box 4060
Ontario, CA 91761
Roses, genetic dwarfs, nectarines, peaches and other fruit trees. 40-page catalog.

Bountiful Ridge Nurseries, Inc.
Box 250
Princess Anne, MD 21853
Specialists in fruit and nuts. 50-page catalog includes a planting guide. Wholesale and retail.

Byland Nursery
1600 Byland Road
Kelowna, B.C. Canada V1Z 1H6
Major suppliers of fruit and berry plants to retail nurseries in western Canada. Retail nursery in Kelowna. Will help locate hard to find varieties. Phone (604) 769-4466.

Buckley Nursery Garden Center
646 N. River Road
Buckley, WA 98321
Fruit trees, shade and flowering trees, shrubs, flowers and ornamentals. 18-page catalog. Retail and wholesale.

C & O Nursery
Box 116
1700 N. Wenatchee Avenue
Wenatchee, WA 98801
Fruit specialists. Exclusive patented varieties. 40-page catalog includes ornamentals and shade trees. Retail and commercial.

California Rare Fruit Nursery Exotica Seed Co.
989 Poinsettia
Vista, CA 92083
Specialists in subtropicals. Mail order seeds. Plants for sale at nursery. Details on culture and use in 16-page catalog; $2.

Columbia Basin Nursery
Box 458
Quincy, WA 98848
Seedling fruit and shade tree rootstock, dwarfing apple rootstock, dwarf and standard budded fruit trees. Color brochure and price list. Wholesale and retail.

Four Winds Growers
42186 Palm Avenue
Box 3538
Fremont, CA 94538
Wholesale grower of dwarf citrus, standard citrus and avocados for California nurseries. Mail order available to other states. Two-gallon and five-gallon-size plants shipped bare root. Over 30 varieties available.

Fowler Nurseries, Inc.
535 Fowler Road
Newcastle, CA 95658
4-page price list of over 200 varieties on request. Commercial price list also available.

J.E. Miller Nurseries, Inc.
Canandaigua, NY 14424
56-page fruit catalog includes garden aids and ornamentals.

New York State Fruit Testing Cooperative Association
Geneva, NY 14456
32-page fruit catalog. $5 membership fee.

Pacific Tree Farms
4301 Lynwood Drive
Chula Vista, CA 92010
12-page catalog features subtropicals and low-chilling apple varieties. Fact sheets available on most plants.

Raintree Nursery
265 Butts Road
Morton, WA 98356
24-page catalog. Specialists in food plants for the Pacific Northwest. Lists include Asian pear, rootstocks and Northwest native plants.

Redwood City Seed Co.
Box 361
Redwood City, CA 94064
19-page catalog of seeds of ornamental and fruiting trees costs $1.

Southmeadow Fruit Gardens
2363 Tilbury Place
Birmingham, MI 48009
Fruit varieties old, new and rare. 112-page, illustrated catalog priced at $8. Condensed, 8-page catalog is free.

Stark Bros. Nurseries
Box B4225A
Louisiana, MO 63353
Illustrated 64-page catalog and guide. Features nearly 400 varieties and assortment of fruit, nuts, berries, ornamentals and other nursery stock for the home gardener.

Van Well Nursery
Box 1339
Wenatchee, WA 98801
Fruit and berries. 28-page catalog. Wholesale and retail.

Dave Wilson Nursery
Box WD
Hughson, CA 95326
Fruit, nuts, berries, grapes. Specializing in Zaiger genetic dwarf fruit trees. Wholesale and retail.

ORGANIZATIONS

American Pomological Society
103 Tyson Building
University Park, PA 16802
Fruit Varieties Journal, a 24-page booklet published four times yearly. Society also offers special rate subscriptions for *Western Fruit Gardener* and *The Goodfruit Grower* magazines.

California Macadamia Society
Box 666
Fallbrook, CA 92028
$12.50 membership includes yearbook, newsletters and notices of upcoming Society events.

California Rare Fruit Growers, Inc.
Fullerton Arboretum
California State University
Fullerton, CA 92634
$10 membership includes quarterly newsletter and a yearbook, plus general meetings, field trips, plant sales, local chapter activities and seed exchange.

Home Orchard Society
2511 S.W. Miles Street
Portland, OR 97210
$5 membership includes subscription to *Pome News*, a 10-page newsletter published four times yearly.

Indoor Citrus and Rare Fruit Society
9823 Mason Avenue
Chatsworth, CA 91311
$10 membership includes subscription to 8-page newsletter published four times yearly.

North American Fruit Explorers
Box 711
St. Louis, MO 63188
$5 membership includes subscription to *The North American Pomona*, a 60-page booklet published four times yearly.

Northern Nut Growers Association
Rural Route 3
Bloomington, IL 61701
$10 membership includes quarterly, 20-page *Nutshell*—report of papers given at annual meeting. Assistance in securing seed, scion and grafted nut trees.

STATE UNIVERSITY EXTENSION SERVICES

State universities offer literature on many aspects of fruit growing. Write to your state university and request a list of available publications. Most extension services discourage out-of-state requests.

ARIZONA
Cooperative Extension Service
University of Arizona
Tucson, AZ 85721

CALIFORNIA
Public Service
University Hall
University of California
Berkeley, CA 94720

COLORADO
Bulletin Room
Colorado State University
Fort Collins, CO 80521

IDAHO
Mailing Room
Agricultural Science Building
University of Idaho
Moscow, ID 83843

MONTANA
Extension Mailing Room
Montana State University
Bozeman, MT 59715

NEVADA
Agricultural Communications
University of Nevada
Reno, NV 89507

NEW MEXICO
Bulletin Office
Department of Agricultural Information
Drawer 3A1
New Mexico State University
Las Cruces, NM 88001

OREGON
Bulletin Mailing Service
Industrial Building
Oregon State University
Corvallis, OR 97331

UTAH
Extension Publications Officer
Library 124
Utah State University
Logan, UT 84321

WASHINGTON
Cooperative Extension Service
Publications Building
Washington State University
Pullman, WA 99163

WYOMING
Bulletin Room
College of Agriculture
University of Wyoming
Box 3354
University Station
Laramie, WY 82070

INDEX

Acknowledgments

This book would not be possible without the generous assistance of:

Bob Bergantz, horticulturist, Placerville, CA
Cal Bream, President, California Rare Fruit Growers, Inc., Fullerton, CA
Dr. Claron O. Hesse, Davis, CA
Bill Nelson, Pacific Tree Farm, Chula Vista, CA
Dr. Robert Norton, Northwest Washington Research and Extension Unit, Washington State University, Mt. Vernon, WA
Fred H. Peterson, Soil and Plant Laboratory, Santa Clara, CA
Dr. C. A. Schroeder, Professor of Botany, University of California, Los Angeles, CA
Dr. C.D. Schwartze, C.D. Schwartze Nursery, Puyallup, WA
Steven Spangler, Exotica Seed Company and Rare Fruit Nursery, Hollywood, CA
Paul Thomson, horticulturist, Bonsall, CA

We also wish to thank:
Wim Boerbom, Research Branch, Canadian Department of Agriculture, Summerland, British Columbia, Canada
Joshua Landis, Rutherford, CA
Dr. Francis Lawrence, USDA horticulturist, Corvallis, OR
Robert Ludekins, L.E. Cooke Co., Visalia, CA
Knox Nomura, Nomura Nursery, Sumner, WA
Dr. David W. Ramming, USDA horticulturist, Fresno, CA
Herman Suter, Suter Nursery, St. Helena, CA
George Vashel, Menlo Growers, Gilroy, CA
The entire staff of Dave Wilson Nursery, Hughson, CA